Fortunate Son

AN AMERICAN PORTRAIT

HILL AND WANG
A division of FARRAR, STRAUS AND GIROUX

Fortunate Son

THE LIFE OF ELVIS PRESLEY

CHARLES L. PONCE DE LEON

HILL AND WANG
A division of Farrar, Straus and Giroux

18 West 18th Street, New York 10011

Copyright © 2006 by Charles L. Ponce de Leon

Printed in the United States of America
Published in 2006 by Hill and Wang
First paperback edition, 2007

The Library of Congress has cataloged the hardcover edition as follows:
Ponce de Leon, Charles L. (Charles Leonard)
    Fortunate son : the life of Elvis Presley / by Charles L. Ponce de Leon.—1st ed.
        p.   cm. — (An American portrait)
    Includes index.
    ISBN-13: 978-0-8090-3042-2 (hardcover : alk. paper)
    ISBN-10: 0-8090-3042-X (hardcover : alk. paper)
    1. Presley, Elvis, 1935–1977. 2. Rock musicians—United States—Biography.
I. Title. II. Series: American portrait (New York, N.Y.)

ML420.P96 P63 2006
782.42166092—dc22

                                                                    2005026894

Paperback ISBN-13: 978-0-8090-1641-9
Paperback ISBN-10: 0-8090-1641-9

Designed by Gretchen Achilles

www.fsgbooks.com

FOR CAROLINE AND CHRISTOPHER

Contents

Fortunate Son

Introduction

IT BEGAN AS an unexceptional incident, the sort of thing that filled police blotters in the crime-ridden 1970s but otherwise attracted little notice. Shortly after midnight on June 24, 1977, two young toughs began roughing up the lone attendant at an all-night gas station in Madison, Wisconsin. Before they could get very far, a limousine pulled up. Its back passenger door swung open, and a large man in a tracksuit and oversize sunglasses jumped out and strode toward them. He assumed a karate pose. Bewildered, the bullies strained to get a better look at the interloper. What they saw made them stop in their tracks. It was Elvis Presley, the singer and movie star. Having just arrived in Madison for a concert that evening, he was on his way to his hotel when he saw the altercation and resolved to help the attendant.

The shock of seeing Elvis completely changed the situation. The young toughs backed away from their victim, who was just as stunned as they were when he recognized his rescuer. Police officers accompanying Presley's limousine then intervened. But Elvis hung around for some time afterward, talking to the officers as well as the victim and his assailants. He shook hands with everyone and even posed for pictures. "He was willing to fight," one of the police officers in his security detail told a reporter. "That was the bad part."[1] The officer's disapproval was understandable. Why would Presley do something so rash and fool-hardy? What business did an entertainer, one of the world's most fa-mous celebrities, have coming to the rescue of a gas-station attendant, especially with the police so close at hand?

This minor incident, one of countless Elvis anecdotes that consti-tute the Presley lore, speaks volumes about the man and the peculiar status he came to acquire during his relatively short yet illustrious ca-reer as a performer, recording artist, and movie actor. As the reaction of the men at the gas station demonstrated, Presley had already become something of a recluse by the mid-1970s—even while regularly ap-pearing before thousands of fans on concert tours that sent him to cities throughout the country. Since the early 1960s he had inhabited a cloistered world outside the public eye, but in recent years his interest in protecting his privacy had become stronger than ever. Stung by press criticism of his poor performances and portly, debauched appearance, Presley rarely went out in public, except late at night, when he knew few people would be around. Even when he was alive, an Elvis sighting was an exceptional occurrence. It was as if he had emerged from a par-allel universe and the rarity of such an event demanded special com-memoration. He was already an icon, a living legend.

Elvis was aware of this, and it was recognition of his iconic power that led him to stop the limo and go to the attendant's aid. Though Pres-ley was in many ways an unpretentious man, he was also convinced that his success was evidence of some divine calling and that he was obliged to use his star power for good. This belief inspired his perception of him-self as a performer and encouraged him to chart a career path that re-mained remarkably consistent in its fixation on mainstream success and conventional show-business values. Over time, it also led him to see his celebrity in more grandiose terms, as a pulpit from which he could reach the public and heal the divisions created by the fractious social and po-litical conflicts of the 1960s. Elvis thought of himself as a "good guy," like the heroes in the comic books and B movies he loved as a boy. And by the early 1970s this understanding of himself had made him sympa-thetic to political conservatism and a self-righteous advocate of law and order. It was no coincidence that when he jumped out of the limo in Madison, he was carrying his badge from the Federal Bureau of Narcotics and Dangerous Drugs, or that in the car was an assortment of firearms that he and his bodyguards took with them nearly everywhere. Like the FBI or the vigilante crime fighters who dominated the era's popular culture, he was protecting the weak from the forces of anarchy that seemed to be engulfing the nation.

As Elvis saw it, he was a "fortunate son," a child of the Depression-ravaged South who had become successful beyond his wildest dreams. Grateful for his success, he was determined to give something back to the nation that had made it possible. Doing so would not only honor America, the land of opportunity; it would also honor his parents. Humble, working-class Southerners, they had struggled to provide him with a decent life. They had also raised him to be "respectable": a wholesome, law-abiding, God-fearing young man. Elvis revered these values. He regarded himself as someone who lived by them, and he was certain they had been instrumental to his success, enabling him to gain the affection and loyalty of fans from a variety of backgrounds. Making people happy with his music, setting a good example for the public, serving the cause of law and order as best he could—this was Elvis's way of paying homage to his upbringing and the respectable working-class culture from which he sprang. It was also a way for him to reconnect with this culture and conceive of himself as its apotheosis, the poor boy from Mississippi who had achieved the American Dream yet remained faithful to his small-town roots.

By the summer of 1977, however, the real Elvis bore little resemblance to this image, and Presley was increasingly troubled by the disjunction between the two. After twenty years as a celebrity, subjected to the pressures of fame and with virtually anything he desired at his fingertips, he had become a self-indulgent libertine, a chronic womanizer, and a man plagued by doubts about the loyalty of his closest friends and associates. Convinced he was a target of "bad guys," he was often armed to the teeth and prone to carelessly firing his weapons, a habit that had already gotten him into minor scrapes and seemed destined to result in a serious accident. He was a drug addict, dangerously dependent on several potent prescription medications, despite his professed hatred for the drug culture and his identification with the police and organizations engaged in the "war on drugs." And he was suffering from depression, a condition exacerbated by his abuse of drugs that heightened his paranoia and eccentric behavior.

Worst of all, these details, which had been published in bits and pieces in the tabloid press, were about to be splashed across the headlines. Three of Elvis's former bodyguards had just finished a tell-all exposé, the first to appear from within Presley's camp, and its impending publication greatly concerned Elvis. He feared that the book would destroy his reputation and, as fans came to learn the truth about him, force him to confront the gulf that had developed between the reality of his life and his revered self-image.

Is it any wonder, then, that Presley jumped out of his limo and rushed to the filling-station attendant's aid? Here was a perfect opportunity to act like the man he liked to think he was, to shore up his faltering self-image, and to remind the public that no matter what they might hear about him in the near future, he was admirable, a good guy.

Unfortunately, less than two months after his escapade in Madison, Elvis Presley was dead, and the unflattering information contained in the dreaded "bodyguard book" became common knowledge. Thanks in part to the publicity sparked by his death, the book became a bestseller, and in the months afterward new questions were raised about the real Elvis and the cause of his death.[2]

But these revelations didn't destroy Presley's image so much as transform it. While some fans refused to believe the sordid and at times exaggerated claims contained in the book and in subsequent exposés, others found ways of accepting them. In due course they were incorporated into a new understanding of Elvis that proved even more compelling than the conventional version that had been widely embraced during his lifetime. It was this new version of Elvis that became the basis for the fervent posthumous devotion displayed by large numbers of his fans, a devotion almost religious in its intensity. And it was this new version that made Elvis a continued object of fascination to the wider public and an all-purpose icon of American popular culture.[3]

Elvis's story, from this perspective, is a tragedy, a story familiar in its essentials to many other accounts of celebrities' lives. At its core is the belief that material success breeds unhappiness and corruption, and that the central drama of Presley's life was an ultimately unsuccessful effort to prevent this from occurring—to ward off the forces that could turn the American Dream into a nightmare. Ironically, Presley's image while he was living emphasized his success at this endeavor. His fans and the wider public were encouraged to believe that despite his fame and riches, he was still the same wholesome, law-abiding, God-fearing man who had risen to stardom so suddenly in the mid-1950s. His lapses were attributed to the difficulties involved in remaining committed to one's values amid the temptations and snares of a secular consumer culture—something large numbers of Americans could readily appreciate.

After his death, the story was turned on its head. His decline into libertinism and moral corruption became further proof that these difficulties were indeed serious. They were particularly serious for celebrities like Elvis, whose very riches and privileged status gave them access to things beyond the reach of ordinary people. Here lay the dramatic resonance of Presley's story, the hook that linked it to one of the master narratives of American culture. It is a story we have been telling and retelling since the era of the Puritans.[4]

Conflating Elvis's story with larger narratives about the pitfalls of success and celebrity is easy. Many of the facts of his life encourage such an interpretation, and it is not surprising that most of his biographers, as well as the vast majority of his fans and the public, see him as a tragic figure, laid low by flaws that epitomize America as a whole.

But the conventional story is too pat, and it downplays Presley's own role as its instigator. Elvis's life took the shape it did because of decisions he made in the course of it, decisions influenced in equal part by his temperament, background, and life experiences. They were also affected, to a degree that hasn't fully been acknowledged, by the times in which he lived. Elvis Presley may have been a singular individual. But he was also a product of history, of a specific time and place.

His tremendous success in the 1950s, as numerous critics and commentators have noted, was a result of his plasticity, his ability to incorporate—in his personal style and public persona as well as in his musical repertoire—a wide variety of influences. This enabled him to attract many different Americans, yet it also made it possible for him to be appreciated in distinct ways. Though Presley appealed to the masses and was one of the quintessential icons of a new national mass culture, it was never in a simple, clear-cut way. He possessed qualities that encouraged particularistic responses, and because of this his following was not merely wide but deeply, personally invested in him.

Some of these qualities can only be attributed to his inborn temperament and psychological disposition, the mysterious things that make individual human beings unique. Smart, naturally inquisitive, and restless, with an intellectual curiosity that, without much formal schooling, found some unorthodox outlets, Presley easily developed great passions and enthusiasms. Among these was an abiding interest in all kinds of music, including the music of African-Americans, an unusual avocation for a poor white man in the Jim Crow South. When inspired by these passions, Elvis did some of his best work. Yet he was also predisposed to depression, and he found it very difficult to persevere in his commitments. As a result, he often fell into routines that were unfulfilling and ultimately self-destructive. This might have happened to him even if he had never become rich and famous. But because he was, and because the routines he fell into were easily rationalized by career strategies that were familiar and personally gratifying, Presley was able to respond to his boredom and frustration in extraordinary ways that undoubtedly contributed to his early death.

Just as important as Elvis's temperament were his family background and his parents' influence. Though Presley, like many Southerners of his generation, spent a lot of time around extended kin, his nuclear family was unusually close-knit. Because of a series of misfortunes during his childhood, he and his parents, Gladys and Vernon Presley, developed an insular, defensive outlook toward the world that Elvis carried with him throughout his life. Within the family circle, Elvis was the cherished only child. His parents spoiled him and convinced him he was special, a belief that would prove useful when he embarked on a career in show business and had to tap wellsprings of ambition and courage his parents had implanted in his psyche. Presley's sense of himself as a unique individual with special talents and powers, worthy of public acclaim and admiration but also besieged by hostile forces on the outside, arose from the dynamics of his nuclear family.

His parents were also determined that Elvis be respectable and achieve a measure of economic security, and so they raised him to be polite, deferential, religious, and clean-living, the antithesis of "white trash." Internalized from an early age, these values remained with him when he became a success, influencing his career decisions as well as his lifestyle. Elvis's commitment to respectability enabled him to overcome the criticism that his music first sparked and gain the approval of the media and important show-business figures. It was the key to his transformation from a controversial rock and roller to a mainstream entertainer. Even as he strayed from this ideal in real life, a development carefully hidden from the public and the press, it remained a source of inspiration and self-identity, a touchstone that allowed him to reconnect to his roots and the emotional security he associated with them.

Equally important, and often overlooked, was the historical context in which he was reared and grew to adulthood. As a child in Tupelo, Mississippi, and as a teenager in booming postwar Memphis, Presley encountered circumstances that had a formative influence on his personality and a decisive impact on the trajectory of his career. These circumstances were temporal as well as geographical—a matter of being in the right place at the right time—and they endowed him with a sensibility that was integral to his success. Owing largely to his unique personality and background, the sensibility he developed was unusually inclusive, democratic, and commercial. It made him receptive to things that most of his peers could not appreciate and eventually allowed him to interpret all kinds of music with a power and sincerity that few performers have matched. Equipped with extraordinary charisma, remarkable talent, and this capacious populist sensibility, which inspired him to move across various musical fields, Elvis appeared on the scene when the major popular culture industries were undergoing dramatic changes and were open to something new.

But if Presley's populism helped him succeed in the 1950s, in later years it held him back. As social, political, and economic conditions in America changed, his continued attachment to it made it difficult for him to adapt. Determined to perform the full range of music he loved, he refused to specialize, unlike the vast majority of other musical artists. By the mid-1970s no other performer had such a diverse repertoire, and while this was crucial in cementing the allegiance of Presley loyalists, who loved him precisely because of his catholic tastes, it made it hard for him to attract new fans, particularly younger ones whose tastes ran to the new post-Beatles rock music that explicitly eschewed many of the show-business conventions Elvis continued to follow. Not exactly an oldies act, but no longer a contemporary performer engaged with the musical trends of the era, Presley came to occupy a unique niche in the popular music marketplace that reinforced the bonds between the singer and his audience and prepared the ground for the latter's transformation into a quasi-religious subculture.[5]

To understand Elvis Presley, we need to begin by exploring this context, and turn our gaze away from the trappings of show business and toward his birthplace in Tupelo and a now-vanished world of sharecroppers, gravel roads, and old-time religion. For it was here, in a world barely removed from the nineteenth century, that his remarkable life and career began.

CHAPTER I

From Tupelo to Memphis

FIRST SETTLED BY WHITES in the 1830s, the wooded hill country of northeastern Mississippi was a magnet for aspiring yeoman farmers and their families for most of the nineteenth century. Boasting rich black soil, abundant stores of shortleaf pine and hardwoods, fish-laden streams, and plenty of game, it was an ideal locale for subsistence farming. Before the Civil War, it was a region with few slave owners, where farm families pooled their resources and worked tirelessly to eke out a crude but reasonably secure living.[1]

After the war, the hill country was gradually transformed. Newly emancipated African-Americans, who had been clustered in the cotton-producing Delta, began moving into the area, hoping to acquire cheap land and become yeoman farmers. Railroads connecting the region to Memphis and the port of Mobile were constructed, and with the railroad came entrepreneurs eager to develop the region's resources. Cotton production expanded, and open, unowned lands used by yeomen for hunting, trapping, and the grazing of livestock were bought and enclosed by speculators and wealthy farmers seeking to enlarge their holdings. Forced to adapt to these developments, many yeomen began producing cash crops, especially cotton, to earn their livelihoods.

Over time, however, the price of cotton declined, and increasing numbers of farmers, black and white, became tenants and sharecroppers, renting their land from their well-to-do neighbors and buying, on credit, many everyday goods from merchants who charged them high rates of interest. As the price of cotton and many other staple crops continued to decline in the closing years of the nineteenth century, most tenants and sharecroppers fell into debt. And through new lien laws designed to benefit creditors, landlords and merchants gained a measure of control over the planting decisions of indebted farmers, which they used to ensure that tenants continued to plant cash crops and became even more dependent on them. In short, the commercial development of the hill country, like other areas of the South, resulted in the impoverishment of many of its inhabitants. Even worse, as these trends played themselves out in the 1880s and 1890s, they were accompanied by an upsurge of racial tensions and the passage of new Jim Crow laws that segregated the races and prevented blacks from exercising their voting rights.[2]

By the early twentieth century, Tupelo, the seat of Lee County, had emerged as one of the region's most important commercial centers. Little more than a dusty crossroads before the Civil War, the town owed its growth to its location at the junction of two railway lines, which gave Tupelo's farmers and businessmen access to markets in four directions and inspired town leaders to establish one of Mississippi's first cotton mills. New neighborhoods were soon built, and the town gained several additional mills and factories, most of them tied to the cotton industry. Tupelo's growth encouraged many rural people to move to the town or to the farmlands on its edge, where they could work as tenants, farmhands, or unskilled laborers. By the 1930s over six thousand people lived within the city limits, and many more lived nearby and were enmeshed in its burgeoning economy. In the eyes of many observers, Tupelo was one of the jewels of the New South, a city that had begun to build an industrial economy out of a foundation in agriculture. It was the first city to be electrified by the Tennessee Valley Authority, and by the late 1930s it had all the hallmarks of an up-and-coming city: large, goods-laden department and variety stores, four hotels, numerous restaurants and taverns, two motion picture theaters, a radio station, public schools, parks, a city pool, and a municipal airport.[3]

BUT FOR ALL its forward-looking features, Tupelo retained a rustic ambience and displayed many of the problems that plagued towns and cities in the early-twentieth-century South. Though one could find a job in Tupelo, even during the depths of the Great Depression, wages in the city, as in the rest of the South, were low, roughly 70 percent of what they were in the Northeast and Midwest. Competition for jobs was also intense, particularly since passage of the Agricultural Adjustment Act. This New Deal law, enacted in 1933, established a system of subsidies to landowners that paid them to take acreage out of production and led large numbers of tenants and sharecroppers to be turned off the land. The need for farm labor also declined as landowners purchased tractors, which enabled them to work their holdings far more efficiently—and with fewer hands—than in the past. These trends not only increased the numbers of applicants for jobs in the factories and mills; they encouraged even more people to move to Tupelo and put pressure on existing housing stock and local relief programs for the unemployed. The economic slump was especially hard on Tupelo's black residents, who made up nearly 40 percent of the population. Confined by law and social custom to segregated facilities and the most menial forms of employment, African-Americans in Tupelo lived in a poor neighborhood called Shake Rag. Most worked as unskilled laborers and domestic servants for middle-class white families. The state's Jim Crow laws were no doubt reassuring to many whites in Tupelo; they certainly kept blacks "in their place," subordinate to whites. But by limiting the aspirations of so large a portion of the city's population, they also limited Tupelo's potential for economic development and ensured that a majority of its residents, including most whites, would remain poor.[4]

Thanks to the region's low wages and the difficulties faced by tenants and sharecroppers, many whites in Tupelo didn't live much better than their African-American neighbors. Aside from the city's entrepreneurial class of professionals, business owners, and well-to-do farmers, the most fortunate whites had jobs in the factories or mills. But during the Depression such jobs were difficult to acquire, and when workers at one of the largest cotton mills struck for higher wages in 1937, the mill's management closed it down, putting hundreds out of work and increasing competition for the jobs that remained. Far more than blacks, poor whites in Tupelo were able to take advantage of local public works jobs made possible by another New Deal agency, the Works Progress Administration. Wage levels for WPA jobs, however, were pegged to local standards and could hardly be counted on to lift a family out of poverty. And with so many people moving to Tupelo from the countryside, there was always somebody willing to work for less or willing to put up with conditions others found objectionable. The same squeeze prevailed in the housing market. By the mid-1930s large numbers of poor whites resided within the city limits, in squalid residential areas near the mills or adjacent to Shake Rag. Others lived on the fringes of town, in small, decrepit shacks they rented from farm owners, for whom they sometimes did odd jobs, including working in the fields during planting or the harvest. Across the railroad tracks was the most degraded residential area of all, the hamlet of East Tupelo, where several hundred sharecroppers and marginally employed unskilled laborers lived in crude shacks without running water or electricity.[5]

It was in East Tupelo, just above Old Saltillo Road, in a crude two-room shotgun shack, that Elvis Aron Presley was born on January 8, 1935. Elvis's parents, Vernon and Gladys Smith Presley, were young, poor, and uneducated. Both had left school at an early age to enter the local labor market. Despite their poverty, Vernon and Gladys came from well-established families, and by all accounts Presleys and Smiths had lived in the region for several generations. Like so many other poor whites, the Presleys and the Smiths were drawn to Tupelo by the economic opportunities that proximity to the city afforded, and by the mid-1930s some of them were doing reasonably well. Vernon's uncle Noah, for example, owned a grocery store, drove the school bus, and would serve as East Tupelo's mayor, while Gladys's uncle Gains Mansell would soon become the preacher of the small Assembly of God church where young Elvis and his parents attended services. Other relatives lived close by and provided the young couple with material and emotional support throughout the early years of their marriage.

Gladys and Vernon were in many ways typical of young Tupelans their age. Born in 1912 on a farm in neighboring Pontotoc County, Gladys was dark, pretty, and vivacious, with an enterprising streak that led her to assume important responsibilities after her father died when she was twenty. When she met her future husband, she was working, alongside dozens of other young women from similar backgrounds, as a sewing machine operator at the Tupelo Garment Plant, a local factory that produced work shirts. Vernon, four years her junior, was quiet, even sullen, a hard worker but seemingly without ambition—not a surprising attitude given the hardships that poor young men like himself encountered as they grew to maturity and recognized the difficulties that lay ahead if they hoped to own their own farm or business, like Uncle Noah. He was very handsome, though, and it was his looks that first attracted Gladys.

They met at a church function and soon after ran off to a neighboring town where, lying about Vernon's age to the county clerk to make him appear older, they were married. She was twenty-one; he, only seventeen. When they returned home, they lived with friends and relatives. Gladys went back to work at the Tupelo Garment Plant until she became pregnant and medical problems forced her to quit. Vernon continued working as a laborer and sharecropper for a farmer named Orville Bean, who owned most of the land around East Tupelo and relied on families like Vernon's to work it for him. Bean later lent them $180 to buy the materials to build a small shack next to the slightly larger one where Vernon's parents, Jessie and Minnie Mae, lived. Constructed by Vernon, his brother Vester, and their father, the small house was completed in December 1934, and a month later Gladys gave birth to twins. The first, Jesse Garon, was stillborn and was buried in an unmarked grave in Priceville Cemetery, not far from the family's home.

The second, Elvis, survived. As he grew up, he was taught to revere the memory of his twin and attribute his own survival to mystical forces that had marked him for a special destiny. In later years Elvis would occasionally visit his brother's grave and contemplate why God had decided that he—and not Jesse—should live.

The Presleys were a close-knit family. And, as an only child, Elvis was showered with attention. They were surrounded by kin who helped them when Vernon was between jobs or was forced to leave the area to secure employment, as he did on several occasions during the late 1930s and early 1940s. The focal point of their life was church and the religious revivals that were often held in Tupelo during the hot summer months before the harvest. The Presleys and the Smiths were Pentecostals, a relatively new denomination that had been popular in the South since the turn of the century. Derided by well-to-do evangelicals as "Holy Rollers," Southern Pentecostals venerated the Holy Spirit, and their faith was expressive and enthusiastic. Pentecostal services involved lots of singing, hand clapping, and emotional reveries in which congregants would speak in tongues. It was a faith that relied on the charismatic abilities of preachers. But with its emphasis on individual experience and the ability of the Holy Spirit to reach the soul of every person, no matter how lowly, it was also democratic and attractive to the poor, promising them deliverance from worldly travails. The Pentecostal movement was also distinctly biracial, and though the small Assembly of God congregation that the Presleys were a part of was all white, in keeping with social custom, the revivals drew blacks, too, and the regular services conducted by white preachers like Gladys's uncle were influenced by African-American religious practices. During the early decades of the twentieth century, the years of Jim Crow and white supremacy, the movement "remained almost uniquely open to exchange between blacks and whites," the historian Edward L. Ayers observes. Through its rituals whites like the Presleys were not merely exposed to black influences; they were immersed in a religious milieu in which black and white elements were hopelessly entangled, though few whites recognized this at the time.[6]

ւg faith like Pentecostalism was useful and compelling to
ӗspecially when they were confronted with hard times.
Іhe young ӷamily experienced a severe blow in November 1937 when
Vernon, Gladys's brother Travis, and another man were charged with altering a check from Orville Bean in order to buy a hog. Lacking money
for bail, Vernon and Travis remained in jail until their trial and conviction in May 1938, when they were sentenced to three years at the noto-
rious Parchman prison. Though Vernon was released in early 1939, in
response to a petition from his neighbors and a letter from Bean, his
eight-month absence was deeply unsettling to Gladys and their son.
Without Vernon's income, they lost their house and had to move in with
relatives. Gladys and little Elvis visited Vernon at Parchman on several
occasions, enduring a five-hour bus ride in order to spend a couple of
hours with him. Yet seeing his father in prison was traumatic for Elvis,
and during Vernon's incarceration Elvis and Gladys became closer than
ever, forging a special relationship that would endure for the next twenty
years. Having Vernon taken away in this fashion upset Gladys, too. She
began to worry constantly, even obsessively, about what might happen
to Elvis if she let him out of her sight. The experience was particularly
humiliating for Vernon. It sullied his reputation in Tupelo and made
the Presleys more determined than ever to achieve a measure of
respectability—to make it impossible for anyone to suggest that they
were "white trash," a stigma that haunted even the most hardworking of
poor whites in the early-twentieth-century South.[7]

When Vernon returned from Parchman, he took a job with the
Works Progress Administration as a laborer on a local sanitation project. The regular paychecks enabled the family to rent their own place
and buy an old truck. As the United States geared up for war, and employers with defense contracts began hiring workers in increasing numbers, Vernon took jobs that required him to leave Tupelo during the
week and return home only on weekends. This widened his horizons
and made him aware of opportunities available to unskilled laborers
outside the northeastern Mississippi hill country, in places like Memphis, Birmingham, and the port cities of Mobile and Gulfport. In 1943,

at the height of wartime mobilization, he moved Gladys and Elvis to the Gulf Coast, where he took a job in a shipyard; homesick, they returned after a month. But with so many men in the service or working in distant cities, there were plenty of jobs in Tupelo—though none paid as much as unskilled work outside the region. Vernon was hired as a deliveryman for a local grocer, and with the addition of income he had earned from out-of-town jobs, the Presleys gained some economic security and were able to buy a small house on Berry Street in East Tupelo.[8]

These were comparatively good years for the Presleys. With Vernon working close to home and Gladys supplementing the family's income by performing odd jobs that still allowed her to look after Elvis, the Presleys were able to put food on the table and provide their son with decent clothing and a few toys. Despite their limited means, they spoiled Elvis and encouraged him to feel special, the center of their little world. Eager to escape the harsh, often unfair judgments of their social betters, they raised him to be polite and deferential, and from an early age he made a good impression on teachers and other authority figures. He played with other children, at home and at school, but he was quiet and shy and often kept to himself. He remained very close to his mother, who always seemed to be watching out for him—and worrying when he was playing away from home. By the time he was twelve, he had already begun to chafe at the restraints she sought to place on his freedom, yet he was reluctant to assert himself. Grateful for the emotional security provided by his parents, he rarely strayed far from home or engaged in behavior he knew his parents would disapprove of. Elvis was a good boy, and his parents had every reason to believe that he would make them proud.

His great passion was music. This was not unusual, for the South in the 1930s and 1940s was awash in it. Emanating from the radio, churches and revival tents, juke joints and honky-tonks, even ordinary people's homes, the strains of hymns, gospel, country, folk music, and the blues were inescapable, as much a part of the atmosphere as the hot, humid summer air.[9] Elvis's first exposure to music was at church and at the Pentecostal revivals that were common in Tupelo during his childhood. Here he learned to sing and to appreciate the stirring sounds of gospel, the music that would always remain his first love. But like other white Southerners, he also became an early fan of country music, which in the 1930s was in its early stages of development and was played by ordinary people as well as professional musicians. Derived from Anglo-American folk tunes, genteel parlor music, and, through the influence of Jimmie Rodgers, black spirituals and blues, country music was ubiquitous in the Tupelo neighborhoods inhabited by working-class whites, and the success enjoyed by professional musicians like Mississippi Slim, a local star who had his own radio show on Tupelo's WELO, inspired many young people to pick up guitars and learn to play.[10] On Saturday afternoons the Presleys would go down to the courthouse to hear such aspiring professionals and regular people like themselves perform in WELO's amateur broadcast show. Among the children who lined up for their turn at the microphone was Elvis, who slowly became accustomed to singing in front of a crowd.

This experience paid off. In October 1945, at the age of ten, Elvis won fifth prize in a children's talent show held at the Mississippi-Alabama Fair and Dairy Show, an annual event in Tupelo. Entered into the contest by his fifth-grade teacher, who had heard him sing at school and was impressed with his voice, Elvis delivered a poignant a cappella rendition of the Red Foley ballad "Old Shep." Several months later, on his eleventh birthday, he received a guitar as a gift and quickly learned to play, getting advice and informal instruction from relatives and from Mississippi Slim, whose radio show preceded the WELO amateur hour. By the seventh grade he was taking his guitar everywhere, even to school, where he would sometimes play for classmates at recess and lunch. They weren't especially impressed, but they did feel sorry for him when some toughs at the school cut his guitar strings, and they took up a collection to buy him new ones.

Music was a refuge for Elvis, providing him with moments of joy and transcendence, a sense of accomplishment, and, when he performed in front of people, an opportunity to stand out from the crowd. Yet it could do little to shield him from the hard economic facts that bore down on his family. By the summer of 1946 the wartime labor shortage that had worked to Vernon's advantage had ended, and he found it increasingly difficult to supplement his pay from his delivery job with extra work. The Presleys lost their house and moved to a rental close to Shake Rag; by the fall of 1947 they had moved again, to another rental designated for whites *within* the black district. Though Elvis, like virtually all white Southerners, had been exposed to African-American culture from an early age, it was during this period, when he lived but a stone's throw from black churches and raucous juke joints blaring blues and R&B, that his familiarity with it deepened. For reasons that remain murky, the Presleys—and especially Elvis—emerged from this experience humbled, with a more tolerant and sympathetic attitude toward African-Americans, particularly the hardworking, God-fearing tradesmen and petty proprietors who were their immediate neighbors. Maybe it came from close contact, closer than most white Southerners in the era of Jim Crow ever experienced. Maybe it came from being poor and seeing themselves reduced to living with African-Americans and recognizing the things they had in common. Or maybe it was simply an accident of nature, the peculiar response of an individual human being to a situation that was highly unusual, that wasn't supposed to happen. Whatever the reason, it made Elvis Presley different from most of his white contemporaries and made it possible for him to become a musical pioneer.[11]

By November 1948 things had not improved much for the Presleys. Vernon was still employed as a deliveryman and Gladys was working as a seamstress, but because of their reduced income the family had been forced to take out a number of small loans to make ends meet. Facing the prospect of continued underemployment, Vernon and Gladys decided to move to Memphis. They had been considering such a move for some time. "One day we just made up our minds," Gladys later told a reporter. "We sold off our furniture, loaded our clothes and things into this old car that we had, and just set out."[12] As Vernon knew from firsthand experience and from relatives who had already moved there, Memphis was booming, even more prosperous than it had been during the war. It was a place where he and Gladys could get decent, secure jobs, and where Elvis might be able to continue his schooling and perhaps even finish high school, something very important to Gladys.

The Presleys were not the only people to come to this conclusion. Since the early twentieth century, and particularly since World War II, Memphis had become an increasingly attractive destination for migrants from all over the Mississippi Valley and the hill country surrounding it. With a vibrant manufacturing sector, rail connections to points throughout the United States, and a growing population eager for goods and services, Memphis offered poor, working-class Southerners well-paying jobs and an environment conducive to small business. It was a real city, with amenities and attractions that made Tupelo seem quite provincial. More important, in the 1940s it was a cultural crossroads, a place where migrants from farms, villages, and small towns, blacks as well as whites, were confronted with new circumstances, and where the customs and values they had brought with them were gradually transformed into a new urban-industrial way of life. Living in densely packed neighborhoods, working in factories and on the myriad construction sites that had sprung up around the city as farmlands were cleared to make way for new industrial and suburban development, buying virtually everything they consumed at local stores, including chain stores like the Memphis-based Piggly Wiggly, newcomers to Memphis experienced a life that differed markedly from the one they had led in rural areas— or even in small cities like Tupelo.[13]

Living in Memphis could prove bewildering, but many newcomers were entranced and excited by the city's opportunities and decidedly modern pleasures. For most, industrial employment meant higher incomes and more free time than was the norm for farmworkers. The latter was especially valuable, allowing working-class Memphians to spend their leisure hours at home with family and friends or patronize the city's many restaurants, diners, nightclubs, bars, and theaters. There was no shortage of things to see and do, and thanks to the city's booming economy, which boosted the wages of blue-collar workers, including the growing number of African-Americans able to acquire unskilled manufacturing and construction jobs, many of its pleasures were within reach of the majority. Of course, the city remained segregated, and there were far fewer economic opportunities for blacks than for whites. But most African-Americans who moved to Memphis from the countryside found the city to be a pleasing new home, far better than the poor, often oppressive hamlets they had left. For blacks, the focal point of the city was Beale Street, a raucous, freewheeling commercial district where businesses catering to African-Americans were clustered and where, at night, the sound of rhythm and blues spilled out from the nightclubs into the street.[14]

The Presleys settled into a rooming house close to where Gladys's brother Travis and his family had also moved, and soon Gladys and Vernon found jobs—Gladys as a sewing machine operator, Vernon as a laborer at a munitions factory. They enrolled Elvis in the eighth grade at Humes High School, where, on his first day, he was so intimidated by the large classes and whirlwind of activity that he returned home after less than an hour, nervous and "bug-eyed," Vernon recalled. But he soon became accustomed to his new surroundings, just as his parents became accustomed to theirs. Tired of living in a cramped single room and having to share a hall bath with the house's other tenants, the Presleys applied for public housing. In September 1949, after a four-month wait and an official interview at their rooming house with a social worker, who judged them "very nice and deserving," their application was accepted, and they moved to the all-white Lauderdale Courts, a large cluster of two-story apartment buildings and grassy courtyards built during the New Deal and run by the Memphis Housing Authority.[15] For thirty-five dollars a month, roughly what they had been paying before, they now had two bedrooms, a living room, and their own bath. "Gladys was so thrilled with the Lauderdale Courts place," Elvis's cousin Billy Smith recalled. The apartment became a gathering place for Presleys and Smiths who had moved to Memphis, and Gladys presided over it with pride and good humor. "She was always jolly. Always laughing and carrying on."[16]

Moving into the Courts also provided the Presleys with a new community of people very much like themselves. The community was full of young families eager to make a success of life in Memphis, raising children and teenagers open to the city's sights, sounds, and experiences. The Courts couldn't have been more conveniently located, particularly for the women, who were responsible for shopping, or for their children, who quickly discovered the exciting new world just beyond their doorstep. Main Street, with its stores and movie theaters, was a mere two blocks away. The city's central commercial district was also within walking distance; a bit farther south, also accessible by foot, was the exotic bustle of Beale Street. And just north of the Courts was a major highway that connected Memphis to cities to the east and the west, making the neighborhood and the entire north end of downtown a natural stopping point for salesmen, truck drivers, and servicemen passing through the city.

It was a vibrant, dynamic place to live, and teenagers like Elvis sought to make the most of it. Though Gladys tried her best to keep him on a tight leash, as she had in Tupelo, this was more difficult in Memphis, where attractions beyond home and neighborhood had a powerful allure, and Elvis found plenty of things to do and see after school and on weekends. He made new friends among the many teenagers who lived in the Courts, and together they played football, explored downtown Memphis, and attended the picture shows. One of their favorite destinations was Beale Street, where Elvis liked to window-shop and was dazzled by the flamboyant styles of clothing for sale at the Lansky Brothers men's store. As he soon learned, this was where many professional musicians bought their outfits. At first, it was mostly black rhythm-and-blues musicians like B. B. King and Rufus Thomas who bought their clothing there, the longtime owner Bernard Lansky noted. But then, when white country artists began noticing what African-American performers were wearing, "they used to come in . . . and buy the same things."[17]

After moving to the Courts, the Presleys enjoyed a period of stability and relative prosperity. Taking advantage of the postwar boom, which encouraged workers to seek better opportunities, Vernon took a new job only a few blocks from home, and in 1951 Gladys was hired as a nurse's aide at a nearby hospital. Elvis also began working, first as an usher at a movie theater after school; then, in the summer of 1951, as a drill press operator at Precision Tool, a munitions plant where his uncle Travis was employed. Eventually, in early 1953, Elvis's senior year at Humes, the Presleys were forced to move out of the Courts; their income exceeded the maximum allowable to qualify for public housing—despite a back injury Vernon had sustained that kept him out of work intermittently. They rented an apartment across the street, enabling Elvis to keep in touch with the friends he had made since his arrival from Tupelo.

Elvis's interest in music deepened while living in Memphis. He was thrilled to discover that several other boys who lived in the Courts also played instruments. And as he became comfortable with them, he began to join their informal jam sessions. He was especially impressed with some of the older guys, who taught him new songs and guitar techniques. His most important source of new music, however, was the radio. The range of music played by Memphis radio stations was a revelation to him. Besides the gospel and country-and-western that had dominated the airwaves in Tupelo, Memphis stations played the mainstream pop music that was the rage in other parts of the country, including the records of crooners like Bing Crosby, Frank Sinatra, and Dean Martin. Elvis developed a liking for such smooth pop, and he soon began to include pop ballads in the small repertoire of songs he enjoyed playing and singing for friends. Memphis was also a center of "Negro appeal programming," radio shows specifically directed at the large number of African-Americans who resided in the city and the region beyond its borders. It was the home of WDIA, the "Mother Station of the Negroes," the first station in the United States to devote all its airtime, every minute of the broadcast day, to music, news, and public affairs shows targeted at a black audience. This was the spot on the dial to which Elvis and his friends turned—often surreptitiously—to listen to B. B. King spin R&B records and play his own music live on the air, or hear spirituals and gospel broadcast from services at the local black churches. For music with an even harder edge, there was the wildly popular *Red, Hot, and Blue,* Dewey Phillips's late-night show on WHBQ, which showcased the latest rhythm and blues. Phillips, a white man with a hyperkinetic, slang-filled delivery, was lionized by Memphis blacks and a celebrity on Beale Street. In the early 1950s his show began to attract substantial numbers of white listeners, mostly working-class teens like Elvis.[18]

During his high-school years Presley listened to just about anything he could get his hands on, making few distinctions about genre or the race of the musicians who made it. He began frequenting the local record stores, including Poplar Tunes, a large store that stocked a wide variety of rhythm-and-blues discs issued by independent labels like Memphis's own Sun Records. But his favorite store was Charlie's, a much smaller establishment three blocks from the Courts. It was owned by a man who appreciated true music lovers, and he allowed Elvis and other teenage boys to hang out and listen to records—even if they didn't have enough money to buy any. This was the place where Elvis really became familiar with R&B and developed the vast knowledge of it that, in later years, would so impress people in the music business. Yet his first love remained gospel, a music that was central to family gatherings and that he and his parents would often sing for fun. He enjoyed attending the monthly All-Night Gospel Singings held at Ellis Auditorium, where the South's most renowned white professional quartets would perform. These concerts were major entertainment spectacles. Deftly combining religiosity with the glitz of show business, they were organized by professional promoters and drew thousands of fans, not unlike the multi-artist tours of country acts that regularly passed through the city. Elvis was especially fond of the Statesmen, perhaps the most innovative of the professional gospel groups. Influenced by black quartets and rhythm-and-blues performers like Roy Hamilton and Clyde McPhatter, the Statesmen put on a dazzling show, complete with flashy suits and an expressive performing style, denounced by conservative preachers, that included leg movements that Elvis later appropriated for his own act.[19]

Presley was unusual in the wide range of his musical tastes. While the majority of his white peers liked country music and gospel and much of the mainstream pop that dominated network radio shows like *Your Hit Parade*, only a small number shared his interest in black music. Yet as music industry commentators like *Billboard*'s Paul Ackerman were beginning to note, white interest in rhythm and blues was increasing. This was particularly true among working-class teenagers who were at least partly drawn to the music by a need to differentiate themselves from their parents. The new interest in black music among working-class white teens may well have encouraged them to alter their racial views and acquire a measure of sympathy for the fledgling civil rights movement, as the historians Pete Daniel and Michael Bertrand have argued.[20] But even if listening to black R&B had no influence on their racial views, the fact that increasing numbers of whites were enjoying music designated for blacks angered conservative white supremacists. As one segregationist—writing in 1956, when white interest in R&B had reached an unprecedented level—put it, "alien forces" seeking to "mongrelize our youth and destroy our American Way of Life" were using the "entertainment field" to carry out their sinister objectives.[21]

The rhythm-and-blues records played by Dewey Phillips and available for sale at many of the local record stores were just what many working-class white teens were looking for, a perfect soundtrack for life in Memphis. Tantalized by the prospects of freedom and the new economic opportunities available to working-class people in the city—symbolized by consumer goods like ranch houses, cars, and fancy clothing—yet constrained by the tedium of high school or menial industrial employment, they eagerly responded to a music that was energetic and expressive, that celebrated good times and provided a release from the psychic fetters of the rule-bound workaday world. More important, as they came of age and sampled the new freedoms available to them, their interest in R&B acquired an additional significance, as a marker that set them apart from their parents as well as from their more straitlaced peers who listened to country, gospel, and pop but were unwilling to defy regional racial etiquette by listening to music made by blacks. Encouraged by their new circumstances to defy parental and community authority and embrace a new, expressive individualism, many working-class white teenagers turned to rhythm and blues not merely for fun but for a kind of transcendence.[22]

Elvis was no different. Once he became comfortable in Memphis and at Humes, the shy, awkward teenager began to assert himself more, escaping from the constraints that the perpetually worried Gladys tried to impose on him. With both of his parents working outside the home, and Elvis earning money from after-school jobs, he had the means as well as the opportunity to achieve some freedom. When he wasn't working as a movie theater usher or at one of the factory jobs he held during his high-school years, Elvis played music with his friends, went to the movies, hung out at record stores, or ogled the flashy menswear at Lansky's. Like many white teens, he hid his interest in rhythm and blues from his parents, and his continued affection for gospel, country, and pop kept them from noticing anything unusual about his musical tastes. Despite the many temptations that beckoned, Elvis stayed out of trouble. He studiously avoided the boozing, carousing, and petty crime that some of the other boys engaged in. Ashamed of his father's prison spell and inspired by his parents' determination to achieve respectability, he was deferential and well behaved at school and in the presence of employers, displaying the humble, respectful manners that poor folk had long used to gain acceptance.[23]

The only unusual thing about him was his looks. By the middle of his junior year, Elvis had begun to cultivate an eccentric appearance. Emulating the truck drivers who passed through the city and Captain Marvel, Jr., his favorite comic book hero, he grew sideburns and began combing his hair into a luxurious pompadour, using lots of Vaseline and hair oil to keep it properly styled. With the extra money he earned after school, he bought flashy clothes—mostly shirts—at local department stores and at Lansky's. His frequent window-shopping expeditions attracted the attention of the stores' owners, and they encouraged his interest in the "high-style" clothing worn by professional musicians and an increasing number of urban blacks. The resulting look defied easy categorization. It was undeniably macho, but not in a proletarian kind of way. Indeed, from the vantage point of the young, denim-clad toughs who embodied working-class masculine style in postwar Memphis, Elvis's look was too swanky and redolent of the black dandies who cavorted on Beale Street. But African-Americans were not his only source of inspiration. He was also trying to pattern himself after certain Hollywood movie stars, especially self-styled "pretty boys" like Tony Curtis, one of his favorite actors. One thing was certain: the look he was struggling to develop was undeniably modern and urban, visual proof of his identification with his new home and the comforts and conveniences he associated with it, a new world of consumer goods that, in the heady atmosphere of postwar America, seemed accessible to anyone, regardless of background or upbringing. Drawing on the welter of new influences he had been exposed to since moving to Memphis, including music and the movies, Elvis's new look allowed him to advertise his sense of individuality without having to act out and risk the opprobrium of authority figures.[24]

If Elvis's new look perturbed his parents—and it may well have, considering its associations and the aura of effrontery it exuded—they didn't pressure him to tone it down. Privately, however, his uncle and aunt Travis and Lorraine Smith expressed their disapproval, and warned their children that Elvis would pay a price for his eccentricity. Their son Billy Smith remembers them predicting, "Somebody's going to beat the hell out of him and peel them nigger outfits right off his hide!"[25] Vernon and Gladys were no doubt aware of this possibility as well, and it probably increased Gladys's fears for his safety. But regardless of his appearance, he remained the apple of their eye, and it is very likely that their unconditional love and devotion bolstered his resolve to proclaim his sense of uniqueness.

Some of his classmates were not so tolerant. His new look was particularly offensive to the jocks who dominated social life at his high school. "It was that hair . . . it got him into all kinds of trouble," said Red West, a Humes student who later became one of Elvis's closest friends. "If he had a regular haircut [a crew cut] like the rest of us, he probably wouldn't have been bothered. But I guess the other kids thought he was trying to show off or something."[26] They teased him mercilessly and threatened to hold him down and cut his hair. Yet Elvis refused to be intimidated. Not a very good athlete—athletics were the key to popularity at Humes—or the kind of student who made the honor roll, he became even more determined to maintain his unusual appearance. According to West, it was as if Presley decided, "If I can't be like you guys, then I'm gonna be someone else."[27] He stuck close to his friends, and his warm, unassuming manner won over some classmates who at first were put off by his appearance. Obedient and polite, he also earned the respect and affection of his teachers, despite being a mediocre student. After graduation, several prospective employers were similarly impressed. Gladys Tipler, the owner of an electrical contracting business, was warned about his appearance by the employment agency that sent him over for an interview. She found him so modest, well-mannered, and devoted to his family, however, that she hired him as a deliveryman on the spot.

Presley was never a popular student at Humes, but during his senior year he gained a reputation for something other than his loud clothing and long, painstakingly combed hair. The occasion was a talent show, the "Annual Minstrel," in which Elvis sang and accompanied himself on the guitar. His performance was well received and surprised most of his classmates, who had never known about his interest in music. After this warm reception, he brought along his guitar and performed again at his homeroom picnic, attracting a small group of boys and girls who clustered around him as he sang plaintive ballads in the style of the popular crooners of the day. For the first time a wider public began to think of Elvis as a musician. And the Humes yearbook, published at the end of the semester, listed him among seniors who seemed destined for careers as "singing hillbillies."

Presley graduated in June 1953, fully expecting to assume the responsibilities of adulthood. The previous year he had already held down what amounted to a full-time job, working the swing shift at a furniture factory, but his parents had made him quit when they heard from his teachers that he was falling asleep in class. In the months before graduation, Elvis filled out some applications and interviewed at a state employment office. In the interviews he expressed an interest in becoming a machinist. His need for full-time employment was pressing. Vernon's back problems had grown worse, keeping him out of work for weeks at a time, and the family needed Elvis to provide a steady paycheck. After several rejections and a short stint as a temporary worker, he landed the position with Precision Tool. Yet he disliked the job and his co-workers, who, like the jocks at Humes, taunted him about his hair. He quit in March 1954 and, a month later, went to work for Gladys and James Tipler at Crown Electric, ferrying electrical supplies to construction sites around Memphis. He became close to the Tiplers, and they encouraged him to go to night school to become an electrician. This was a real opportunity for Elvis, a potential route to middle-class respectability. Some of the older boys he knew from the Courts were already well on their way toward such a future, and it is conceivable that if Elvis had applied himself to his work and to night school, his life would have turned out like theirs: hard work and steadily increasing pay, perhaps even the assumption of supervisory responsibilities, and maybe, if he worked hard enough, a chance to start his own business, like the Tiplers. For working-class Southerners from Tupelo, this was success, and it was precisely the future that Gladys and Vernon had hoped for for their son when they moved to Memphis.

Presley's inclinations to settle down and apply himself to work were reinforced in the spring of 1954 by his having his first serious girlfriend, Dixie Locke, a sophomore at a rival Memphis high school. Elvis met Dixie in January at a function at the First Assembly of God Church in South Memphis, where he and his cousin Gene Smith attended worship services and Bible classes. Though the Presleys prayed at home and considered themselves devout, they had not gone to church regularly since moving to Memphis, and it is not surprising that Elvis, the family member most comfortable in their new surroundings, was the first to seek out a congregation that his parents might also eventually join. The principal reason for Elvis's and Gene's interest in going to

church, however, was not religion. It was to meet girls. The congregation they joined was large and still growing; among its members were
the renowned Blackwood Brothers gospel quartet—Gladys's favorite
singing group—and the congregation's choir was well known throughout the city. The minister specialized in fiery denunciations of worldli-
ness and sin, and encouraged congregants to display their faith openly,
in the ecstatic, enthusiastic manner common among Pentecostals.
Dixie's family were committed, God-fearing people, and their approval
of Elvis as a suitor was attributable to his modesty and sobriety, and the
interest he expressed in leading a wholesome Christian life. These professions of faith were not hypocritical. As much as Elvis enjoyed the
worldly pleasures available in Memphis and saw church as a means of
enhancing his love life, he was also serious about religion and committed to trying to live up to evangelical standards of respectability.[28]

Elvis and Dixie began dating and soon were very close. Vernon and
especially Gladys accepted her into the family, and she spent a lot of
time at the Presley home. She and Elvis went roller-skating or to the
movies and on the weekends enjoyed picnics at local parks. Elvis would
often bring along his guitar and serenade her. "He sang songs that were
popular and a lot of the old blues-type songs; he did some of the old
spirituals, too," Dixie told Elvis's biographer Peter Guralnick. Occasionally, his singing attracted the attention of friends and bystanders,
including some of Dixie's friends who thought he was strange. "Right
from the start it was as if he had a power over people . . . It wasn't that
he demanded anybody's attention, but they certainly reacted that
way—it didn't matter how rough they were or whether they even acted
like they were going to be interested or not, they *were*, once he started
singing . . . He loved being the center of attention."[29] Elvis and Dixie
shared a love of gospel music and regularly attended the All-Night
Gospel Singings at Ellis Auditorium, sometimes with Elvis's parents,
where the Blackwoods would perform. From time to time they would
also sneak off with some of the other kids from Bible class to a nearby
"colored" church to hear the impassioned singing and oratory. Elvis

took Dixie to her high-school prom, and they were soon talking about getting married after Dixie graduated from high school in 1956.

It was to Dixie that Elvis confessed his dream of becoming a professional musician—though at the age of nineteen, with full-time work and the prospect of night school and a career as an electrician on the horizon, it was no more than a dream, the sort of fantasy that young people often entertain on the eve of their entry into a life of adult responsibilities. In fact, Presley had begun fantasizing about it long before he met Dixie. It may have first occurred to him when he and the other boys at the Courts began to play music together and he became aware of the thriving music scene in Memphis, where opportunities for professional musicians were plentiful and country and gospel stars were local celebrities who embodied an altogether different ideal of the good life—a life in the spotlight, as the center of attention, with all the material rewards that postwar America had to offer. The chances of ever making it in the music business, however, were so remote that Elvis never did anything about it—not until his performance at the Humes "Annual Minstrel," which finally inspired him to seek out opportunities that might get him a break. Energized by the positive response he had received, and the fact that so many of his classmates now thought of him as a musician—not just some quiet guy with loud clothes and a weird hairstyle—he decided to give the music business a shot. Fearing rejection and the disapproval of his parents, who were determined to see him go into a secure and respectable line of work, he didn't tell anyone about his plans, and during the last few weeks of his senior year, as he began plotting how he might be discovered, he went about looking for full-time employment as if nothing had changed.

In the summer of 1953, shortly after graduation and during a period when he hadn't yet found a full-time job, Elvis paid a visit to the Memphis Recording Service, a studio not far from his neighborhood where anyone could record an acetate for the modest fee of $3.98 plus tax. In later years, Elvis would suggest that his intent was merely to make a record for his mother's birthday, and this account would become central to the myth of his serendipitous "discovery." Yet as Peter

Guralnick has noted, Gladys's birthday had passed several months before, and if all Elvis had wanted to do was make a record of his own
voice, he could have gone down to the department store on Main Street
where his musician friends from the Courts made theirs. In Guralnick's
view, Presley's visit to the small studio on Union Avenue was a calculated act inspired by ambition. He went there to be noticed, to attract
the attention of a man who had recently been written about in the
Memphis papers—the proprietor of the Memphis Recording Service
and of a fledgling label, Sun Records. Not content to wait passively for
his lucky break, he went to impress Sam Phillips.

Phillips, a native of rural Alabama, was a true visionary, but in the
summer of 1953, when Elvis first visited his small storefront studio, he
was struggling financially and frustrated by the hackneyed conventions
of the music business, which discriminated against any music that devi-
ated from the commercial mainstream. Only thirty, Phillips had grown
up around black people on his father's farm and from an early age had
developed a deep affection and fascination for their music and culture—
an interest that gave him a reputation as a crank and eccentric in the
years before World War II, when the vast majority of white Southerners
eschewed the music of blacks and embraced country music instead. As
a teenager, he had gotten into the radio business, and when he moved
to Memphis in 1945, he landed a job as an announcer and programming engineer at the local CBS affiliate. But Phillips soon grew tired of
playing big-band music and began looking for new opportunities. Convinced that audiences in the South could be made to share his love for
the music of African-Americans, he opened a recording studio in 1950
that specialized in it. With the dedication of an archivist and the savvy
of an entrepreneur, Phillips began recording all kinds of black music,
from ragged country blues no different from what he had heard as a boy
to the new electrified R&B that had become the rage on Beale Street
and in the black districts of Midwestern cities like St. Louis, Kansas
City, and Chicago. He leased some of these recordings to independent
labels like Chess and RPM that produced "race music" for the growing
African-American market; others he kept for posterity, relics of a South

that was being obliterated by postwar suburbanization and economic development, what the historian C. Vann Woodward called the "Bulldozer Revolution." To make his new business pay, he hustled for work providing sound systems for public events and encouraging people to come in and use his facilities. "We record anything—anywhere—anytime," his business card read. "A complete service to fill every recording need."[30]

Derided by fellow whites for his interest in "nigger music," Phillips eventually left his radio job to devote all his time to his studio. In 1953 he started his own label, Sun Records, to capitalize on the increasing popularity of rhythm and blues—not just among blacks but also among working-class white teens. Among Sun's first releases were records by Rufus Thomas and Little Junior Parker, and Phillips was confident he could make a profit by tapping into the same market that was proving so successful for other independents. Expecting the market for white pop to continue to grow, the major labels—RCA, Columbia, Decca, Capitol, Mercury, and MGM—were not especially interested in making "race records" anymore, even though demand for them was growing. So the establishment of Sun made economic sense. With so much of the market conceded to independent labels, there was plenty of money to be made there. But founding the label also provided Phillips with a venue to articulate his vision and help musicians express feelings that were often stifled by the pressures to conform to existing formulas. "I went into the studio to draw out a person's innate, possibly unknown talents, present them to the public, and let the public be the judge," Phillips told a journalist in the early 1970s, after he had become a legend. "I went with the idea that an artist should have something not just good but totally unique. When I found someone like that, I did everything in my power to bring it out."[31]

BY 1953 Phillips had become convinced that black R&B held a special allure for many white teenagers and that the racial boundaries that segmented the popular music market—and encouraged Southern whites to see country as "their" music—were beginning to crumble. When they crumbled, he believed, white Southerners would not only listen to black music but come to appreciate its rich heritage, just as he had. This process of discovery, in turn, would spark a broader reconciliation between the races and allow all Southerners to acknowledge their distinctive regional culture, a culture that was a product of blacks as well as whites and defied the segregationist logic of Jim Crow laws. When pressed by business associates to cite evidence for his bold, seemingly foolhardy predictions, Phillips often mentioned the popularity of radio programs like Dewey Phillips's *Red, Hot, and Blue* and the increasing numbers of young whites who were buying race records and venturing into the clubs on Beale Street. (Sam Phillips and Dewey Phillips were not related.) But were these anything more than passing fads? And would they have such far-reaching consequences? As Phillips himself recognized, the white South remained implacably racist. Even before the Supreme Court's landmark 1954 decision in *Brown v. Board of Education*, which compelled the desegregation of Southern schools and gave impetus to the civil rights movement, conservative whites had begun to resist the renewed efforts of Southern blacks to achieve equal citizenship. And white leaders committed to maintaining the racial status quo were acutely sensitive to developments—like white interest in R&B—that might imperil their ability to keep the races apart. In other words, for all the forces arrayed in Phillips's favor, seeming to point toward an increase in the white audience for R&B, others were arrayed against him.[32]

Yet, like a true evangelist, Phillips remained undaunted. After all, the country music popular with whites already bore the influence of blacks, even if few whites realized it, and he was certain that the impediments to white acceptance of black music were artificial and would eventually fall, enabling all Southerners to embrace their shared cultural heritage. Before this could occur, he conceded, the color line in music would have to be blurred. Given the power of white racism, only a white musician could accomplish this, someone "with the Negro sound and the Negro feel," who could effectively express the passion and originality of black R&B and put it into music so infectious that reluctant whites would have no choice but to accept it. If Phillips found such a person, he and his label would profit handsomely. "I could earn a billion dollars," he was alleged in later years to have quipped, in interviews in which he stressed his business acumen. Such remarks have not only become part of the lore of Presley's career; they have also given Phillips an undeserved reputation as a cynical mercenary and have obscured the fact that making money was not his sole objective. Though eager to make a success of his studio and provide for his family, Phillips was also, in his own way, committed to remaking the South. And part of the frustration he felt in the summer of 1953 was prompted by a recognition of the obstacles that lay in his path. Would he ever find a white musician who could help him realize his vision?

When Elvis Presley, guitar in hand, first appeared at the Memphis Recording Service, there was nothing about him that made Phillips or his assistant, Marion Keisker, think he was the one Sam was looking for. It was a hot Saturday in July, and, without air-conditioning, the small waiting room was stuffy and uncomfortable. Elvis was greeted by Keisker, a local radio personality who had become Phillips's devoted friend and accomplice. He asked about making an acetate and, while waiting for his turn, inquired whether she knew of a band that needed a singer. "What kind of singer are you?" she asked him. "I sing all kinds," he replied. "Who do you sound like?" His retort took her by surprise: "I don't sound like nobody." It was an unusual answer and might have been taken as cockiness were it not for his modest, deferential manner, which instantly endeared him to Keisker.

When his turn arrived, she ushered him into the studio, while Phillips manned the controls in the booth. The first song he sang was a pop ballad, "My Happiness," a hit from the late 1940s that he had played regularly for friends. The second was another ballad, which the Ink Spots had made popular in the early 1940s, "That's When Your Heartaches Begin." Neither suggested the range of Elvis's tastes, and his singing was merely adequate. But there was something unusual about his voice, and after he finished, Phillips conceded he was an "interesting" singer. "We might give you a call sometime," he told Elvis as the latter was leaving, and he had Keisker take down his name and address, noting beside it that the young man was a "good ballad singer."[33]

Yet weeks and months passed and Phillips never called. In the fall Elvis would stop by from time to time to make small talk with Keisker and ask again about bands needing a singer. In January 1954 he came in and made another acetate, hoping perhaps that this would remind Phillips of his talent and availability. Once again, however, Elvis's hopes were dashed as time passed without any word from him. Phillips was not Elvis's only option. In the spring, as his romance with Dixie was blossoming, Presley tried out for a spot with the Songfellows, a junior gospel quartet composed of boys he knew from church, including the younger brother of one of the Blackwoods. Much to his dismay, he was rejected. The experience was deeply disappointing to Elvis; one of the Songfellows even had the temerity to tell him that he couldn't sing. And it was several weeks before he mustered the courage to tell Dixie. Despite this setback, Presley tried yet another option. In May he heard from a musician friend whose country band was looking for a singer. He and Dixie went down to a local nightclub, where he auditioned for the bandleader, Eddie Bond. He performed two songs alone, accompanied only by his guitar, and though Dixie thought he did very well, the result was another rejection. In later years Elvis would claim that Bond told him he would never make it as a singer and should stick to driving a truck. "Man, that sonofabitch broke my heart."[34]

By June 1954, then, Elvis Presley's hopes for a career in music were fading. He had pursued several possibilities, but none had panned out, and his new job with Crown Electric had opened his eyes to the prospect of becoming an electrician, a potentially lucrative career during the construction boom of the 1950s. With a steady girlfriend and the strong likelihood of marriage within the next couple of years, Presley had reached the end of his youth. Yet Vernon and Gladys's boy had not merely grown up. Having moved from Tupelo to Memphis, he had become a different person from the one he would have been if the family had stayed in Mississippi. And it was this new person—forged in the crucible of postwar Memphis—that would soon rocket to fame and help to transform American culture. Though still anonymous, one of thousands of young working-class Southerners who dreamed of a career as an entertainer, he had already absorbed many of the influences that would shape his career. Even more important, he had developed the unique sense of self that, with the right encouragement, would blossom onstage and on-screen.

CHAPTER 2

The Hillbilly Cat

HIS HOPES FOR A CAREER in music seemingly dashed, Elvis returned to the routine of everyday life. As the spring of 1954 turned into summer, he spent most of his time behind the wheel of the Tiplers' truck, driving up and down the city's long, straight thoroughfares, delivering supplies and, when possible, making the rounds of his favorite hangouts. After getting off work, he usually went out with Dixie, most often to the movies but also to Riverside Park, where many Memphians gathered on warm summer evenings. He would pick her up in his 1941 Lincoln, which Vernon had bought for the family in 1952, then return her later in the evening, sometimes after a late-night snack of burgers and fries at K's Drive-In on the south side of town, not far from Dixie's house. He would then drive back uptown to the rental unit on Alabama Street that his family had occupied since their departure from Lauderdale Courts, say good-night to his mother, who was usually waiting up for him, and hit the sack.

It wasn't a bad life, and Presley knew it. And every indication suggested that it would remain relatively unchanged, at least until he and Dixie were married. But on Saturday, June 26, he received a call from Marion Keisker, who asked him to come down to the studio. He was there within minutes, eager to demonstrate what he could do.

Sam Phillips had thought of "the boy with the sideburns" who kept hanging around—and whose name he couldn't remember—after receiving a new song from a Nashville publisher, but he didn't have great expectations when he and Presley went into the studio and began working on it. It was another ballad, called "Without You," and they worked on it throughout the afternoon. When it became clear to Sam that Elvis couldn't get it right, he stopped taping and had him try some other songs to get a sense of his range. Phillips sat in the control booth and listened, encouraging the young singer, identifying his influences, trying to discern whether Elvis possessed the spark of originality that he always looked for in a performer.

When they finished, three hours later, Phillips still wasn't sure. Most of the time the boy's singing was conventional, even trite, particularly when he sang the ballads he appeared to prefer. But on several occasions Phillips had glimpsed something else buried amid the pop clichés that Elvis had picked up from the crooners he heard on the radio. What was it? And how might it be released?

After mulling over his options, Phillips decided to see what Presley could do with some additional instrumental backing. He called Scotty Moore, a twenty-two-year-old guitarist. Moore, the leader of a local country band, the Starlite Wranglers, had approached Phillips in the spring about putting out a record, and the two men had become good friends. Scotty would often stop by the studio after his day job at a dry cleaner's, and he and Sam would sit and talk for hours at the restaurant next door, discussing trends in the music business and speculating when the big "crossover" that Phillips had predicted would finally occur. Phillips actually mentioned Elvis during one of these conversations, when he and Moore were talking about potential vocalists for the Wranglers. But this was in May, before Elvis's callback to Sun, and Scotty never followed up. Phillips recorded the Wranglers, and their first Sun record was released in June. When it failed to sell, Moore again became interested in adding a new singer, and after Presley's lengthy session in the studio Phillips suggested that Moore and one of his fellow Wranglers, the bassist Bill Black, get together with Elvis.

On July 3, Moore, identifying himself as a representative of Sun Records, called the Presley home looking for Elvis. Elvis wasn't there—he was at a local movie theater—but Gladys went to fetch him, and when he called Scotty back, they agreed to meet and play some music the following day at Scotty's house.

When Elvis appeared—in a black shirt, pink pants, and white shoes, with his long, greasy hair combed into a ducktail—he made quite an impression. Very quickly, though, Moore and his wife recognized that beneath the loud exterior lay a shy, awkward, painfully insecure young man. Scotty called Bill Black, and after the latter's arrival Elvis began to run through bits of virtually every ballad he knew, with Scotty and Bill falling in behind him. They played for a while before calling it quits, and Moore phoned Phillips later that day to give him a report on the session. Scotty's estimate wasn't much different from Sam's. Elvis had a pretty good voice, but he was nothing out of the ordinary. But Phillips wasn't yet ready to give up on Presley. Despite Moore's middling assessment, he scheduled a recording session for the next evening, Monday, July 5, with Elvis, Moore, and Black. He wanted them to come into the studio so he could hear for himself.

They arrived at about seven, and after some joking and conversation, during which Elvis seemed nervous, they began to play. This time, however, they worked for some time on two ballads, recording one, then the other, over and over again, as Phillips encouraged them and listened to the result from the control booth. He went out periodically to reassure Elvis and help him feel comfortable in the studio, but then it was back to work, back to recording. After several hours it seemed as if they had hit a wall. Everyone was tired and frustrated; Phillips called a break. As Moore and Black relaxed and drank sodas, Phillips occupied himself in the booth. "All of a sudden," Scotty recalled, "Elvis just started singing this song, jumping around and acting the fool, and then Bill picked up his bass, and he started acting the fool, too, and I started playing with them." Phillips immediately pricked up his ears, poked his head out of the booth, and asked them to start over and play it again.[1]

The song Elvis had broken into—Arthur Crudup's "That's All Right," an R&B tune from the 1940s—was very familiar to Sam. He was surprised, however, that Elvis knew it, since Elvis hadn't played any rhythm and blues in his auditions, perhaps believing that as a white singer he was limited to a "white" repertoire of pop and country ballads. Yet it wasn't merely Presley's choice of song that struck Phillips. It was how he sang it, the exuberant playfulness he put into his rendition—a spirit that hadn't been apparent in any of the other songs he had sung and could only come from an appreciation of black music as fervent as Sam's. They worked on the song again and again, Phillips providing instruction from the booth, the musicians tearing into the tune with abandon, and Elvis at last expressing himself in an entirely unaffected way. When Sam played the tape back for them, they were shocked to hear the fruits of their efforts. It was a blues song, to be sure, but done like no blues song ever before. "We thought it was exciting," said Scotty, "but what was it?" It certainly wasn't country; it wasn't the kind of music that white musicians were supposed to make. And right away, Scotty, Bill, and Elvis were aware of this. When people hear this, "they'll run us out of town," they joked nervously.[2] But if they were apprehensive about how their music might be received by white audiences, Phillips was euphoric. This was precisely the sound he had been searching for, a sound he had vaguely imagined and now was hearing for the first time. Here, he was convinced, was the breakthrough that would open the world of African-American culture to Southern whites and unify the twin streams of the region's musical culture, artificially separated by Jim Crow.

They all reconvened at Sun the next evening to work on some new material, but after the previous night the session seemed anticlimactic. Besides, Phillips's mind was elsewhere. He was trying to figure out how to promote the recording of "That's All Right," how to ensure that it reached the widest possible audience. This was more vexing than one might assume. The song was clearly a blues number, and Elvis's version would be immediately familiar to African-Americans and the small but increasing number of white Memphians who listened to R&B. But it was not minstrelsy, not simply a white man doing a credible version of the blues. The song was also indebted to country music, and the strangeness of its sound—strange to blacks as well as to whites—was attributable to its felicitous blending of these influences. The most obvious course was to take it to Dewey Phillips, the host of WHBQ's popular R&B show, *Red, Hot, and Blue*. Dewey and Sam were good friends, and Dewey could always be counted on to provide Sun recordings with airplay.

After a call from Sam, Dewey stopped by the Sun studios after his show, and Sam played him the tape of "That's All Right." Its unique sound startled Dewey, and even after listening to it again and again and talking about it with Sam for several hours, he was uncertain if he should play it on the air—and run the risk of alienating his largely black audience of hard-core R&B fans. By the next morning, however, he had made up his mind. He called Sam and asked for two acetates, which Sam delivered to the radio station later that day. Sam then called Elvis and told him his song would be played on the radio.

That evening Elvis set the radio dial and told his parents not to change stations, but then abruptly went to the movies. "I guess he was just too nervous to listen," Gladys later surmised.[3] But his parents and grandmother Minnie Mae Presley, who had moved in with them, stuck close by the radio as *Red, Hot, and Blue* began. Finally, after a half hour or so of talk and spinning records, Dewey announced he had a new record from Sun that he was sure was going to be a hit, a record by Elvis Presley. Hearing her son's name on the radio was mesmerizing to Gladys, so mesmerizing that she barely paid attention to the song itself.

Yet other Memphians were listening, and the response was like a bolt of lightning. Immediately the station's phone lines lit up with queries about the artist and demands that Dewey play the song again. Dewey happily complied, playing "That's All Right" again and again, as the phone calls and telegrams kept pouring in. In the end, nobody knows exactly how many times in a row he played the song, or how many airings it received before his show ended at midnight. But one thing was certain: people, white and black, had heard the music and responded without knowing the race of the singer. As Sam Phillips put it years later in an interview, savoring his triumph, "They didn't give a fuck about classifying him . . . they liked what they heard."[4]

By midnight, however, the boldness of their gambit had been revealed. Shortly after the calls began coming into WHBQ, Dewey had called the Presley home looking for Elvis, hoping to get him down to the studio for an interview. When he heard that Elvis was at the movies, he dispatched Gladys and Vernon to the theater, a few blocks from their home, to find their son. After going up and down the aisles, they finally located him and sent him to the studio, housed downtown at the Hotel Chisca. Elvis was terrified—"scared to death," he later recalled.[5] After all, he had gone to the movies to sit in the dark and avoid all of this, hoping that when he emerged it would be over. But rather than pass unnoticed—or attract ridicule, as he had feared—his record had become an instant sensation, and he was now being dragged into the limelight.

Dewey sensed Elvis's nervousness and put him at ease by engaging in casual conversation, indicating that he would let him know when the actual on-air interview would begin. But Dewey turned on the mike and never gave him the signal, and before Elvis knew it, the interview was over. During the course of their conversation, Dewey had made a point of asking Elvis where he had gone to high school, knowing full well that the reply, "Humes," would reveal to listeners that the singer of "That's All Right" was white, not black, as the vast majority had probably assumed. So by the end of the evening many Memphians had not only heard the breakthrough Sam Phillips had been plotting for several years. They were aware that it was a breakthrough, and perhaps even aware of what it signified for the regime of Jim Crow.

The success of "That's All Right" dictated that they quickly record a B-side so the single could be released and sold to the public. On July 9, the night after Elvis's radio debut, Presley, Moore, and Black went back into the recording studio. The results were not very promising, with Elvis again displaying a predilection for ballads. Then Black began fooling around, as Elvis had a few nights before, with a classic. This time it was Bill Monroe's bluegrass standard "Blue Moon of Kentucky," a song that Monroe and country musicians covering the tune usually played in a stately waltz time. Black sped it up, and when Scotty and Elvis joined in, the song was transformed into a rousing, up-tempo number. Sam sensed the direction they were going in right away, and he coaxed them to refine the ragged sound they had spontaneously developed, to move it further away from its "hillbilly" roots. Phillips's intervention was crucial. While most producers would have been content with something merely different, a novel take on a song familiar to white listeners, Phillips encouraged them—pushed them, even—to develop an entirely original sound. Some musicians Phillips worked with resented this obsession of his and disliked the "strange" versions of songs he favored. Yet others, like Elvis, came to appreciate his determination and intuitively recognized that at Sun they were not just making music; they were making history.

Presley's first record—with "That's All Right" as the A-side and "Blue Moon of Kentucky" the B-side—was released a few days later and began receiving airplay throughout the Memphis area. When Dixie and her family were driving back into Memphis from Florida, where they had been on vacation for two weeks, they heard "Blue Moon of Kentucky" on the car radio. Many other people who had known Elvis from the Courts or from Humes heard the record, too, and soon realized it was the shy boy to whom they had hardly paid attention. Sales of the single outpaced the ability of the manufacturing plant to produce it, and by the end of October the Memphis *Commercial Appeal* would report that over six thousand copies had been sold in and around the city, to blacks and whites alike.[6] Well before then, in late July, as the local record shops were deluged with orders, Elvis had signed a contract with Sun. It required him to record no fewer than eight songs during the next two years. In return, he would receive a royalty of 3 percent of the wholesale price for every record sold.

Brisk sales and extensive radio airplay in Memphis didn't surprise Phillips, for the ground there had already been prepared thanks to shows like *Red, Hot, and Blue.* It was going to be much harder to generate sales and airplay outside Memphis, particularly in the towns and small cities of the Deep South, where the changes of the postwar era had not been as sweeping and where racial segregation was firmly woven into the social fabric. This suspicion was confirmed in August and September, when Phillips began traveling throughout the South trying to get Elvis's songs played on radio stations and stocked in record stores and on jukeboxes. Though disc jockeys at stations targeting African-Americans were the most receptive, he encountered many who were disturbed by the originality of "That's All Right." It sounded "too white," they told him repeatedly. Disc jockeys at country stations were even more hostile. Most found Presley's music "too black," and some were outraged by his blasphemous version of "Blue Moon of Kentucky." As Phillips later suggested, much of this resistance was unconscious, something "they probably didn't quite understand." Even when many young whites heard Elvis's early Sun sides on the radio or on jukeboxes, they were often confused and uncertain about how to respond. "They liked the music, but they weren't sure whether they ought to like it or not."[7]

These problems confirmed Phillips's belief that only live performances and touring could overcome the obstacles that kept Presley's music from reaching the majority of white Southerners, who remained reluctant to embrace it because of its racial connotations and because, early on, its principal audience was black. Sam first began to explore the possibility of turning Elvis, Scotty, and Bill into a live act in mid-July, around the time the first single was released, arranging for Presley to appear with Moore and Black as the opening act for the Starlite Wranglers at a Memphis nightclub, the Bon Air. Presley made his performing debut on July 17, before a crowd of hard-drinking country music fans. Extremely nervous before taking the stage, he still performed well, and his surprisingly confident manner onstage was a revelation to Phillips, who hadn't yet thought about how Presley and his music would come across as a live act. Despite his inexperience, Elvis had charisma, a kind of presence that enhanced his songs. If he could get Elvis out on the road, Phillips thought, they could build quite a following.

Phillips contacted Bob Neal, a local disc jockey who had been playing Presley's songs on his country-and-western program on WMPS, and Neal agreed to put Elvis on the bill of a "hillbilly hoedown" he was promoting on July 30 at the Overton Park Shell, an amphitheater in a leafy Memphis park. The headliner was Slim Whitman, a veteran of the *Louisiana Hayride* radio program, and the other acts, aside from Presley, were country performers cut from the same cloth. To prepare for the show, Elvis, Scotty, and Bill rehearsed after work, often under Phillips's watchful gaze, and they played again at the Bon Air. A few days before, to give him some much-needed publicity, Marion Keisker took Elvis to one of the newspapers for his first official interview. Eager to push Sam's agenda, Keisker made a point of telling the reporter, Edwin Howard, that Presley's single had become a hit "on popular, folk, and race record programs." Sun's newest discovery had "something that seems to appeal to everybody."[8] This was an important point to emphasize, for Phillips had no interest in forsaking the African-American market in his quest to generate a white audience for his new act. The real significance of Elvis's music, in his view, was that it could appeal to both.

Despite the preparations, Elvis was still terrified on the day of the show. Though Dixie, his parents, assorted relatives, and some of the young people he and Dixie knew from church were there, the audience was much larger than at the Bon Air. And it was an all-white "hillbilly" crowd that might not respond well to his songs. By the time Phillips arrived, just before Elvis, Scotty, and Bill were about to go onstage, Elvis was in a near panic, convinced the audience would hate him. Phillips attempted to reassure him, and after an introduction by Neal the trio came out of the wings and began playing "That's All Right."

After a few moments of clutching the microphone and staring out at the crowd, Elvis began to move with the music. Rather than tapping his toe in the fashion of country musicians, he bounced around the stage jiggling his knees, movements that came naturally as he worked out his nervousness and embraced the spirit of the occasion. In some ways, his leg-shaking resembled the stage movements of Big Chief, the bass singer of the Statesmen. Yet because he was playing an up-tempo song, Elvis's movements were more dramatic and eye-catching. They were further accentuated by his loose-fitting pants, which billowed and flapped wildly—and, as Moore later recalled, "made it look like all hell was going on under there."[9]

The crowd was startled. Many teenagers whooped and hollered in response to his gyrations. At first Elvis thought they were laughing at him, but when the musicians began their second song, "Blue Moon of Kentucky," he realized it was ecstatic approval, and he became more confident. Called back for an encore—another take of "Blue Moon of Kentucky"—Elvis, Scotty, and Bill were even more relaxed and uninhibited. And, Elvis noted, the wilder he got, the wilder the crowd became in response to him. That afternoon Slim Whitman discovered what many other performers would soon learn—that Elvis Presley was a tough act to follow.

Elvis's triumph at Overton Park was followed by performances at another Memphis nightclub, the Eagle's Nest. These shows were also successful, drawing larger and larger crowds and prompting the club's manager to hire Elvis, Scotty, and Bill to play weekends for the rest of the fall. The Eagle's Nest gigs—which his parents, relatives, and the Tiplers often attended—helped Elvis increase his confidence and gave the band additional opportunities to perfect their act and add new songs to their repertoire, usually contemporary rhythm-and-blues hits like Ray Charles's "I Got a Woman." As Presley assumed a new identity as a performer, his flamboyant dress—mostly pink and black—and exuberant stage demeanor began to complement each other, coalescing into a style that differed radically from that of country musicians. Along with his music, it gave him a strange, unclassifiable air, and over the next few months concert promoters and disc jockeys would struggle to categorize him. Not surprisingly, almost all of their attempts emphasized the hybrid nature of his music and performing style. The nickname most commonly applied to him, "The Hillbilly Cat," was most emphatic in highlighting this potentially controversial feature. But such publicity did not dampen interest in him. It made him exotic and more attractive to the increasing number of white Memphians looking for something new.[10]

Meanwhile, sales of Presley's first record remained brisk as both songs continued to receive extensive airplay on both country and R&B programs throughout the city. The record also received a glowing review from *Billboard*'s editor Paul Ackerman, who praised Elvis as a "strong new talent" and noted that his songs appealed to blacks as well as whites.[11] This kind of institutional approbation was vital for Phillips, giving him much-needed ammunition in his campaign to convince radio program directors and disc jockeys outside Memphis to play the new music. Nevertheless, most jocks remained reluctant to play Presley's records, and Phillips was increasingly discouraged as he traveled from city to city and failed in his quest.

Back in Memphis, however, word of Elvis's performances was beginning to get around. In early September he agreed to play at the grand opening of a suburban shopping center, and after advertisements trumpeting his appearance were posted around the city and aired on local radio stations, hundreds of white teenagers descended on the new complex to hear Elvis, Scotty, and Bill play on the back of a flatbed truck—teenagers who had heard Presley on the radio but, like Dixie, weren't old enough to get into the Bon Air or the Eagle's Nest. The response was even more frenzied than at Overton Park; here was clear evidence that their music was reaching a whole new crowd. It was a crowd that had come not for the country music that their parents listened to and that many patrons at the Eagle's Nest preferred. They were there for the new music that Elvis and Scotty and Bill had stumbled upon almost by accident, and that Phillips had coaxed from them and then helped them to refine—a music rooted in tradition yet quintessentially new, driven by a propulsive beat that evoked the vitality and sense of possibility that reverberated throughout Memphis and other booming metropolitan areas during the prosperous 1950s.

Hoping to get Elvis more exposure, Phillips persuaded the manager of the Grand Ole Opry, a weekly concert of country acts broadcast live throughout the South and Midwest, to give Presley a spot on the bill. For white musicians in the South, this was a shot at the big time, and Elvis, Scotty, and Bill were nervous and excited at the prospect of playing the legendary Ryman Auditorium in Nashville and rubbing shoulders with the famous performers who appeared on the show.[12]

Their performance, on October 2, 1954, went smoothly enough, but the audience's response was only lukewarm, and at the end of their act Phillips was informed that while Elvis and the boys weren't bad, they wouldn't be invited to appear on the program again. This was no surprise to Phillips, who had become accustomed to rejection and appreciated whatever attention he could get, "even from people that hated what I was doing."[13] So long as they couldn't ignore Elvis, he knew that sooner or later the disc jockeys and concert promoters who were keeping his music from reaching a wider public would relent.

Sam's determination and confidence were rewarded two weeks after the Opry appearance, when Presley, Moore, and Black were warmly received by the audience and the promoters of another weekly live radio concert program. The *Louisiana Hayride* was broadcast every Saturday night from Shreveport, a long day's drive from Memphis. It was a kind of "junior Opry" known for booking new acts, and exposure on the program had been important for a number of established country stars, including the late Hank Williams. This was a more appropriate venue for Elvis and the Blue Moon Boys, as Scotty and Bill had begun to call themselves, and Phillips was relieved when the program's manager offered them a contract for weekly appearances over the next year. Regular gigs on the *Hayride* gave them an opportunity to meet and impress other performers. They also provided them with a new platform from which to extend their appeal throughout the Deep South.[14]

To take advantage of such exposure, Phillips began working with the Memphis deejay Bob Neal, who had produced the Overton Park show, to get the band bookings in towns and small cities in the large geographical region that the *Hayride* reached—Louisiana, East Texas, Arkansas, Mississippi, Alabama, and Tennessee. Conscious of their appeal among teenagers, Neal supplemented bookings on the nightclub circuit with concerts in high-school auditoriums and other venues that made it easier for younger fans to attend.

By early 1955, when Neal became the band's official manager, these gigs had become more frequent and were attracting large and enthusiastic crowds, and increasing numbers of white disc jockeys had begun to play Presley's records. Some of these deejays, like Neal, were also local and regional promoters, and with their help Elvis and the Blue Moon Boys began to appear on package tours of country performers, often composed of fellow *Hayride* regulars, in locales even farther from their home base. It was through such intermediaries that Elvis, Scotty, and Bill got a chance to tour West Texas and influence young musicians like Buddy Holly and Roy Orbison. Placing Presley on bills with established country acts was a shrewd move. It gave him a measure of legitimacy in the eyes of white audiences and made it "safe" for white teenagers intrigued by his music to become full-fledged fans.

As Presley's career as a performer began to take off, he and Moore and Black returned every few weeks to the Sun studios in Memphis to record new material with Phillips. The two songs on their second single—"Good Rockin' Tonight" and "I Don't Care If the Sun Don't Shine"—were recorded in September 1954 and released shortly afterward. "Good Rockin' Tonight," the R&B classic that served as the A-side, immediately became a staple of their live act. The flip side was a novelty song popularized by Dean Martin that Elvis, Scotty, and Bill completely reworked and infused with a buoyant, carefree energy. Their third single was recorded and released in December. Once again, it featured an R&B tune, "Milkcow Blues Boogie," on one side and an upbeat country-pop song, "You're a Heartbreaker," on the other. Two more singles were released in 1955, and additional songs were recorded during these sessions that would only appear later. Thanks to their constant touring, each single received more airplay than the previous one. Yet while sales were relatively strong, and the singles became substantial hits in a number of urban markets in the South, the label's limited distribution network kept them from reaching very high on the regional charts kept by trade publications like *Billboard* and *Cash Box*.

Their modest sales, however, should not lead us to underestimate their importance. If Presley and the Blue Moon Boys had faded into obscurity after making these recordings, they would still occupy a central place in the history of American popular music. Some of the songs they covered were already well known, and their sound was recognizable to country and R&B listeners, particularly those who preferred the offbeat material issued by independent labels like Sun, Chess, Peacock, and Specialty. Phillips's strategy of pairing country and blues songs was designed to exploit this fact and appeal to both markets. Yet the music they developed at Sun, at laborious sessions directed by Phillips, was also unusual, and often wantonly defied the conventions of both country and R&B. The best of it—"That's All Right," the insouciant "Baby Let's Play House," the eerily hypnotic "Mystery Train," the deeply affecting "Tryin' to Get to You"—was astonishingly original, blurring generic boundaries that, the critic Greil Marcus notes, all white performers "had been raised to respect." What Elvis developed during these early sessions, Marcus suggests, was the nerve and commitment to cross such "borders," and "once that was done . . . those borders dissolved as if they had never existed—for Elvis."[15] In short, while their music drew on the familiar, it was also entirely new, and its originality stemmed not from a serendipitous accident but from hard work and a unique artistic vision.

Even on their more conventional material, country-pop ballads like "I Don't Care If the Sun Don't Shine" or the ebullient "I'm Left, You're Right, She's Gone," there was an energy and an irreverent spirit that distinguished their work from the records of mainstream country performers like Hank Snow, Ernest Tubb, and Lefty Frizzell. As Marcus argues, that same playfulness, and a good deal of humor, infused Presley's interpretations of rhythm-and-blues songs like "Good Rockin' Tonight," "Milkcow Blues Boogie," and "Baby Let's Play House." Reworking the lyrics, injecting a bit of country corn, adding assorted hiccups, whoops, and hollers, Presley made these songs his own and helped to forge a new musical genre, rockabilly, that enraptured many young would-be country singers and sent them on the trail blazed by Elvis.[16]

But it wasn't simply the music Presley and his comrades recorded at Sun that makes them important historical figures—though, on its own, the music was enough. It was also their influence on other musicians, their role in sparking the pilgrimage to Sun Records that Carl Perkins, Jerry Lee Lewis, Roy Orbison, and countless others embarked on after hearing "Blue Moon of Kentucky" or "Good Rockin' Tonight" or seeing Elvis and the Blue Moon Boys play in a nightclub or high-school auditorium. With his expressive performing style, loud clothes, and intoxicating fusion of country and R&B, Presley established a new template for white performers, an alternative to the more conservative and self-contained styles available in the world of country music.

And while this template was clearly influenced by Delta bluesmen and urban R&B "shouters," it was not just a case of whites appropriating the culture of blacks. The rockabilly developed by Presley, Moore, and Black at Sun—and perfected by Perkins and especially Lewis, whose "Whole Lotta Shakin' Goin' On" is perhaps the quintessential rockabilly anthem—was, as Marcus has argued, "as authentically new as any music can be," proof that white boys "could be as strange, as exciting, as scary, and as free" as the black rhythm-and-blues performers who were attracting an increasing number of white listeners. Unlike the infamous "covers" of R&B hits that the major labels were beginning to produce in response to the growing appeal of black music among white teenagers, a campaign designed to soften and "whiten" such material, the best rockabilly was wild and menacing, openly displaying its R&B roots and celebrating a life of excess.[17]

This authentically new sound owed a great deal to the vision and patience of Sam Phillips. Phillips spent hours in the studio with Elvis, Scotty, and Bill, encouraging them to experiment and rework conventional material, pushing them to develop new angles and approaches, setting a mood that kept them on track yet did not confine them. As Dave Marsh has suggested, it is unlikely that Elvis and his band would have been able to conjure this sound outside the privacy of Phillips's studio, which "freed them from the inhibiting effects of audience disapproval."[18] By the time they began playing live, they had already gained confidence in the material, a confidence that Phillips worked hard to bolster.

Phillips was especially careful when dealing with Elvis, whose insecurity made him easily intimidated. Yet as they worked together more and more, Phillips came to the conclusion that Presley's insecurity was an asset, the source of the innocence and authenticity that he brought to virtually any music he sang—a quality Sam had also noted among some of the black blues singers with whom he had worked. During these sessions Elvis revealed a nearly photographic memory for every song he had ever heard, including many obscure blues songs that Phillips was surprised he knew. Sam became increasingly impressed with Presley's instincts, and convinced that the young nineteen-year-old was, in Peter Guralnick's words, a kindred spirit, "someone who shared with him a secret, almost subversive attraction not just to black music but to black culture."[19] These sentiments remained unspoken, but they were part of the bond that developed between Phillips and his protégé, and they helped them to reach the heights they achieved at Sun.

By February 1955, when Presley and the Blue Moon Boys played on a country music program at Memphis's Ellis Auditorium, Elvis had become an established regional star and local celebrity in his hometown. Much of his success was attributable to exposure on the *Louisiana Hayride,* which he and Scotty and Bill played nearly every Saturday. But it was also a result of their nearly constant touring throughout the South, which, as Phillips had hoped, increased public demand for his records. With a regular income from the *Hayride* and bookings several days a week, Presley, Moore, and Black quit their day jobs to devote themselves full-time to music. Before expenses—gasoline and automobile maintenance, hotel bills, and commissions to promoters and Bob Neal—they were now earning in excess of a thousand dollars a week, which they split 50-25-25. This was the formula they had settled on back in August, when they had begun performing regularly, and by early 1955 Moore and Black saw no reason to ask for more, since it was clear that Elvis was the star and that the other two were riding on his coattails. Quitting their day jobs enabled them to accept gigs much farther from Memphis. More important, it gave them more time to record and made possible the long sessions that brought out the best in Elvis and the band.

The money Elvis earned from music—not just his pay from concerts but royalties from Sun as well—was far more than he had been making at Crown Electric, and Vernon and Gladys applauded his success and were happy to see him improve the family's financial status, particularly since Vernon was still plagued by back problems. Elvis was glad to contribute; he had fantasized since childhood about relieving the poverty and economic insecurity that had long dogged his parents. Thanks to his earnings, the family rented a home on Lamar Avenue, in a middle-class neighborhood on Memphis's south side. He also bought them a brand-new Ford Crown Victoria sedan and bought himself a pink-and-white Cadillac, the first of dozens of automobiles that he would purchase over the next twenty-two years. The Cadillac was "a perfect symbol" of his ambitions and working-class sensibility, of having made it on his own terms.[20]

Yet from Gladys's perspective, there was a downside to his success. She felt this from the beginning, and in the early days she often confided to Dixie that she was worried about her boy. Gladys had always been very protective of Elvis, and even during his teenage years had tried to maintain a watchful eye over him. But this became ever more difficult when concert appearances took him away from Memphis several nights a week, and then for days at a time once he and Scotty and Bill began touring more extensively. Though he telephoned his parents nearly every day, this was little comfort to Gladys. She was especially terrified of car wrecks. Her fears were heightened when, in March, a woozy Bill drove Elvis's Lincoln into the back of a truck on one of their return drives to Memphis and again when, three months later, Elvis's Cadillac burst into flames en route to a concert in Texarkana.

Then there were the crazed teenage girls who shrieked at his concerts and sometimes even pursued him offstage. As he developed his act in the fall of 1954, their response to his performances became increasingly frenzied. Elvis, who had always liked to flirt, now had young women clamoring for his attention, and with their attention came many new opportunities for sex and romance. Unfortunately, he found himself the object of ire as well as adulation, since many young men resented the effect the flashy singer had on their girlfriends. Gladys was afraid her son might be injured or even killed by a jealous boyfriend. Or he could find himself "in trouble" with a girl he met on the road. To be sure, Gladys was proud of her son's accomplishments and derived great satisfaction from his success, which she assiduously cataloged in scrapbooks. These feelings, however, were accompanied by a powerful undercurrent of anxiety that only grew as his popularity increased.[21]

Dixie felt much the same way, though she had her own reasons for worrying. They had tried to keep their relationship the same after the success of "That's All Right," and there were times, particularly when Elvis was back at home, when it seemed as if nothing had changed. They went to the movies or to Riverside Park, or spent time at Elvis's house, listening to the new pop and R&B records he was constantly buying. Yet when she saw him perform, she quickly realized the power of the new life that had opened up for him, and by early 1955, as he began to spend more time on the road, she felt it pulling him away. It wasn't simply the bevy of girls that competed for his attention; she knew he fooled around with them. What was drawing him away was less tangible, the seductive lure of show business, a world of glamour and excitement where the moral compass that guided "respectable" folk lost its capacity to provide reliable directions. She saw it in the swagger he gradually acquired offstage, and in the delight he took in being the center of attention, and in the fits of jealousy that would sometimes overtake him, during which he accused her of seeing other guys when he was on the road. For Dixie and Gladys alike, it was as if the world at large were taking him away. "It grew hard for [Gladys] to let everybody have him," Dixie suggested years later, when asked about the impact of Elvis's popularity on his family and their relationship. "I had the same feelings. He did not belong to [us] anymore."[22]

This feeling became more palpable when Elvis, Scotty, and Bill began traveling even farther afield with country performers as part of package tours. These tours were arranged by Bob Neal and Jamboree Attractions, a booking agency run by the country star Hank Snow and a veteran promoter and manager, Tom Parker. They placed Elvis and the Blue Moon Boys on programs in large venues throughout the South, where Elvis shared the bill with Snow, one of country music's most popular singers, and such well-known artists as Faron Young and Mother Maybelle and the Carter Sisters. With the extensive promotional resources of Jamboree Attractions behind him, these concerts were widely publicized in advance, and with Presley's Sun recordings receiving more and more radio airplay, increasing numbers of people came out to see "The Hillbilly Cat."

Elvis never let them down. He was a sensation wherever he played, even before thoroughly "country" crowds, and he continued to refine his act in response to the audience's reaction, adding gestures that went over well, jettisoning those that fell flat. On these tours he observed Snow and the other musicians on the show, and eagerly sought them out for advice and pointers. His enthusiasm and sincerity impressed his fellow performers, compensating for the bruised egos that resulted when he stole the show. To maximize Presley's impact yet keep Snow and the other established stars happy, the promoters put Elvis and the Blue Moon Boys at the end of a program of "younger" talent, right before an intermission.

By May 1955, Elvis's popularity as a live act had swelled, bringing him to the attention of show-business insiders who were coming to recognize his potential. The crowds at his concerts, now composed largely of teenage girls, screamed and moaned at his every gesture, sometimes storming the stage at the conclusion of his act. The wildest scene occurred in Jacksonville, Florida, at a concert in the brand-new Gator Bowl. After finishing his last song, Elvis flippantly told the crowd of fourteen thousand people, "Girls, I'll see you backstage." The result was pandemonium as hundreds of young women ran after him, tearing off his clothes and his shoes before the police were able to sequester him in the stadium locker room. The Jacksonville incident was unusual in the large number of fans involved, but near riots occurred at other Jamboree-sponsored gigs in the spring and summer of 1955, demonstrating Presley's star power. As Elvis gained experience as a performer, he acquired an air of poise and self-possession onstage that enabled him to blow away the well-established country musicians with whom he appeared.

One of the show-business insiders most impressed with Presley was Jamboree's Tom Parker, a mysterious figure who had worked on the circus and carnival circuit in Florida before becoming the manager of the country star Eddy Arnold in the 1940s. The quintessential self-made man, Parker was Dutch, and his real name was Andreas Cornelis van Kuijk. He had come to the United States as an illegal immigrant in 1929, taking the name Parker to protect him from expulsion. After a stint in the U.S. Army, during which he was stationed in Hawaii, he settled in Florida and eventually moved into show business, working for circus companies and coordinating personal appearances for some of the film and country music stars who spent winters there. These contacts eventually led him to become a full-time manager of talent, and during the early 1940s he became involved with Grand Ole Opry stars like Roy Acuff and Ernest Tubb. In 1944 he began managing Arnold, a handsome, accomplished country singer with a voice and look that, Parker sensed, had potential mainstream appeal. Dropping all his other commitments, he devoted himself completely to promoting Arnold, bringing all the bluster and conniving tricks he had learned in the carnival industry to the realm of show business. No manager was more determined and relentless on behalf of his client. Parker's vulgarity and unabashedly crude down-home style led many adversaries to underestimate him in negotiations, an advantage he knowingly exploited. But driving hard bargains was the least of his gifts. In his own way, he was just as much a visionary as Sam Phillips, and his adroit handling of Arnold's career revealed an uncanny ability to discern—and develop strategies for capitalizing on—the emerging trends of the day.[23]

THE TREND that Parker exploited in his promotion of Arnold was the growth of America's emerging "national culture." Through the innovative institutions of commercial popular culture—feature syndicates, newspaper wire services, mass-circulation magazines, radio networks, major record companies, and Hollywood studios—it was now possible to achieve a new level of fame and material success. But as Parker recognized, reaching these heights required satisfying the tastes of a broad national consumer market, a market that transcended local and regional tastes and was composed of people eager for stories, programs, music, and movies with high production values and familiar narrative and musical motifs. To appeal to this national market of consumers, one often had to smooth the edges off material that had played successfully to local and regional audiences. The idea was not to make everything the same but to make it familiar, part of a larger world of high-quality, brand-name products that were attracting increasing numbers of Americans who liked to think of themselves as forward-looking and up-to-date. From this vantage point, the success one could gain from dominating a peripheral field like country music—the epitome of "making it" for the vast majority of Southern musicians and their managers, who still thought in local and regional terms—was small-time, a mere stepping-stone to the larger rewards of mainstream acceptance offered by the national radio networks, the pop music charts, and Hollywood.[24]

Under Parker's guidance, Arnold quickly topped the country charts and began achieving some crossover success. But for Parker, this was only the beginning of the ambitious plan he had developed for his only client—a plan he worked on with a zeal and dedication that surprised even Arnold. By the early 1950s, through Parker's ceaseless labors, Arnold had become affiliated with the William Morris talent agency and had appeared in several Hollywood films; he had been a guest on the wildly popular Milton Berle television program; and he had played Las Vegas, an up-and-coming gambling resort that was seeking to attract high rollers from around the United States.

These moves into the entertainment mainstream were unprecedented for a country performer, and Parker's estimate of the importance of the new medium of television as a means of exposing artists to a wider public was a stroke of genius. Parker was also shrewd in appreciating the place Las Vegas would soon occupy in the emerging national culture of show business. The owners of the new hotel-casinos were determined to provide their well-heeled guests with lavish shows featuring the most famous and accomplished performers. In Parker's view, the support of such high rollers—many from the Hollywood and show-business establishment—was crucial to gaining access to the full complement of opportunities provided by the national popular culture industries. In a few years, he correctly surmised, the imprimatur of Las Vegas would distinguish performers who had reached the "big time," achieving elite status across various media.[25]

Parker and Arnold eventually had a falling-out, however, and in 1953 Arnold stunned his manager by firing him. Chagrined by his reversal of fortune, Parker returned to booking package tours of country acts, establishing a partnership with the singer Hank Snow. It was in this capacity, as the promoter and manager of Jamboree Attractions tours, that Parker encountered Elvis Presley. Bob Neal was eager to have Elvis, Scotty, and Bill join one of Jamboree's tours; he had heard of "Colonel" Parker (the title was an honorary commission conferred by the governor of Louisiana, an old show-business chum), and he was certain that Parker's promotional acumen could enhance the group's visibility, enabling them to get better bookings and boosting sales of the Sun releases.

Accordingly, he arranged a meeting in February 1955 between Parker and his Jamboree associates and Elvis, Scotty, Sam Phillips, and himself. At the meeting Parker agreed to add Presley and the Blue Moon Boys to Jamboree tours, and in the ensuing months he had an opportunity to see for himself what the young singer was capable of. Here, he soon discovered, was a talent more prodigious than Eddy Arnold. But it wasn't Elvis's music so much as his charisma and effect on audiences that aroused Parker's interest and convinced him he had found a figure even better suited than Arnold for mass appeal.

At first Parker worked through Neal, who remained Presley's manager and assumed the task of securing bookings outside the South. Not long after their first meeting with Parker, Elvis, Scotty, and Bill drove to Cleveland—where large numbers of Southerners had moved since World War II and a thriving hillbilly and R&B music scene had developed—for their first concert in the North. It was a rousing success, even though Sun's distribution network didn't reach that far and Presley's records were known to fans only through radio airplay. Elvis's performance impressed Bill Randle, a well-connected Cleveland deejay who helped Neal get Presley an audition for *Arthur Godfrey's Talent Scouts*, a weekly television program that showcased unheralded artists. The audition required a plane trip to New York City, an experience that was exciting and somewhat intimidating for Elvis and the boys. But the tryout, held on March 23, 1955, was a failure. The Godfrey people found Elvis nervous and poorly prepared, and they were disturbed by his appearance. Disappointed, Elvis, Scotty, and Bill returned to Memphis and continued touring for the rest of the spring and summer. Back on their home turf, their popularity only grew, and Parker became convinced that with the right promotion and management, Elvis could succeed in New York and become a national sensation.

By the end of the summer Bob Neal had begun to receive inquiries from some of the major record labels. Several scouts had heard Elvis's records and seen him perform, and they shared Parker's optimism about the young singer's potential. Neal responded to these inquiries by asserting that Sam Phillips had no interest in selling Presley's contract. In a sense, this was true. Sun was enjoying real success, and Elvis's breakthrough had inspired many young musicians to flock to the studio to work with Phillips and produce music in the same vein. But as Neal was aware, there were real limits to Sun's promotional capacities, and even with the money Phillips was now making from Elvis's records, the label's limited distribution network restricted Presley's reach, particularly in the Northeast, a region Neal was sure Elvis could conquer.

Parker had pointed out these problems back in February, at his meeting with Elvis, Neal, and Phillips, and over the course of the summer he kept emphasizing them to Neal, who was soon convinced. Phillips, who took an instant dislike to Parker, disagreed, but by the fall his resistance to selling Presley's contract had weakened—particularly since interest among the majors had grown markedly. It was clear he stood to make a lot of money from any deal.

Meanwhile, Parker and Neal worked out an arrangement in which Neal remained Elvis's manager but Parker, as a "special adviser," assumed control of booking performances and long-range planning, seemingly ensuring a key role for Neal. In fact, this agreement paved the way for Parker to take over management of Presley's career, something Neal didn't realize until several months later.[26] Until then, Neal encouraged Elvis to put his faith in Parker and trust the decision both older men had reached—that it was in his best interest to leave Sun and sign with a major label.

At first Elvis was reluctant. He was comfortable with Sun, and he appreciated the way Phillips had nurtured his talent. Yet he could not deny the facts that Neal laid out before him. When he continued to dither, Parker went around Neal and appealed to Vernon Presley, who quickly jumped on the bandwagon. Vernon's enthusiasm for signing with one of the majors helped to undermine Elvis's resistance. But Gladys remained obstinately against the move and fiercely suspicious of Parker. Vernon, too, continued to have reservations about the gruff, cigar-chomping promoter, but he was won over by Neal's endorsement of Parker's arguments for signing with a big label. To mollify Vernon and especially Gladys, Parker dispatched Hank Snow to convince them of the Colonel's business acumen and honorable intentions. These small gestures sealed the case, though Gladys never got over her distrust.

On November 21, 1955, executives from RCA Records, a firm Parker had dealt with extensively, arrived at Sun Studio and bought Elvis Presley's contract from Phillips for the princely sum of thirty-five thousand dollars. In exchange, RCA received not simply Elvis's services for the next year—and potentially longer, since the company had the option to renew—but all the tapes and masters he had recorded for Sun. Elvis received a five-thousand-dollar bonus and a 5 percent royalty, for which he was expected to produce eight sides per year.

It was an extremely lucrative contract for a performer with only a regional following, and several of the RCA people worried that Parker had induced them to make a colossal blunder. After all, Presley was a performer from the South, a cultural backwater, making a new music that derived from marginal influences that seemed far removed from the high-gloss pop that dominated the musical mainstream. What if he fell flat before audiences outside his native region? What if the music he specialized in was a passing fad? What if this naive young man lost his head amid the pressures of a national buildup?

For Phillips, the sale of Presley's contract to RCA evoked mixed feelings. On the one hand, it gave him a much-needed infusion of cash to pay off debts and develop the new talent that had come to Sun since the breakthrough of July 1954. He was also able to invest in production and distribution, allowing Sun records to be purchased in areas outside the South. These developments enabled Carl Perkins, Johnny Cash, and Jerry Lee Lewis to acquire followings throughout the country, and paved the way for Lewis to become a national sensation whose Sun sides battled with Presley's RCA recordings for supremacy on the pop charts. Yet handing a talent like Presley over to a crass promoter like Parker rankled. There was no denying the Colonel's brilliance, as the RCA negotiations revealed. Phillips had asked for a sum almost 50 percent larger than any major had ever paid for an established singing star, and Parker had gotten RCA to agree. And there was no doubt that under Parker's guidance, Elvis would become very rich. But what about his gift? What about that innocence and intuitive feeling that Sam had discerned and helped to bring out? Would Parker appreciate it? Would he even recognize it? Would it be sacrificed to the bottom line?

Sam Phillips's feelings about Parker eventually came to be shared by many of Presley's fans, inspiring a myth about Elvis's "corruption." In this account, a version of the proverbial Faustian bargain, Parker seduced Elvis by promising that he could make him a mainstream success. In the process, Presley's unique talents were squandered, and Elvis himself became frustrated and unhappy. According to the myth, only Gladys, Elvis's anchor and closest confidante, could see through the Colonel's snow job; only she understood what would be lost when Elvis became a huge star.

Like many myths, this one contains more than a kernel of truth. Gladys was, in fact, the lone holdout against her son's signing with

Parker. And she was genuinely fearful about what would happen to him if he became as successful as Parker predicted he would. There were also pitfalls in the strategy Parker devised to make Elvis a successful mainstream entertainer. In less than three years Elvis would be complaining to friends that he felt trapped into following the course laid out by his manager, a course he might not have followed on his own.

But the myth does not comport with all the facts, and it encourages misleading impressions of Presley and Parker alike. As Peter Guralnick has persuasively argued, Elvis's ambitions were much grander than those of most white singers in the postwar South. Bob Neal, for one, knew this, and this was the principal reason why he thought Elvis would be well served by Parker's management. He had seen Presley work hard to improve his act, learning tricks from other performers, striving to outdo them in a fashion that was rare and revealed a burning hunger to succeed. And on the long drives back to Memphis from gigs, Elvis had confided to Bob's wife, Helen, that he hoped to one day become a movie star, to "go all the way."[27] Presley, an obsessive movie fan and a longtime reader of comic books, began his career with hopes and expectations that were already influenced by the products of a national mass culture, that looked beyond the local and the regional, that defined success in terms that were not merely national but unabashedly mainstream—at a time when, as Parker recognized, the mainstream was in the process of being enlarged and was open to new influences.

Thus it was perfectly natural for Elvis to be attracted to the kind of mainstream success that Parker seemed able to guide him toward, since Elvis's vision of a successful career was in many ways similar to the Colonel's. Indeed, considering Parker's track record with Eddy Arnold, perhaps no other show-business manager at the time was better suited to help him realize his grandest ambitions. No other manager was as savvy about negotiating the largely uncharted currents that could sweep a performer from the margins into the commercial mainstream, or could see so clearly how nascent trends, like the development of television or the emerging purchasing power of teenagers, were changing the rules of promotion and marketing. And if, in the end, the result turned out to be less fulfilling than Elvis had hoped, this was no fault of Parker's. He did his job. Not only did he make Elvis Presley a successful singer; he also helped him achieve his wildest dreams.

For Elvis, the urgent, irrepressible rockabilly of the Sun era was his entrée into the mainstream, not an end in itself. The Hillbilly Cat was but a temporary incarnation, and the musical revolution that Presley and his fellows inaugurated was a mere prelude to a career that would take him to Nashville, New York, and eventually Hollywood, far beyond the world of rock and roll.

CHAPTER 3

Elvis the Pelvis

IT DIDN'T TAKE LONG for Colonel Parker to swing into action. Within days of Presley's signing with RCA, his new manager began issuing a steady stream of letters, telegrams, and phone calls from his office outside Nashville, where he lived with his wife, Marie. Pulling out all the stops, he pressured his partners and associates to exploit *all* their connections on behalf of his newest client. He was in constant contact with RCA officials, offering advice on the rerelease of some of Elvis's Sun records and making arrangements for Elvis's first RCA recording session, scheduled for early January in Nashville. He was also busy planning new tours for the winter that Presley would headline and that would take him beyond his regional base. But his most determined efforts were directed at his contacts at the William Morris Agency, to whom he had entrusted the job of getting Presley on television, a more feasible prospect now that Elvis had signed with the industry powerhouse RCA.[1]

Television was the key, the vital medium that Parker was certain could catapult Elvis to stardom. Far more than most managers and talent agents, he recognized that America had entered a new era that would be shaped by television, and that all the other popular culture industries—mass-circulation journalism, radio, the major record labels, even the big Hollywood studios—would have to revise their products in its wake. Invented in the 1930s but introduced only gradually over the course of the 1940s and early 1950s, television had already become a fixture in the majority of American homes. Thanks to technological innovations, vigorous competition among manufacturers and retailers, and rising incomes, even many working-class families could afford a set, and by the end of the 1950s nine out of ten households would have at least one of them.[2]

Television provided Americans from different regions and backgrounds with a common source of entertainment and shared experiences, encouraging viewers to see themselves as part of a single national audience. With its wheels greased by abundant advertising revenues, its programming crafted by the same executives and creative personnel who had dominated network radio and had perfected strategies for attracting a broad mainstream audience, and its wares distributed through a system of affiliate stations that reached from coast to coast, television was the perfect platform for any performer seeking mass appeal.[3]

Parker's efforts bore fruit in early December, when the producers of *Stage Show*, a variety program hosted by the bandleaders Jimmy and Tommy Dorsey, agreed to have Elvis appear on their show for four consecutive weeks beginning in late January. Presley would receive $1,250 for each appearance, with a chance to earn even more if the Dorseys and their producers exercised their option to have him return for additional performances. The Dorsey show, broadcast on Saturday evenings on CBS, was a ratings laggard, but it provided Presley with a chance to get some much-needed national exposure. Parker was hopeful it would attract interest among Hollywood executives, and as the date of Elvis's first appearance neared, he implored his William Morris contacts to ensure that prominent movie producers would be watching.

Even while Parker was in the process of negotiating the terms of Elvis's first television appearances, the two of them flew to New York for a meeting with RCA officials. The purpose of the trip was for the top brass to meet their newly signed singer, and for Elvis and the Colonel to begin working with the marketing and publicity staff who would now assume a major role in promoting him. The meetings were productive and informative for both parties and continued in January, when Presley returned to New York to appear on the Dorsey show. Anne Fulchino, RCA's publicity director, was impressed: "He was a very quick study . . . This was a kid who knew where he wanted to go, and he was very single-minded about it."[4] Taken with Presley's intuitive grasp of the business and of the kinds of things that would be expected of him, she gushed about their meetings when she reported back to Steve Sholes, RCA's point man in Nashville and the person responsible for getting new material from him. But Sholes was still plagued by doubts. Until he had some potential hits on tape, he couldn't be sure that the label hadn't made an expensive mistake. And when, early in that same January, Sam Phillips released Carl Perkins's "Blue Suede Shoes," which quickly began to rise on the charts, his doubts deepened. The new Sun release seemed destined to be a huge crossover hit. Had RCA signed the right man?

Sholes's apprehensions, which were shared by some other RCA people, were heightened by a growing sense that the pop music market was in flux, and that the conventional formulas RCA and the other big labels had followed for most of the 1940s could no longer guarantee success. To be sure, over the past year the sweet pop of the McGuire Sisters had attracted a large audience, and the year's biggest hits included Mitch Miller's "The Yellow Rose of Texas" and Dean Martin's "Memories Are Made of This," the epitome of pop conventionality. But 1955 had also seen some big surprises. For example, among the year's biggest sellers was a mambo-influenced instrumental recorded by the Cuban bandleader Pérez Prado, and in the fall the country singer Tennessee Ernie Ford topped the pop charts for several weeks with "Sixteen Tons," a remake of an old folk tune. Publicity from the film *Blackboard Jungle* had lifted a song featured in the movie, Bill Haley and the Comets' "Rock Around the Clock," to No. 1 during the summer. Haley's song, deeply influenced by the R&B of Big Joe Turner, was more pop than rhythm and blues, but its success among teenagers was a revelation to music business executives like Sholes and helped to convince RCA to make the investment in Elvis.

Despite a raft of covers by white artists like the Crew-Cuts and Pat Boone, sales of rhythm-and-blues records had increased during 1955, especially among whites. Fats Domino, a veteran of the New Orleans music scene, had a huge hit with "Ain't That a Shame," while Chuck Berry, newly signed to Chess, rose to the top of the R&B charts and to No. 5 on the pop charts with his first single, "Maybellene," a song as lively and original as the best of Presley's Sun sides. Richard Penniman, a young Georgian who went by the name Little Richard and had released some little-noticed records for RCA in the early 1950s, also burst onto the scene. His first single for the Los Angeles–based indie label Specialty, "Tutti Frutti," didn't sell as well as Berry's first single, reaching No. 2 on the rhythm-and-blues charts and only No. 17 on the pop charts, but he brought a wild new sound to the market that influenced many performers, including Elvis. The vocal group the Platters did best of all. Inspired by the example of the Ink Spots, who achieved great success on the pop charts in the 1940s with a smooth, romantic sound, the Platters developed a unique doo-wop music that was purposely designed to attract a crossover audience. Their first big hit, "Only You," made the top five, but it was their next one, "The Great Pretender," that really shook up the industry. Released near the end of the year, it quickly shot to No. 1 on both the pop and the R&B charts.[5]

New styles were clearly emerging, and they were beginning to outsell the kind of music that had dominated the pop charts—and earned huge profits for the majors—since the end of the war. And they were doing so by expressly catering to teenagers and finding a place on the playlists of disc jockeys who were not afraid to tailor their shows to the tastes of youth. One of these deejays, Cleveland's Alan Freed, who had been playing music by black and white performers on his highly rated show since the early 1950s, began calling the new music "rock and roll," and soon enough the name began to stick. But it was still unclear whether it would last or was merely a fad, as many music business veterans secretly hoped.[6]

Steve Sholes's worries were only partially allayed by the results of Presley's first RCA recording session, held in Nashville on January 10 and 11, 1956, at the studio where Sholes recorded his stable of RCA country acts. Elvis, Scotty, and Bill were joined by D. J. Fontana. Fontana, a drummer who had played with them at their *Louisiana Hayride* shows and at some gigs during the fall, soon became a full-fledged member of the group. Also present were some well-regarded session men that Sholes kept on retainer, the pianist Floyd Cramer and the guitarist Chet Atkins. The addition of Cramer and Atkins gave the group a fuller sound, while Fontana's drumming provided a rhythmic anchor that had been missing from the music they made at Sun. Several of the songs they recorded were already staples of their live act, but they also produced two ballads and an offbeat blues tune that Sholes had sent to Elvis in advance of the session. The latter, a Mae Axton song called "Heartbreak Hotel," was unlike anything Elvis had ever recorded, and when they were done, it sounded even stranger, a haunting piece that would leap out of the radio when it was issued as his first single at the end of January.

But Sholes wasn't happy; nor were RCA officials in New York. The masters revealed that Sholes hadn't come close to capturing the distinctive sound that Phillips had gotten out of Elvis at Sun. To hedge their bets, Sholes arranged another session in New York in late January. Here Elvis recorded additional material that would be on his first album—and give RCA additional product should "Heartbreak Hotel" fail to capture the public's fancy.

On Saturday, January 28, Presley made his television debut on *Stage Show* before a relatively small studio audience that was mostly unacquainted with him. Introduced by Bill Randle, the Cleveland-based deejay who had gotten him the audition for the Godfrey show, Presley burst out onto the stage, where Scotty and Bill were waiting, and began a rollicking version of Big Joe Turner's "Shake, Rattle, and Roll." At the instrumental break, he moved away from the microphone and started shaking his legs and hips wildly. The crowd was surprised, even shocked, and some people in the audience laughed at his movements and frenetic delivery. Without pausing, the band segued into another of Turner's R&B hits, "Flip, Flop, and Fly," also played at breakneck speed. Then it was over, and with a bow Elvis left the stage almost as quickly as he had entered. It was a powerful performance. But only the Memphis papers took notice, and it hardly seemed to mark a breakthrough.

In hindsight, however, it was one. It gave Elvis a much-needed dose of confidence, which he then brought to his recording sessions, his live act, and his subsequent Dorsey appearances. His performances on the program over the next few weeks got better and better. At his third, he finally sang "Heartbreak Hotel," though with Scotty and Bill virtually hidden in the shadows and the Dorseys' big band adding in- strumental accompaniment, it didn't sound much like the single. He also performed a rousing rendition of Perkins's "Blue Suede Shoes," which had already become a regular feature of his live act. At his fourth appearance, on February 18, he sang one of his recently recorded bal- lads, "I Was the One." By this time, "Heartbreak Hotel" had begun to get nationwide radio airplay, and demand for the record had sharply in- creased. In early March it would finally enter the pop charts, rising to No. 1 by mid-April, much to the relief of Sholes and his superiors at RCA. Noting Presley's increased popularity, the producers of the Dorsey show decided to sign him for two more performances in March. Soon other television programs were calling Parker to see if Elvis was available.

Everything, so far, was working according to Parker's plan. Elvis's first RCA album was released in late March and quickly rose to No. 1. As national airplay fueled demand for Presley's records, the audience for his television appearances grew. And with each television appear- ance, the buzz surrounding Elvis intensified, drawing new fans to his records and concerts, which Parker had adroitly scheduled between *Stage Show* appearances.

Elvis was also terrific with the press, submitting to lengthy inter- views during his tours and while staying in New York. As reporters dis- covered, Presley's wild, sensual, and exotic demeanor, which so excited audiences, completely vanished when he stepped offstage. In inter- views he came across as modest, well-mannered, and very eager to please. His gracious behavior when in the company of journalists was much appreciated by Parker, who recognized that the success of their plan depended, in large part, on Elvis's ability to ingratiate himself with the press and project a wholesome image that offset—and complemented—the more "dangerous" one he projected while performing. Parker rarely had to remind Elvis to behave, and Presley's intuitive understanding of media relations led his manager to develop a new respect for him. By the end of May, after "Heartbreak Hotel" had topped *Billboard*'s pop and country charts and reached No. 3 on the R&B charts and Presley's next single, "I Want You, I Need You, I Love You," was also selling at a rapid clip, the people at RCA had become believers, too. As Parker had predicted, they had signed not just another country act but "America's Newest Singing Sensation."

Elvis was overjoyed. So were his parents, who avidly followed his career and were amazed at the large sums of money he now earned. They had already moved from the Lamar Avenue rental to a larger home a few blocks away, in Sam Phillips's neighborhood, before Elvis signed with RCA. And in May 1956, flush with money from royalties, they moved again, purchasing a large five-bedroom ranch house on Audubon Drive, in one of the city's affluent upper-middle-class neighborhoods. For the first time they had lots of space, and Elvis was pleased to have been able to buy such a home for his parents. They bought new furniture, redecorated, and even put a pool in the backyard.

By the spring of 1956, with Elvis on television and his records reaching the top of the charts, the Presleys were very comfortable. Vernon managed the family's finances, a role that enabled him to make up for the many months he had spent unemployed. Gladys presided over their spacious new home. In her well-appointed kitchen she prepared Elvis's favorite meals, and when she was not keeping house or watching her favorite programs on television, she worked on the scrapbooks that documented her son's illustrious achievements. More important, she continued to offer Vernon and Elvis reassurance and emotional security.

Elvis remained the dutiful son, but he displayed greater interest in spending money and entertaining himself. He bought more cars for his parents and himself, including a series of Cadillacs. He also bought lots of clothes at Lansky's and records at Poplar Tunes, indulging himself to a degree unimaginable only two years before. It was a wonderful life, and one that had been realized with extraordinary speed. Working-class people less than three years removed from public housing, the Presleys were now homeowners in an affluent neighborhood inhabited by Memphis's professional and business elite. And though their snooty neighbors may not have welcomed them with open arms, they could not prevent them from moving in. For the Presleys, for all their hillbilly airs, were white and had the requisite admission ticket: enough money to purchase a house in that particular neighborhood.[7]

Unfortunately, Elvis spent even less time at his new home than he had at the rentals. Besides trips to New York and weekly appearances on the *Louisiana Hayride*, from which Parker finally freed him at the end of March, Presley continued performing throughout the South and mid-Atlantic region during the first half of 1956, playing large venues—usually municipal auditoriums seating several thousand people—as a headliner. With his new RCA releases zooming up the charts, his visibility enhanced by television guest spots and, by late spring, notices in national publications like *Time* and *Newsweek*, these concerts attracted huge crowds and inspired a new level of hysteria among fans. At most gigs the screaming was so loud the musicians couldn't hear themselves play and had to rely on Elvis's movements for cues. "It was like being in a sea of sound," recalled Scotty Moore.[8]

The tours were organized and overseen by Parker, who assumed control over even the smallest details, from the opening acts—no longer musicians, who might distract the audience from the supposed center of attention—to the color of the publicity posters. Everything was more businesslike, which was especially disconcerting to Moore and Black. With revenues increasing weekly, the Colonel quite consciously kept them and D. J. Fontana on small salaries—two hundred dollars a week when they were touring and a retainer of a hundred dollars a week when they were not—and he made it clear that he would have axed them had it not been for their relationship with Elvis. In response to heightened interest in his "boy," Parker also upped the fee that he demanded for television appearances and continued badgering his contacts at William Morris about getting Elvis a Hollywood screen test.[9]

Finally, the film producer Hal Wallis, impressed with Elvis's stage presence on the Dorsey show, agreed to pay him to come out to Los Angeles at the end of March. Wallis saw Presley as a natural for the emerging teen market, which had begun to attract resources from the major studios and independent producers and would soon lead the industry to produce a new genre called "teenpics."[10]

Elvis was delighted, and it was with high hopes that he flew to the West Coast and appeared at the Paramount lot. The screen test took place over three days and required him to perform dramatic scenes as well as lip-synch and dance to his own music. He performed well enough, "like a lead in a high school play."[11] His abilities as a dramatic actor, however, weren't of much interest to Wallis. Elvis's popularity was his principal asset; in the short run, it would certainly draw large numbers of teenagers to any movie in which he appeared.

The question was whether his charisma would translate to the big screen and make it possible for him to have a career as a movie star who appealed to a wider audience and specialized in roles that included singing and dancing, a path followed most successfully by Bing Crosby. That question was answered almost instantly when he began lip-synching and dancing to "Blue Suede Shoes." According to an eyewitness, "The transformation was incredible . . . electricity bounced off the walls of the soundstage." Elvis was clearly movie-star material; he oozed charisma and sex appeal. Now it was a matter of finding the right vehicles for him, films that would build on his teenage fan base but point him toward the mainstream.

From the start, though, Elvis had other things in mind. He informed Wallis of his interest in playing straight dramatic roles, even suggesting himself as the lead for a biopic about the late James Dean. But awestruck by Hollywood and eager to please, he did strictly what Wallis and the others asked of him, unwittingly encouraging them to believe that he would be happy to work in any kind of picture, at least for the next few years. Wallis had encountered many aspiring actors who expressed such ambitions, and his response to most of them was a bemused indifference. Who were they to judge their talents and marketability? To overcome this indifference, actors had to be assertive, opportunistic, even pushy—hardly traits that an easily intimidated neophyte from the South was likely to possess. Ironically, Wallis's inclinations to dismiss Presley's ambitions were reinforced by Elvis's inclinations to be deferential and pliable, especially in a new, unfamiliar arena like Hollywood.

At the end of April, after several weeks of brutal negotiations in which Parker pressed Wallis relentlessly, Presley signed a contract with the producer and Paramount. It was a one-picture deal, with Elvis receiving fifteen thousand dollars, but it gave Wallis the option to have Presley make as many as six more films, with Elvis receiving increasing payments for each project, culminating in a hundred-thousand-dollar payment for the seventh, and final, film. The contract also gave Presley the right to make one picture a year with another studio, unless Wallis paid him a comparable fee not to. It was a brilliant strategic maneuver by the Colonel. By arranging Elvis's movie deals to avoid binding, long-term commitments that would limit his options, Parker ensured that the major studios would compete for Presley's services. He and his client were now poised to reap a fortune from movies well into the 1960s.

Even more farsighted was Parker's decision to book Elvis for a two-week engagement at the New Frontier Hotel in Las Vegas beginning at the end of April. Parker knew it was a long shot, but he was eager to see how Elvis would fare in front of an older, well-heeled crowd. Presley and the band were nervous, particularly at their first few shows, but they did their best, with Elvis adding self-deprecating humor between songs to loosen up the audience. The engagement was still a disaster. Most patrons were more interested in gambling, and some audience members who did listen expressed shock and bewilderment at the "noise" emanating from the stage. Yet there was an upside. Elvis absolutely loved Las Vegas. During the long days before their two short evening shows, he and his cousin Gene Smith, who had accompanied them as a roadie, spent hours hanging around the pool and flirting with waitresses and showgirls. He met the singer Johnnie Ray and the flamboyant pianist Liberace, one of his mother's favorite performers, and saw as many shows as possible. At one, a performance by Freddie Bell and the Bellboys, he heard a cover song he thought might work in his act, Big Mama Thornton's R&B hit "Hound Dog." With entertainment of one sort or another available virtually around the clock, Las Vegas was an ideal playground for the energetic, irrepressible Elvis. "Man, I really like Vegas," he told a newspaper reporter when he returned to Memphis after his engagement. "I'm going back there the first chance I get."[12] True to his word, it became one of his favorite vacation spots.

Capitalizing on Presley's mushrooming popularity, Parker continued to solicit offers from television producers and soon arranged for Elvis to appear on two episodes of Milton Berle's variety show. Nicknamed "Mr. Television," the former Catskills comedian was one of the most popular performers of the day, and his NBC show earned high ratings. Presley's first appearance, for which he received three thousand dollars, coincided with his screen test in Hollywood. Broadcast from the deck of an aircraft carrier moored in San Diego Harbor, the show increased Elvis's national visibility and revealed that he had reached a new level of self-assurance as a performer. Elvis and his band played bang-up renditions of "Heartbreak Hotel" and "Blue Suede Shoes," and he also appeared in a comedy sketch with Berle.

The second appearance, broadcast from Berle's regular NBC studio in Burbank, California, was on June 5. Once again there was the usual comedic banter with Berle, but this time Elvis performed his latest single, the ballad "I Want You, I Need You, I Love You," and a blistering version of "Hound Dog," now the showstopping finale of his live act, adding suggestive bumps and grinds to the ending. It was yet another tour de force, and the show garnered high ratings, winning its time slot for the first time that season.

But in the wake of the second Berle appearance, Elvis became the object of fierce criticism. Television critics for the national press led the way. His leg movements and pelvic gyrations, declared a critic for the New York *Daily News,* were more appropriate for "dives and bordellos" than for a network television show.[13] Most of his critics were no more charitable about his singing, which was assailed as vulgar and unintelligible. Writing in *The New York Times,* Jack Gould insisted that Presley had "no discernible singing ability."[14] And many critics expressed concern about the response he elicited from his audiences. Teenagers at his shows went wild, they reported in tones that mixed shock with earnest self-righteousness.

These attacks continued throughout the rest of the year as prominent politicians, clergymen, and newspaper columnists around the country joined in. Older performers added their voices to the swelling chorus. "Rock 'n' roll smells phony and false," Frank Sinatra, himself a former teen idol, asserted in a *Time* article on the new music in 1957. The musicians who played it were "cretinous goons," and its "sly, lewd . . . dirty lyrics" were inspiration to "every sideburned delinquent on the face of the earth."[15]

By today's standards, the criticism seems shrill. But Sinatra's comments were typical and reveal some of the deeper anxieties stoked by the rise of rock and roll. Expressed in the stilted language then preferred by press agents for serious remarks on issues of the day, they not only cast rock and roll as an inferior musical form but also linked it to the lower rungs of the socioeconomic ladder and the widely publicized problem of "juvenile delinquency." As a self-styled representative of the entertainment mainstream, Sinatra was drawing a line in the sand, suggesting that the new music coming to dominate the pop charts—and displacing the smooth, Tin Pan Alley pop that had defined the musical mainstream since the decline of swing in the early 1940s—lacked artistic value. It was a simplistic, formulaic music cynically crafted to appeal to the lowest common denominator, the worst example of "mass culture." Wrapping himself in the mantle of middlebrow gentility, a sensibility that greatly influenced the educated public and vast numbers of aspiring middle-class Americans in the 1950s, Sinatra relegated rock and roll to the cultural trash heap.[16]

Beyond rock and roll's aesthetic qualities, many critics condemned

Elvis and his fellow rock and rollers for the tremendous influence that the new music and its unorthodox stars were having on teenagers. Here lay the significance of Sinatra's allusion to sideburned delinquents. Viewed as a serious social problem in the years after World War II, juvenile delinquency was, in fact, no more widespread in this era than in previous ones. But for a variety of reasons it became a widely publicized issue, a lightning rod for adults and other authority figures concerned about the rise of youth culture.[17]

For most of American history, people between the ages of thirteen and twenty had identified with their parents, extended families, and ethnic and local communities. Few institutions segregated them by age or encouraged them to identify with their peers. Before the early twentieth century even public schools mixed pupils of different ages together in classrooms, and work and family responsibilities kept most young people, many into their twenties, from enjoying much personal autonomy. What money they earned went back to the family, and the low wages paid to the vast majority of workers made it very difficult to live independently, encouraging obedience and loyalty to parents and kin. Before World War II, the lone exception to this pattern of dependence and identification with family was the "sub-deb" set—affluent, upper-middle-class teens who were disproportionately represented in many of America's high schools and the dominant group at most colleges and universities. Constituting less than 10 percent of young people their age, these teenagers were the first targets of advertising and marketing campaigns that emphasized their youth, and the first to assert their autonomy from their parents and families. But the youth culture they developed in the late 1920s and the 1930s was exclusive and had little influence on the vast majority of teenagers.[18]

By the late 1940s, however, a different, more inclusive youth culture had begun to emerge. It embraced a far wider array of teenagers, and its tone was frequently set by working-class teens, to whom some middle-class teens now looked for inspiration and tips on being "cool." This new culture was made possible by a number of developments. The first was the grouping of large numbers of teenagers from a variety of backgrounds in new, comprehensive high schools. These began to appear in the 1930s but proliferated after World War II as the number of high-school-age Americans increased and more and more working-class families, because of rising incomes, were able to keep their children in school. Though students in such schools were segregated, with the college-prep track dominated by middle-class teens and the vocational track dominated by the sons and daughters of factory workers, the sheer number of working-class students gave them an unexpected influence over the tenor of student life and created new opportunities for contact with middle-class students in the hallways, in the cafeteria, and during after-school activities.[19]

The second development that made the new youth culture of post-war America more inclusive was affluence. Teenagers in the 1950s had little memory of the Great Depression, and their formative experiences occurred during the economic boom sparked by World War II. The boom continued after the war, fueled by government spending on the emerging Cold War and a host of new social programs created during the 1930s and 1940s that made the majority of Americans more economically secure. Rising incomes and abundant jobs encouraged working-class families to leave their children in school and provided teenagers with opportunities for after-school and weekend employment and a better shot at keeping a large share of their earnings. As teenagers from a variety of backgrounds began to earn money from their own jobs, and parental demands that older children contribute to the "family wage" declined, teenagers emerged as consumers in their own right, becoming attractive to businessmen eager to tap into the new "teen market," which now included large numbers of more prosperous lower-middle-class and working-class Americans. By the mid-1950s, when Elvis arrived on the scene, an increasing number of products were being crafted for teenage consumers, and the habit of buying these products led many young Americans to identify with one another as much as with their parents.[20]

The third development was subtle but just as important. Far more than mainstream consumer culture, which had become more restrictive and conformist since the advent of the Cold War, the new youth culture celebrated pleasure, instant gratification, and "kicks," an ethos that could spark conflict between teenagers and their parents, most of whom had little experience with the kinds of peer-group pressures that now affected American teens. From the teenagers' point of view, cruising in cars with their friends and listening to rock and roll at dances, concerts, or even alone in their bedrooms were declarations of independence announcing the importance they placed on their own tastes and desires. These declarations were not necessarily rebellious, and by the early 1960s experts were encouraging parents to view them more tolerantly, as an inevitable phase of adolescence. Yet in the 1950s they were interpreted as an affront to both tradition and the new ideal of "togetherness" that psychologists, social workers, advice columnists, and educators were promoting to ensure that the nuclear family remained the linchpin of morality and the social order. Middle-class parents were especially concerned. The new youth culture encouraged mingling across lines of class, ethnicity, and even race, and its defining ethos and cultural style were influenced in part by working-class teenagers.[21]

These parental concerns were galvanized by the official outcry over juvenile delinquency. Predisposed to be wary of "mass culture," which was widely thought to resemble propaganda in its capacity to narcotize and brainwash ordinary consumers, many educated adults were quick to blame the mass media for making their teenagers more willful and defiant. And, in some respects, who could blame them? Since World War II the products of commercial popular culture—everything from movies, network television programs, and *Life* to comic books, lurid pulp fiction, and new publications like Hugh Hefner's *Playboy*—had become even more visible and easy to acquire. They were now widely available in many small towns and once-insular neighborhoods, and they offered consumers there, including the young, alternatives to the provincial norms that had long prevailed in such communities.

The stakes, moreover, seemed unusually high. The Cold War had inspired fears that a nation besotted with affluence might not be strong enough to withstand the threat posed by Soviet totalitarianism. As numerous commentators noted, meeting this threat required resolve and moral fiber, not only among ordinary Americans but especially among leaders and future leaders. With so many hopes invested in middle-class youth, the fear that they were being corrupted by an ethos of care-free self-indulgence resonated widely and acquired the stature of a genuine social problem.[22]

For many middle-class parents, rock and roll appeared to be one of the most dangerous conduits through which this ethos spread. Marketed at a biracial audience that was increasingly peer-oriented, the music exuded a vitality and irreverence that alarmed adults concerned about its cumulative effects. Had its popularity remained confined to a small subculture of young, dissolute working-class males—a group long relegated to society's margins by teachers, social workers, employers, and the police—there might not have been much of a controversy. But when rock and roll began to appeal to a much larger white teen audience, an audience that included girls as well as the middle class, the music became a more serious threat, and its producers became the targets of criticism and official inquiries.

In response to this outcry, record labels began to produce sanitized covers of R&B hits by white artists like Pat Boone and encouraged their black artists to "sweeten" their sound. The appearance of covers, however, did little to slacken demand for the real thing—not least because obstinate disc jockeys like Alan Freed and Bill Randle continued to play the original versions. And though the new, "sweeter" pop sound achieved by black groups like the Platters and the Drifters was less offensive to rock and roll's critics, it made their music even more popular among whites and created a larger African-American presence on the pop charts. By early 1956, in the wake of Elvis's Sun records and the first efforts of black artists like the Platters, Fats Domino, Chuck Berry, and Little Richard to appeal to the crossover market, the new styles that Freed called rock and roll were not only taking over the popular music market. They were inspiring musicians to develop even more novel hybrids that combined elements of R&B, doo-wop, country-and-western, swing, and Tin Pan Alley pop. These musicians were white as well as black, and their music was consciously designed to appeal to teenagers of all races. By 1957 some of them—Berry, Domino, Buddy Holly, the Coasters, and the Drifters—were appearing as part of "package" shows featuring black *and* white acts, or were playing before integrated audiences.[23]

Even more disturbing than working-class influence, then, was the degree to which, through crossover products like rock and roll, the new youth culture displayed the influence of African-Americans, particularly the urban black working class. Long associated in the middle-class mind with riotous living, this was the worst possible group for whites and blacks alike to emulate. Unlike the African-American middle class, which embraced the self-help ideology popularized by Booker T. Washington, a certain portion of the black working class had responded to discrimination and limited opportunities by at least partially rejecting the values of self-control and self-improvement that were central to the ideal of middle-class respectability. In many communities, especially in the urban North but also in Southern cities like Memphis, working-class African-Americans created a lively subculture that revolved around nightlife, alcohol consumption, and sexual gratification.[24] Vividly evoked by Malcolm X in his *Autobiography,* this was the subculture from which rhythm and blues emerged, and though the vast majority of black and white artists making rock and roll offered teenagers mere hints of such earthy pleasures, it was altogether too much for many adults, arousing nightmares of illicit pleasures and "mongrelization." The fact that large numbers of white teenagers were listening to music that was "black" in origin and often brought blacks and whites together sparked fears that support for white supremacy might wane. Such concerns were most acute in the South, where the civil rights movement had begun its assault on the legally sanctioned racism of Jim Crow. Yet they also pervaded much of the North, where racial prejudice was just as strong.[25]

These concerns about race, class, and youth were accompanied by a growing sense that the sexual values of middle-class America were under attack. Since the 1920s and increasingly after World War II, advertisers and other agents of consumer culture had relied on titillating sexual imagery to sell products, and by the mid-1950s such imagery had spread throughout much of the nation's popular culture. The new visibility of sexuality in the culture reflected important changes in sexual behavior. Encouraged by social and geographical mobility, which removed many Americans from the direct oversight of parents and extended families and gave them a new degree of freedom, rates of nonmarital and premarital sex had increased since the early twentieth century; so had the incidence of teenage pregnancy, which after World War II rose the fastest among middle-class whites. The widely publicized Kinsey Reports, which were published in 1948 and 1953, appeared to confirm that many Americans—not just those on the social margins—were violating the traditional values of sexual self-control. Postwar affluence and the self-indulgent ethos of consumerism, as well as recurrent fears of nuclear war, which sharpened public interest in the pleasures of private life, led large numbers of Americans to embrace a more expressive, informal, leisure-oriented style of life.[26]

Yet even as most Americans were moving along this path, others resisted it, organizing boycotts and pressure groups that focused on the most blatant examples of immorality. Often led by well-heeled religious conservatives like the Cincinnati businessman Charles Keating, these groups had little hope of turning back the tide of consumerism, which would create a far more permissive social milieu by the 1970s. But their protests and boycotts compelled politicians and other civic leaders to take notice. More important, their focus on the potential impact of a sexualized popular culture on teenagers and children won them the support of many Americans who were ambivalent about their own self-indulgent inclinations.

For conservatives and the substantial number of middle-class Americans who shared at least some of their views, Elvis Presley embodied their worst fears. He was unabashedly proletarian, a poorly educated former truck driver who was clearly entranced by his newfound wealth. And he displayed indifference toward traditional middle-class standards of taste and notions of upward mobility. To the consternation of his critics, Presley expressed no interest in literature, current events, or the "responsibility" of entertainers; unlike Pat Boone, who attended

Columbia University, he revealed no burning hunger to go to college or become a "cultured" person. Even his manners and respectful demeanor were unorthodox, betraying the insecurity and bewilderment of an un-lettered country boy, not the polish and self-command of a middle-class gentleman.[27]

He was also from the South, a region Northerners and the New York–based media elite had long viewed as a degraded cultural cesspool, and a representative of a social group widely ridiculed by many Ameri-cans, including middle-class Southerners embarrassed by their poor kinsmen. Newspaper criticism of Elvis dripped with contempt for "hill-billies" and his native region; many published interviews quoted him in dialect, a treatment most commonly reserved for blacks.[28]

Then there were the racial echoes he exuded. Presley's music ex-plicitly displayed the influence of African-Americans, and his popular-ity among blacks, demonstrated by the success of his records on the R&B charts, far exceeded that of any other white performer.[29] With the heavy makeup he had taken to wearing during his concerts and flashy Beale Street–inspired wardrobe, Elvis even looked racially ambiguous, reinforcing fears that rock and roll might contribute to race mixing and miscegenation. To the dismay of many of his critics, many young men—and smaller numbers of young women—were soon imitating his dress and hairstyle, as the "Presley look" became a feature of the new youth culture.

Finally, there was the matter of his performance style. Onstage, "Elvis the Pelvis," as some newspapermen called him, exhibited an ex-pressiveness that was utterly foreign and off-putting to whites accus-tomed to the restrained mannerisms of mainstream pop or country performers. It was an expressiveness that was frankly sexual, and thus easily linked in the minds of his critics to other assaults on the culture of reticence. At a time when advertisers were becoming wary of of-fending the sensibilities of conservative consumers, when pressure groups like Charles Keating's Citizens for Decent Literature were on the offensive, sparking official investigations and threatening boycotts, and when the nation's mainstream popular culture industries were engaged in a blatant program of self-censorship designed to improve their reputation in the eyes of the public, Presley not only offered Americans a very different kind of music; he was also a different kind of star.

This was, of course, exactly what led many teenagers to embrace him. He seemed new and refreshing, and when he came under attack and it became an act of rebellion in some homes to listen to his records and openly declare oneself an Elvis fan, he was transformed into a symbol of youth culture, a figure many teenagers claimed for their own because of the reaction he elicited from parents. Being an Elvis fan became yet another way for them to declare their independence from their parents. Ironically, then, press criticism of Presley, rather than limiting his popularity, made him bigger than ever and helped to inspire scores of imitators—fellow musicians who soon joined him at the top of the charts, and countless teenagers who made the Elvis look, precisely because of its rebellious connotations, ubiquitous in high schools around the country. The extent of his influence, in turn, amplified the threat he seemed to pose and made many adults all the more hysterical about him.

Elvis was shocked and dismayed by his critics. As he explained in countless interviews, he wasn't doing anything out of the ordinary. Black R&B musicians had been playing music similar to his for years, and he was simply following in their footsteps and responding to public demand. "I enjoy rock and roll," he admitted to a New Orleans disc jockey in the summer of 1956, shortly after his second Berle show appearance. "A lot of people like it, a lot of people don't. But as long as it lasts, as long as it sells, I'll continue doing it, as long as that's what the people want."[30] Presley hated the nickname Elvis the Pelvis and was especially distressed by charges that his pelvic gyrations were vulgar and calculated to arouse the libidos of female fans. He insisted that his movements were perfectly natural; he moved his body in rhythm with the music "because I enjoy what I'm doing." In an interview with a writer for *TV Guide* a few weeks later, Elvis proclaimed, "I'm not trying to be vulgar, I'm not trying to sell sex." Noting that scantily clad actresses regularly appeared on television and sparked little controversy, he suggested his critics had a double standard.[31]

But he most avidly defended his fans, occasionally showing rare flashes of anger. During his *TV Guide* interview, Elvis lashed out at a Miami columnist who had condemned his fans as hysterical morons. Those screaming teenagers were "somebody's decent kids, probably . . . raised in a decent home," Presley noted. "If they wanna pay their money to come out and jump around, and scream and yell, it's their business. They'll grow up someday and grow out of that. But while they're young let them have their fun." He insisted that the notion that listening to rock-and-roll music could lead to juvenile delinquency was ridiculous.

For Elvis, rock and roll had no overtly rebellious connotations. Though his parents didn't listen to R&B and had frowned on his interest in it, regarding it as "lowdown," their objections were mild, and they did nothing to stop him from listening to it and playing it once he began performing. They were so happy to see him succeed. Accordingly, Vernon and Gladys were as dismayed as Elvis by the criticism directed at him. During his rise to stardom as a regional performer, many older country music fans had been alienated by his version of "nigger music," but the only controversy he had sparked in the South was over crowd control and his own personal safety. But when the national press began to attack him, many Southern newspapers, politicians, and civic leaders joined the assault as well, giving the original critique a distinctive regional spin. With segregationists denouncing the new music as a menace to Jim Crow, other institutions of the Southern establishment were compelled to voice their objections.[32]

Technically, Elvis and his parents were right: he was doing nothing out of the ordinary, only trying to make a living in a fickle, highly competitive field and drawing on sources that were native to his region and ought to have been familiar to any white Southerner. However, a white man playing a hybrid music for a biracial audience in the mid-1950s was too much for many Americans, even Southerners who, under different circumstances, might have been proud of his success and defended him against Northern critics whose digs at Elvis were also digs at the South. What the Presleys missed was this new context, and the still-potent cultural authority enjoyed by the Northeastern media elite, who had the power to determine when a phenomenon constituted a social problem. It was this media elite that objected to Elvis Presley, and when they did so, other institutions of the "official culture," including those in the South, followed suit. Of course, their claims would have fallen on deaf ears if elements of the American public had not shared many of their concerns. Whipped into a frenzy by the Cold War, the rising tide of hedonism unleashed by postwar affluence and the new youth culture, and the escalating African-American challenge to white supremacy, many white Americans were prepared to believe that rock and roll posed a mortal threat to the American way of life.

Colonel Parker, for his part, saw only dollar signs in the controversy. The focus on Elvis might be unfair, as the Presleys insisted, but it also gave him a tremendous advantage. By the summer of 1956 there were many performers who might have become the most popular and successful rock and roller; because of the publicity he was attracting, however, it was Elvis. But managing the controversy in a way that would enable them to profit from it was still a tricky business that sometimes required a tactical retreat. For example, when NBC executives expressed concern about Presley's upcoming appearance on *The Steve Allen Show*, Elvis and Parker were forced to play by Allen's rules, an experience that proved humiliating to Presley. On the program, broadcast on July 1, Elvis appeared in a tuxedo and sang "Hound Dog" to a basset hound; he also took part in a comedy skit lampooning Southern culture. The show achieved high ratings and impressed the William Morris people, who were more concerned about the controversy than Parker, but it also inspired some of Presley's New York fans to protest with signs reading, "We Want the GYRATIN' Elvis."

Buoyed by such support, which was as gratifying to the Colonel as it was to Elvis, Presley displayed more confidence than ever when he returned to the studio to make a record of "Hound Dog" and a jaunty

Otis Blackwell tune, "Don't Be Cruel." He took charge of the session, relegating Steve Sholes and RCA's studio personnel to the sidelines, a position to which they would quickly become accustomed. Determined to achieve the perfect sound, Elvis led the musicians through take after take, listening carefully to the tapes and making changes in their approach to the songs. His resolve was rewarded when the new single was released and immediately shot to the top of the charts, with "Hound Dog" and "Don't Be Cruel" both reaching No. 1. By the end of 1956, four million copies of the single had been sold, and Presley "product"— singles, EPs collecting material other than the singles, and his first two albums, both of which reached No. 1 on the charts—accounted for 80 percent of RCA's revenues for the year.

By midsummer, with Elvis's double-sided hit receiving continuous airplay and his records, even the Sun reissues, selling at an unprecedented rate, Ed Sullivan approached Parker about having Presley appear on his Sunday-evening variety show. After Elvis's second Berle appearance, Sullivan had vowed never to allow the singer to be a guest on his top-rated program, but Elvis's good showing on *The Steve Allen Show*, a Sunday-night rival, convinced Sullivan that Presley was simply too popular to pass up. Negotiating from a position of strength, Parker insisted that Elvis be granted complete control over the selection of songs and his manner of performing them, a condition the Sullivan people were forced to accept.

Elvis's first appearance was on September 9. Introduced by the actor Charles Laughton, who was filling in for Sullivan, Presley performed "Don't Be Cruel," "Hound Dog," Little Richard's "Ready Teddy," and "Love Me Tender," a new ballad he had just recorded for his first movie. Initially subdued, Elvis became more and more animated and self-assured during his set, and as he moved away from the microphone to rock out during "Ready Teddy," the camera moved away from him, keeping the viewing audience from seeing his trademark leg movements. But the studio audience, packed with teenage Elvis fans, went wild, screaming and moaning with a delight that made it very clear what was going on outside the camera's range. The show garnered historic ratings, with over 80 percent of the viewing public tuning in, and though it elicited the usual critical barbs, it was widely talked about and soon acknowledged as one of the seminal events of the television era.

Elvis's subsequent appearances didn't attract quite so many viewers, but they inspired widespread press coverage and public commentary. His second one, on October 28, occurred on the eve of the release of his first movie, and he used the occasion to once again sing the title song and remind viewers that it would soon be in theaters. His performance was as kinetic as ever, and he displayed even more confidence and good humor.

The third appearance, in early January, was the coup de grâce. Wearing a gold lamé vest, Presley performed a wider array of songs, from "Don't Be Cruel" and "Too Much," his new single, to a poignant version of Thomas A. Dorsey's gospel classic "Peace in the Valley," which he gladly sang at the network's request. To minimize controversy, during his up-tempo songs CBS photographed him from the waist up. At the end of the performance, Sullivan thanked him and paid him a high compliment: "This is a real decent, fine boy . . . We've never had a pleasanter experience on our show with a big name than we've had with you."[33] Dogged by controversy for most of the previous year, Presley had begun the task of winning over the show-business establishment.

The high ratings earned by the Sullivan show enabled Parker to increase the fee he demanded for television appearances. Elvis had received $50,000 for the three Sullivan guest spots, but in early 1957 his manager informed the three networks that it would take no less than $300,000 to purchase Elvis's services and that any agreement to appear as a guest on a network show would have to include a full-hour Presley special. These terms were far in excess of what the networks were willing to pay, and Parker knew this. But he was happy to see Presley off television as he built up his movie career. As he made clear in numerous arguments with William Morris executives, Parker was convinced that frequent appearances on the small screen would result in overexposure and reduce public demand for Elvis's concert appearances and movies.

This was one of several shrewd strategic gambits orchestrated by the Colonel as Elvis's career took off. In July 1956, Parker negotiated an agreement with the marketing wizard Hank Saperstein to sell a variety of officially licensed Elvis Presley merchandise. Aimed mostly at teenage girls, these items—from charm bracelets, lockets, and lipstick to more expensive products such as jeans, shoes, and record players—were soon available at department and novelty stores around the country and produced a windfall of revenue for Elvis and the Colonel.[34] Not long afterward, Parker began using this merchandise as bait to draw teenagers to newly established Elvis Presley fan clubs. Most of these organizations sprang up spontaneously and were organized by enterprising young women like Kay Wheeler, whose Dallas-based Elvis Presley Fan Club had seven thousand members by the end of 1956. But very quickly they fell under Parker's influence as he plied them with "official products" and used the clubs as a base from which to pitch the latest Elvis music and movies. Eager for information about and access to their idol, most fan club presidents were happy to establish close ties to Parker, and as the controversy over Elvis persisted, it took little prodding from the Colonel to inspire fan club members to spring to Elvis's defense.[35]

Though Elvis had become the very embodiment of rock and roll, his commitment to the music was more pragmatic than principled. As he noted frequently, while he liked playing rock and roll, he feared it was a short-lived trend and that its popularity would wane. "When it's gone, I'll switch to something else. I like to sing ballads the way Eddie Fisher does and the way Perry Como does."[36] In his first auditions for Sam Phillips, Presley had sung nothing but ballads, and it was only on a lark that he had revealed to Phillips his deep affinity for rhythm and blues. Phillips, disdainful of the bland crooners who dominated the pop charts, had discouraged him from recording such material; Steve Sholes was less of a purist. He included some country-influenced ballads in the first batch of demos he sent for Elvis to consider, and Presley was very proud of his versions of these tunes, particularly "I Was the One." Most of the songs that Elvis recorded for RCA in the first few months after his signing, however, were rhythm-and-blues covers and original rock-and-roll songs like Otis Blackwell's "Don't Be Cruel," written expressly for a crossover audience.

When Elvis went to Hollywood and began making movies in the fall of 1956, his musical horizons expanded. Though he was expected to attract teenagers to theaters, Presley was first cast in a period drama set during the Civil War, limiting the kinds of music he could perform in the film. The title track, "Love Me Tender," which topped the pop charts after its release in September, a few weeks before the movie's opening, was a reworking of a traditional nineteenth-century folk tune, and the other songs on the soundtrack were also folk-inspired. His next three films, made in 1957 and early 1958, before his induction into the Army, had contemporary settings and provided him with plenty of opportunities to rock out on-screen, but they also included ballads and pop novelty tunes, a harbinger of the mix that would characterize Presley soundtracks for most of the 1960s. Elvis's success with these kinds of songs led RCA and Hill and Range, the publishing company that provided him with much of his material, to widen the array of songs they offered to him.

By the end of the 1950s Presley was already more than a rock and roller, and his ability to sing a variety of styles made him one of the most versatile and accomplished performers in the history of American popular music. His repertoire included rock and roll, R&B, country-inflected ballads, and conventional pop songs. He even recorded a Christmas album and several stirring gospel songs, which appeared on an EP released in April 1957. All this material was given the "Elvis treatment": arranged in the studio, through rehearsals and multiple takes, according to his precise specifications and the high production values characteristic of RCA. The result was music with a distinctive sound, instantly recognizable as Presley's.

Sales of his records remained strong throughout the 1950s. "Too Much," released in January 1957, reached No. 1 on the pop charts and sold 2 million copies. Its follow-up, "All Shook Up," did better, selling approximately 2.5 million copies and holding down the top spot on the charts for eight weeks. "Teddy Bear," "Jailhouse Rock," and "Don't" also reached No. 1. Sales dipped slightly in 1958 and 1959, when Presley was in the Army, but his singles remained top-five material, and in June 1959 he once again reached the top of the charts with "A Big Hunk o' Love." His albums were also very popular; by the late 1950s they included greatest-hits packages and soundtracks from his films. Elvis's conquest of the pop charts was accompanied by a gradual decline in his presence on the country charts, because conservative radio programmers and country listeners eschewed many of his songs—especially the fast-paced rockers—in favor of more conventional fare. But he remained very popular with African-Americans and continued to place records near the top of the R&B charts through 1963, when *Billboard* stopped keeping a separate black singles chart.

Some of the songs Elvis recorded for RCA in the 1950s were banal, but many others were first-rate, equal to the best of his recordings from the Sun era. The RCA singles were certainly polished, lacking the grittiness of the music he made with Sam Phillips. Yet they were also powerful and accomplished, with Presley's voice displaying self-confidence and his band—usually Scotty Moore, Bill Black, D. J. Fontana, assorted studio musicians, and the vocal group the Jordanaires—providing rhythmic punch and a tight backing. Up-tempo rockers like "Hard Headed Woman" and "Jailhouse Rock" had a sharp edge and an almost volcanic energy. The latter remains one of the most explosive songs in the history of rock music. Much of Presley's smoother, pop-rock fare, however, was just as impressive. Songs like "All Shook Up" and "A Fool Such as I" were lively and infectious, and Elvis's blues-influenced songs continued to demonstrate his mastery of the idiom. His cover of Smiley Lewis's "One Night" was riveting. Despite cleaned-up lyrics, it exuded a swagger and carnality that could be found only in the most "lowdown" R&B.

Far more than that of most other artists recording during the 1950s, Elvis's music had an edge. Indeed, aside from Jerry Lee Lewis and Little Richard, no rock-and-roll performer of the era could convey such energy. But Presley combined this with an uncanny pop sensibility that enabled him to master many different styles. Rock and roll may have been what first made Elvis popular, yet the stardom it enabled him to achieve created new opportunities for him to display his vocal skills and powers of interpretation—powers that grew over time as he became more comfortable with Steve Sholes and the session men and facilities at RCA. On balance, signing with RCA opened up new creative vistas for Presley. As the critic Dave Marsh has argued, rather than ruining him, as some purists claim, it liberated him.[37]

Presley was no musical lightweight, as many Americans raised on 1960s rock believe. Able to play guitar, piano, even the electric bass, without formal musical training, he impressed the studio musicians and songwriters with whom he worked and made it very clear that he was the person in charge. Mike Stoller and Jerry Leiber, two young New York–based songwriters who had worked closely with black R&B groups like the Coasters and were the authors of "Hound Dog," had a very low opinion of Elvis before collaborating with him on the soundtracks of *Jailhouse Rock* and *King Creole*. They hated his version of "Hound Dog" and viewed him as a disingenuous interloper seeking to profit from the popularity of R&B. But after meeting him, they instantly recognized a true aficionado.

Elvis's knowledge of R&B and gospel was encyclopedic, and he liked to warm up for recording sessions by singing spirituals with his fellow musicians. Sessions with Presley were loose and informal. "The thing that really surprised us," Mike Stoller noted, "was that there was no clock."[38] When RCA officials tried to impose order and efficiency, Elvis balked, insisting that sessions be conducted his way or not at all. Presley may not have been a songwriter, the hallmark of a true artist in the eyes of most rock fans since the era of the Beatles and Bob Dylan, but many of the songs he chose to record were imprinted with his influence, and his material from this period displayed the distinctive sound of a gifted and dedicated vocal stylist.

Presley's ability to reach these heights was not only a result of his catholic tastes and intuitive feel for different styles of music; it was also a result of Colonel Parker's willingness to let Elvis handle the musical end of their partnership. Unlike many managers, Parker kept his distance from the studio, a practice that endeared him to Elvis and convinced his client that Parker respected his talent.

Aside from establishing a streamlined pipeline for songs, which required songwriters to share publishing royalties with Presley, Parker let Elvis choose his own songs and record them in the manner he saw fit. He did not intervene when RCA officials objected to Presley's informal methods of recording, and he was farsighted enough to see the potential benefits of Elvis's dynamic performance style, despite the controversy it sparked. And though Parker was not always happy with the material produced by Elvis—he complained, for example, that the instrumental backing to songs recorded at a session in 1958 drowned out Elvis's voice—he invariably deferred to him. As Presley explained to a reporter, "Colonel Parker knows the business end and I don't. He never butts into record sessions, I don't butt into business."[39]

By trusting Presley's talent and musical instincts, Parker helped him develop the skills and artistic vision Sam Phillips had kindled at Sun. And by making adroit use of television, he made it possible for a nationwide audience to recognize Elvis's musical gifts. Television amplified Presley's unusual combination of traits—his smoldering sensuality, his relentless energy, his self-deprecating modesty, and his eagerness to please. Combined in a single personality, they made him attractive to a wide range of Americans—but not necessarily in the same ways. For every Elvis fan drawn to the "bad boy" who seemed to defy the norms of middle-class propriety, there was one drawn to the "good boy" who sang romantic ballads and impressed Ed Sullivan with his manners and fundamental decency. No other performer embodied such disparate features.

In the end, Elvis himself was most responsible for his astounding success, capitalizing on the opportunities Parker steered his way. Trusting his instincts and building on every triumph, he conquered television just as resoundingly as he had the concert stage. And when the chance came to go to Hollywood and take a screen test, he made the most of it, convincing veteran executives to invest a sizable sum in a man without a whit of acting experience. But what sort of a movie star would he be? And would he be able to succeed in motion pictures and still hold on to his position in the music industry?

CHAPTER 4

The Next James Dean?

THE FAME that made it possible for Presley to go into movies, however, had a price. And a vacation he took in July 1956, even before going to Hollywood to make his first film, offered a glimpse of what was to come. After months of touring, television appearances, and recording sessions, Elvis, his cousins Gene and Junior Smith, and two friends, Red West and Arthur Hooton, drove from Memphis to Biloxi, Mississippi, to visit a young woman Elvis had begun seeing. It was Presley's first significant break from performing and recording since Christmas and his ascent to national stardom, and it occurred during a period when criticism of him was snowballing. But any hope of a quiet, event-free idyll was quickly dashed. Within hours of their arrival word had spread that Elvis Presley was in town. Before long a large crowd had gathered in the courtyard of his hotel, and his white Cadillac convertible was covered with mash notes, addresses, and phone numbers, some written in lipstick, some scratched into the car's paint.

This was a foretaste of the attention, curiosity, and frenzied adulation that Presley would inspire as he gained national stature as a singer and movie star. With his enormous success came celebrity—and changes that Presley and his family never anticipated and for which they were completely unprepared. In some respects, his newfound celebrity was an amplified version of the notoriety he had enjoyed in Memphis following his success with Sun and his early concert appearances. But the national celebrity he achieved in 1956—and maintained for the rest of his life—was different. Now instantly recognizable to the vast majority of Americans, he was subjected to new pressures and forced to decisively alter his activities and daily life. If the youthful, self-assured Elvis of 1956 was a product of his upbringing in Tupelo and Memphis, the aging, debauched Elvis of 1977 was a product of his celebrity and the bizarre lifestyle he adopted in response to it. This transformation was by no means sudden or inexorable. It would take years to occur. It was prefigured, however, by developments relatively early in his career. Once these were set in motion, it became progressively more difficult for Presley to change the course of his life, to become someone other than "Elvis Presley."[1]

To be sure, Presley reveled in his popularity and, more often than not, was enthralled by the attention he received. He was especially grateful toward his fans, and went out of his way to chat with them, sign autographs, and return their attention. They were, after all, the ones responsible for his success, and in the wake of the controversy that erupted over him, he came to value their affection and loyalty more than ever. When the Presleys moved to the house on Audubon Drive, he often went out front to socialize with the people who regularly gathered there, a ritual that made the spot a mecca for Elvis fans. "I just wish there was some way to go around to every one of them," he insisted.[2] He couldn't understand stars who resented and avoided their fans. This attitude contributed to his appeal and reflected values that distinguished Elvis from many of the rock musicians who would follow in his wake. Despite Presley's gifts as a singer and his determination to maintain control over his music, he viewed himself as an entertainer, not an artist. He equated success with popularity and viewed pleasing his fans as the highest priority. Making music that appealed to them was his *job*.

He was also very happy with the attention he received from young women. Even though he generally had a steady girlfriend, when Elvis was on the road he fooled around a good deal, and he often had friends like George Klein, a Humes classmate who had become a local disc jockey, scour the crowd at gigs for women who were "Elvis's type." Presley had sex with many of them, but he was careful to avoid an accidental pregnancy. As his pickups discovered, Elvis liked to talk and lie in bed as much as he liked having sex, and much of his interest in women was sparked by his need for intimacy and companionship. The Memphis girls who became his steadies were even more fortunate. Usually reigning beauty queens or aspiring actresses introduced to him by Klein, they basked in his attention and tried to convince themselves that he was serious about them. In a sense, he *was* serious about them, bringing them into his insular family circle, calling them pet names, and expressing a desire to settle down in a few years, once his career solidified. But such displays of commitment didn't put much of a dent in his womanizing, particularly when he was in Hollywood or on the road, as most of his steadies realized. Nevertheless, bringing a woman home to meet his parents was a kind of threshold for Presley, separating his myriad casual dalliances from relationships that were more meaningful. Once admitted into his home, girlfriends like Barbara Hearn and Anita Wood were not only accorded special treatment but also linked to Elvis in the press, something that opened many doors and heightened their stature in Memphis.

Presley's most serious relationship was with June Juanico, a young woman from Biloxi he first met on tour in the summer of 1955. They became reacquainted nearly a year later, when June and some friends, on vacation in Memphis, joined the crowd outside Elvis's Audubon Drive home and he recognized her. They spent the next week together as he showed her the town, including the places that had been significant to him growing up: Lauderdale Courts, Humes High, Lansky's, Crown Electric, the Sun studios. They were reunited again during Elvis's vacation in Biloxi and became very close—so close that rumors that they were engaged spread widely. In fact, Elvis and June discussed marriage, but Elvis told her he had made an arrangement with Parker to postpone any such decision for three years. By then, his career would be secure or have faded; either way, he would be free to step out of the limelight, marry, and resume a normal life.[3]

In hastily arranged interviews with disc jockeys and reporters, Elvis and June denied the rumors of an engagement, but they acknowledged their relationship, with June doing so in a tone that affirmed its seriousness. Colonel Parker was furious. The interviews had been done without his knowledge or approval, and he admonished Presley for acting without consulting his manager. More important, he made it clear to Elvis that any serious relationship with June was a threat to his career. Stung by his manager's reaction, and distracted by the resumption of touring and his Ed Sullivan appearances, Elvis drifted away from June. And in late December she was enraged to read in the newspaper that Presley had spent Christmas in Memphis with a new flame, a showgirl he had met in Las Vegas.

Parker's objections to Juanico were not personal. He would have blown his top no matter who the girl was. The problem with Elvis's getting serious about any woman was that it might shatter the illusion, held by many of his female fans, that he was available, an illusion that Parker reinforced through the "personal notes" from Elvis sent out through the fan clubs. According to Parker's reasoning, if Elvis married or became attached, his appeal among teenage girls, his most loyal fan base, would decline. Until he had established a new base of support among adults, his relationships had to remain low-key and beyond public scrutiny. Parker had no objection to Elvis's dating lots of women, particularly those he picked out of crowds. It reinforced the illusion of availability and created another incentive for female fans to attend his concerts. As long as he stayed out of "trouble," Elvis could consort with whomever he pleased. Indeed, Parker greatly admired Presley's prudence and common sense when dealing with women. The goal was a carefully balanced image that played up Presley's interest in women without making him seem like a lecher.[4]

Female attention was only one perk of celebrity. Elvis soon found that merchants were willing to open after hours to make it easier for him to buy clothes, cars, and jewelry. When he walked around downtown Memphis, he was treated like a hero, and the local press fawned over him. His presence at charity events and other public gatherings elicited cheers and screams of delight. In December 1956, for example, thousands of African-Americans attending a WDIA-sponsored charity concert at Ellis Auditorium went wild when, led onstage by fourteen-year-old Carla Thomas, the daughter of the disc jockey and musician Rufus Thomas, Elvis displayed one of his patented "wiggles." He and his parents were even invited to dinner by their well-to-do neighbors on Audubon Drive, an experience that proved less painful and awkward than they had feared.

By the end of 1956, however, these advantages had begun to be offset by new problems. First evident on the road, fan reaction to his performances swelled to new heights of hysteria, and soon Elvis required police escorts to ferry him away from venues. He began to be mobbed whenever he appeared in public, including in Memphis. Going to the movies, eating in restaurants, or attending public events attracted undue attention, almost always creating a scene. Elvis found it impossible to oblige all the fans who clamored for his autograph, and his efforts to disentangle himself from the crowds that seemed to materialize out of nowhere created misunderstandings and bad feelings all around. Being recognized sometimes even led to potentially embarrassing public incidents. For example, in October 1956 Elvis stopped at a local gas station and a crowd quickly gathered, preventing him from driving away. The station's manager became angry. Believing that Elvis wasn't doing enough to clear the spot for other customers, he reached inside the car and slapped Elvis on the back of the head. Not one to take such affronts, Presley jumped out of the car and slugged the manager, who promptly pulled a knife. Fortunately, the police arrived and restrained the manager and his attendant, who had joined the fight. All three were charged with assault and battery and disorderly conduct. "It's getting where I can't even leave the house without something happening to me," Elvis complained to reporters.[5]

Deeply resented by many jealous boyfriends, Presley also had to be on guard for young men eager to punch him out. "Many times," he explained in a telegram to a soldier who had accused Elvis of insulting his wife, "there have been people who came up to me and stick [sic] out their hands to shake hands with me and they hit me or I have had guys . . . come up and ask for autographs and hit me and then take off for no reason at all."[6] This was particularly true when he was on the road, and out of concern for his own safety Elvis had begun traveling with Red West, a former football player from Humes who served as a bodyguard as well as a companion. But by the end of 1956 it was happening even when he went out in public in Memphis. As Elvis and his family gradually realized, there was such a thing as too much attention. And because of his controversial reputation, everything he did was of interest to a national press predisposed to report critically on his activities.

The crowds outside the Presley home grew larger, and while he and his parents did their best to accommodate them, by the fall of 1956 things were getting out of hand. The large crowds not only annoyed their neighbors; they also attracted vendors and created a circus-like atmosphere. Hoping to reclaim their block, several of Presley's neighbors offered to buy him out. Elvis and his parents were not insensitive to their neighbors' complaints; by everyone's standards, the situation on Audubon Drive had become intolerable. So, shortly after the first of the year, the Presleys began thinking about moving to a new house that would afford them more privacy.

With the assistance of a real estate agent, Gladys and Vernon discovered Graceland, a fourteen-acre estate in rural Whitehaven, about eight miles south of downtown Memphis and near the Mississippi border. Named after the great-aunt of the woman who had it built in 1939, and anchored by a stately colonial mansion set back about a hundred yards from Highway 51, the estate was just what the Presleys were looking for. They called Elvis, who was making a movie in Los Angeles, immediately after seeing it to tell him they had found the perfect home. When Elvis returned from the West Coast and saw the place, he agreed and put down a deposit. On March 25, 1957, the Presleys purchased the estate for $102,500, trading in their Audubon Drive home for $55,000, adding a $10,000 deposit, and taking out a mortgage for the rest.

Elvis was ecstatic. He contacted the interior decorator who had recently remodeled Sam Phillips's new home, and within days the interior of the house was being redone. Elvis had big plans for the place. "This is going to be a lot nicer than Red Skelton's house when I get it like I want it," he told a Memphis newspaperman, referring to a Hollywood mansion widely known for its lavishness.[7] The result was a testament to his aspirations—but also to his sensibilities as a working-class Southerner. Decorated in a style that promiscuously mingled the classical and the modern, Graceland resembled the mansions of Hollywood movie stars, with decorative touches that exuded an over-the-top opulence that, as Karal Ann Marling has noted, was very much in vogue during the 1950s and 1960s. The rooms and the furniture glimmered in resplendent colors more common to movie sets than to real life. Unlike old-money WASPs, whose postwar consumption was governed by an aesthetic of restraint, the Presleys openly displayed their good fortune through eye-catching consumer goods—like the custom-built fifteen-foot white couch in the living room—that epitomized the new comforts and conveniences available to wealthy consumers during the prosperous 1950s. Elvis had a soda fountain and a jukebox installed in his basement playroom, and Gladys's appliance-laden kitchen was right out of an ad for General Electric. Outside, the Presleys built a chicken house and planted a vegetable garden, enabling them to enjoy some old-fashioned amenities as well. Within a stone's throw of these vestiges of East Tupelo, however, were a sunken patio, a kidney-shaped swimming pool, and front gates emblazoned with musical notes. Over the years, Graceland would undergo additional renovations as Elvis earned even more money and his tastes became more defiantly idiosyncratic. Building a home exactly to his liking—wasn't that what success was all about?[8]

Comfortably ensconced at Graceland, the Presleys resumed the life they had led on Audubon Drive. The estate's walls and gates, which were manned by relatives like Vernon's brother Vester, kept fans and curiosity seekers off the grounds and gave the family some much-needed privacy. Gladys tended her vegetable garden and chickens, while Vernon continued managing the family's finances. Assorted relatives came for extended visits, and when he was home, Elvis spent most of his time entertaining his friends, mostly Memphians like George Klein, Red West, and Anita Wood, whom he began dating in the summer of 1957. But there were also some new people, friends Elvis had made since becoming famous, who were as eager to join the inner circle as he was for constant companionship. They included Cliff Gleaves, Lamar Fike, and Alan Fortas, all young men roughly his age who were torn between their own responsibilities and the prospect of a "career" hanging out with Elvis Presley. When Elvis was in Memphis, the Presleys still spent a lot of time together, watching television or singing spirituals around the baby grand piano that Elvis had installed in the music room. And despite the near-constant presence of his friends, the atmosphere at Graceland remained family-oriented. "It never got wild at Graceland," as Alan Fortas later noted. This was largely due to Gladys, whose presence kept Elvis from straying emotionally too far from home and family.[9]

Gladys's role in keeping him tethered to Graceland was important, since other forces were pulling him in the opposite direction. The most compelling of these was his career. Recording, touring, appearing on television, and making movies in Hollywood put heavy demands on his time. His schedule was so hectic that he spent relatively little time at Graceland during the first year his family lived there. And when he was around, he found it hard to get out of the unusual rhythms of a performer. Keyed up after shows, Elvis had gotten into the habit of staying up all night and going to sleep in the morning. When he began to encounter problems in public, this penchant for leading a nocturnal life was reinforced. What better way to avoid the scenes that occurred when he was out on the town than by confining his outings to when few people were awake? And being Elvis Presley, he found that business owners, restaurateurs, theater managers, and even the managers of the local amusement park were happy to accommodate his peculiar hours. A phone call was all it took to get a store owner to open his shop so that Elvis could engage in a late-night shopping spree, or to arrange an after-hours screening of the latest Hollywood film for Presley and a dozen of his friends and assorted hangers-on. Whenever the spirit moved him, Elvis would take his friends out to the fairgrounds after closing, and they'd ride the bumper cars or the roller coaster to their hearts' content, or he'd rent the local roller rink and have skating parties. Gradually, Elvis began to inhabit an alternative universe governed by his whims and predilections.

Presley's immersion in this world was reinforced by the group of male friends that had begun to gather around him. By the summer of 1957 an inner circle composed of Klein, Hooton, Gleaves, Fike, Fortas, and Presley's cousins Gene and Junior Smith had formed. Red West, Presley's first traveling companion, had left for the Marines but would later rejoin the group after his discharge. These men were almost nightly visitors when Presley was home at Graceland, and as he became more famous, Elvis began to want them around all the time, even when he was on tour or making movies. Their presence was reassuring, particularly when he was in Hollywood and his insecurities were amplified. Though respectful of Gladys and Vernon, Elvis's friends encouraged his interest in adolescent fun and games, and in their company he assumed an exaggerated macho swagger. This acting-out only continued as his circle grew larger and came to resemble a full-fledged entourage. It often resulted in his being rude or possessive toward his girlfriends, behavior that differed markedly from the thoughtful sensitivity he exhibited when alone with them. To be sure, Presley tried to be a good influence on "the boys," admonishing them for swearing and setting an example by eschewing alcohol. And because they were so eager to stay in his good graces and keep enjoying the benefits that came with being his friend, they were susceptible to his influence. But their dependence and his unrivaled position as the leader made it difficult for any of them to stand up to him. Those who did quickly discovered that deference to Elvis was the price of remaining in the group. Sadly, the peculiar dynamics of the group recast many of Elvis's true friends into sycophantic yes-men.[10]

All of this happened gradually. Most of the time it seemed as if the only thing that had changed was the size of the checks Colonel Parker forwarded to Vernon and the range of things the family could now buy. But there were occasions when the Presleys recognized how much their lives had changed. Gladys dwelled on it the most. Though she was happy to have found Graceland and eager to make it a home, she was never completely comfortable there. Always fearful of what might happen to her son, she felt helpless as his career took him further and further away from her and changed him. "She hated the way Elvis looked on his brief visits home, how pale he seemed from lack of sleep and overwork, how hyperexcited he seemed all the time, and how edgy and nervous," recalled Fortas.[11]

According to friends, as Elvis became famous, he and his mother began to argue more often, and during his absences she began drinking heavily. She spent most of her time in the kitchen, often staring out the window, deep in thought. The biographer Elaine Dundy has argued that Elvis's success drove Gladys to drink and began her slide into alcoholism and depression. Many of his friends agree. "She was very proud of Elvis, but his stardom scared her," Lamar Fike insisted. "It drove her over the edge . . . and hastened her death."[12]

Even Elvis, for all his kid-in-a-candy-store excitement, had moments of doubt. Hounded by a largely hostile press, prevented from going out in public, pulled away from home and family for extended periods by the demands of his career, Presley found himself living a fishbowl-like existence that was taxing and, at times, dispiriting. Attending Easter services in April 1957, the first time he had been to church in months, Elvis told the minister, "I have got more money than I can spend. I have thousands of fans out there, and I have lots of people who call themselves my friends, but I am miserable."[13] A good deal of the misery resulted from the pressures of responsibility, which Elvis felt acutely. Happy and proud to be able to provide for his parents and share his success with friends and extended kin, he sometimes felt his new role as provider like an ox's yoke. When Dixie, now married, saw him again in August 1958, he startled her by expressing a desire to walk away from his new life. When she urged him to do so, he shook his head and responded glumly, "It's too late for that . . . There are too many people that depend on me . . . I'm in too far to get out."[14]

Most of the time, however, Elvis was simply too busy to think about the costs of success and celebrity. The tours continued. In the spring of 1957 he played big cities in the Northeast, the upper Midwest, and eastern Canada. At the end of the summer, he traveled to the Pacific Northwest for the first time, appearing before stadium-size crowds in Spokane, Vancouver, Seattle, Tacoma, and Portland. And later in the fall, he performed in California and Hawaii, where Colonel Parker had been stationed while in the Army and still had friends. Parker also received offers for Presley to play in London and perhaps even undertake a European tour. Elvis was excited, but the Colonel turned the offers down, claiming the terms were not sufficient. Europe, he told Presley, would have to wait. Parker conveniently hid from Elvis another reason for his lack of interest in a European tour: his status as an illegal immigrant and his fears that travel abroad would result in his real identity being discovered.[15]

Controversy continued to dog Presley. Fans rioted at several concerts, worrying civic officials in cities where Elvis was scheduled to appear. In Vancouver, thousands of fans, their movements unrestrained by security, surrounded the stage on which he was performing. Terrified, Parker stopped the concert and brought Elvis backstage, where he implored him to tone down his act for his own safety. But Elvis, captivated by his power over the audience, refused, and at the end of the show fans turned over the makeshift stage as he fled into the wings and a waiting automobile. The protests and criticism also continued, despite Elvis's best efforts in interviews to reassure the public that he meant no harm. The Catholic Church was especially hostile toward him. Priests told their parishioners to boycott Presley's music, movies, and television appearances. Some teenagers, mostly boys jealous of his sex appeal and eager to please authority figures, threw eggs at him during his concerts and wore buttons that said "I Hate Elvis."

Things came to a boil in late October, when Presley played a gig at the Pan Pacific Auditorium in Los Angeles before a crowd that included large numbers of Hollywood big shots, their families, and representatives of both the local and the national press. After a particularly wild performance, Elvis was assailed by the press and some of the celebrities who had attended, usually parents who had brought their children to the show. One newspaper columnist likened his music and movements to "darkest Africa's fertility tom-tom displays"; another suggested that the scene was reminiscent of "one of those screeching, uninhibited party rallies which the Nazis used to hold for Hitler."[16] The Los Angeles vice squad warned Parker that Elvis would have to reduce his movements and dancing, and at the following show the police filmed the proceedings in case they needed evidence for a criminal prosecution. Sensing the seriousness of the situation, Presley was more restrained, and the experience, after months of increasing tension and public criticism, finally convinced Parker that perhaps tours were more trouble than they were worth. Accordingly, when Elvis and Parker returned from Hawaii, Parker refused to book any more live appearances. Over his William Morris contacts' objections, the Colonel persuaded Elvis that additional concerts would only contribute to overexposure and make it more difficult to keep him at the top.

Presley's move away from live concerts was possible because of his emerging success as a movie actor. After negotiating the contract with Hal Wallis and Paramount, Parker took immediate advantage of the provision that allowed Elvis to make a movie with another studio and arranged for his client to appear in a 20th Century–Fox production. And when a suitable Paramount vehicle for Elvis was delayed, Wallis had no choice but to let the young star make his first picture for the other studio. Produced by David Weisbart, the executive responsible for James Dean's *Rebel Without a Cause*, it was filmed in August and September 1956 and originally titled *The Reno Brothers*. A drama set during the Civil War, the movie cast Elvis as the youngest brother of a close-knit family, a central but supporting role. Eager and excited when he flew out to Hollywood, Elvis memorized the entire script, hoping to impress the director, Robert Webb, and his co-stars, Richard Egan and the starlet Debra Paget, whom Elvis had met at his first appearance on

Milton Berle's show. In order to capitalize on his popularity, the studio changed the script to allow him to sing several songs and the movie was retitled *Love Me Tender*. Elvis's performance was decent for someone with so little experience, though he was embarrassed by the final cut and resolved to improve. Nevertheless, the film was a smash when it was released in November. It earned over half a million dollars during its first week, second only to *Giant*, a big-budget blockbuster starring Elizabeth Taylor and the late James Dean that was released simultaneously.

Presley loved Hollywood and was awestruck during his first visits to the studios. Having grown up a movie fan, he enjoyed meeting famous people in the business and impressed many of them with his seriousness and courtesy. He quickly became friends with Nick Adams, a young actor who had been close to James Dean, and through Adams got to know rising young stars like Dennis Hopper, Russ Tamblyn, and Natalie Wood. Though Elvis was often accompanied in Los Angeles by his cousin Gene Smith and at least a couple of friends from home, he at first spent a lot of time with this Hollywood clique. They attended parties and hobnobbed on the weekends. Presley became particularly close to Adams, inviting him back to Memphis for a visit after the conclusion of shooting. A week later Natalie Wood joined them. Elvis showed Nick and Natalie around town, pointing out the familiar places that by now had become part of the regular tour. It was almost a surreal experience for Wood, who had been in the limelight since the age of five and had settled into a routine that involved avoiding crowds and potentially awkward public situations. "When we went out on Elvis's motorcycle," she recalled, "we had an instant motorcade behind us. I felt like I was leading the Rose Bowl parade."[17] All of this seemed perfectly normal to Elvis, whom she found naive, sweet, and exceedingly polite—a far cry from the jaded young people she was used to.

Presley made his first film for Paramount in early 1957. Titled *Loving You*, it was a thinly veiled fictionalization of his own rise to stardom, perfect for his first starring role. Elvis's performance reflected how much more comfortable this film was for him to make than *Love Me Tender*. The musical numbers were inspired, and his acting displayed marked improvement. During the filming, Vernon and Gladys came out to Hollywood to visit their son, even appearing in the audience during one of the musical interludes. Taking advantage of *Love Me Tender*'s success, Colonel Parker was even able to wrangle a fifty-thousand-dollar bonus for Elvis. The film opened in May and quickly became one of the most popular of the season.

By this time Elvis had already completed work on his next picture, a film for MGM called *Jailhouse Rock*. This was the third studio Presley worked for, and the deal negotiated by Parker—a $250,000 fee plus 50 percent of the profits—made Hal Wallis recognize he would have to up the ante if he wanted to keep Elvis working for him. Filming began in May, with Elvis playing a singer who experiences a reversal of fortune that includes a spell in a penitentiary. With songs by Jerry Leiber and Mike Stoller, some sensational dance routines, including a riveting version of the title song, and Presley's best dramatic performance yet, the movie was a triumph for Elvis. It opened in November, peaked at No. 3 in *Variety*'s weekly survey, and wound up fourteenth on the magazine's list of the year's most successful films, ahead of *Loving You*.

The fourth, and final, movie Elvis made before enlisting in the Army began filming in January 1958. Based on a Harold Robbins bestseller and set in New Orleans, *King Creole* was Presley's strongest performance to date. The film, produced by Hal Wallis at Paramount, was directed by Michael Curtiz, a veteran responsible for classics like *Casablanca* and *Mildred Pierce* as well as the successful Jerry Lewis–Dean Martin comedies. Elvis's co-stars included Walter Matthau, Dean Jagger, and Carolyn Jones, and the film once again featured songs by Leiber and Stoller. Elvis again played a singer, but the role was his meatiest yet. The result satisfied not only the ever more discerning and self-critical Elvis but even many critics and movie people who hadn't expected very much from him. The movie, which opened in July, after his induction into the Army, was another box-office success, reaching No. 5 on *Variety*'s charts.

Before he entered the Army, Elvis took his acting very seriously. As usual, he listened to and learned from the more experienced people he met, and with each film he became more competent and polished. After what he regarded as an embarrassing performance in *Love Me Tender*, he began studying the mannerisms of actors like Marlon Brando, Robert Mitchum, and the late James Dean, incorporating them into his own technique. And by the time of *King Creole*, he had developed the rudiments of his own style. As Walter Matthau recalled, Elvis wasn't just a natural, "he was very intelligent." He knew how to play a character "simply by being himself *through* the means of the story."[18] He also became more concerned about his appearance. Shortly before making *Jailhouse Rock*, he had his teeth capped and underwent minor plastic surgery to smooth out pockmarks on his face. Concluding that he looked better with black hair, he began having it dyed regularly. Elvis had always dreamed of a movie career, and when he first went out to Hollywood, he told people about his interest in becoming a serious actor. At first this was little more than a pipe dream, the sort of bravado that Wallis and other movie veterans often heard from newcomers to the field. Yet by 1958 it had become a more realistic possibility. His talent and potential for growth had been recognized, even by producers who had dismissed him as a teen heartthrob, and he had shown the drive and commitment to improvement that were necessary to break into serious dramatic roles. Even Parker was on board, informing his William Morris contacts in Los Angeles that Elvis was keen to appear in a nonmusical picture.

However, a big obstacle remained. Back in January 1957, only two days after Elvis's final appearance on *The Ed Sullivan Show*, the Memphis draft board had announced that the singer was eligible for induction into the armed forces, and by the end of the year it had become apparent that his career would be interrupted, to one degree or another, by military service. But what kind of service? Would it provide him opportunities to continue making music and the occasional movie? Elvis was soon flooded with proposals from various branches of the military, each offering different perks that would allow him to keep a foot in show business. For example, the Air Force proposed that he become a recruiter and tour the country, while the Navy suggested he lead a specially trained "Elvis Presley company" that would serve a promotional, rather than purely military, function. Presley was interested in these prospects, but Parker soon convinced him that, given the criticism directed at him during the previous year, the best course was to enlist in the Army as an ordinary private, just like everyone else. In Parker's view, this would finally exorcise the controversy that had dogged Presley since his emergence as a national star.

Elvis grudgingly accepted Parker's advice, and he put up a brave front before the press, much to Parker's delight. "Millions of other guys have been drafted, and I don't want to be different from anyone else," Elvis told reporters on the morning of his induction, a line he would reiterate like a mantra during his two-year stint in the Army.[19] But privately he was upset, and his anger at Parker and fears about his career steadily escalated in his last few weeks as a civilian. What if Parker was wrong and his fans forgot about him? Was he throwing away his career? The only break he got was a deferment to complete *King Creole*, preventing Paramount from losing all the money it had sunk into the project. After finishing the film, he returned to Memphis. In the few remaining days, he spent as much time as possible with family and friends, renting out the local roller rink and staying up all night listening to records and singing gospel songs in Graceland's music room.

On March 24, 1958, in the early morning, Presley arrived at the draft board offices in downtown Memphis, along with a caravan of friends, relatives, and his parents, who appeared despondent. Also present were about two dozen reporters and photographers. He and twelve other inductees were then sent by bus to a nearby VA hospital for processing. The caravan, now including the press, followed closely. After a lengthy delay, during which a crowd gathered and Colonel Parker began handing out promotional materials for *King Creole*, Presley said his goodbyes and left by military bus for Fort Chaffee, Arkansas. Once again the press followed him and were present for his official induction, when he received the standard GI haircut, was issued his olive-drab uniform, and was assigned to the armored division formerly commanded by George S. Patton. Elvis, still followed by the press, was then sent to

Fort Hood in Texas, where his new unit was stationed. After indulging the press—and Parker, who was orchestrating most of the coverage— for four days, Army officials finally drew the line and declared Elvis off-limits to reporters.

Elvis's induction into the Army was the epitome of a relatively insignificant event transformed into a lavishly publicized media spectacle, the sort of pseudo-event that had become quite common in the United States since the advent of tabloids and visually oriented mass-circulation periodicals like *Life*—and would become even more common as television news departments expanded and fell under the entertainment ethos that dominated much of American journalism.[20] But the symbolism of Presley's induction was important, regardless of how it was covered. By submitting to the draft and entering the Army as an ordinary private, Elvis accepted the discipline of an institution that had come to play a vital role in transforming men from assorted backgrounds into soldiers and "Americans." For the next two years he would live by the Army's rules and conform to its standards of manliness. Nothing brought this home quite as vividly as his highly publicized haircut and appearance in uniform, both effacing his visual distinctiveness. The look that had made him "cool" to some and subversive to others had been erased, sacrificed at the altar of national conformity.[21]

Military service had become a rite of passage for most American men, and Presley's willingness to go through it as well made him more acceptable to many people who had mistakenly regarded him as a rebel. Moreover, as Parker often reminded reporters, by going in as an ordinary soldier rather than in a capacity that would have allowed him to continue to perform, record, and perhaps even appear in movies, Elvis was making an enormous financial sacrifice and putting his career at risk. Unlike the vast majority of young men his age, who hadn't yet embarked on careers, Elvis had a lot to lose.

At first, Presley was very homesick, but he adjusted quickly and soon won over his fellow soldiers. Allaying their suspicions with his sense of humor and willingness to endure every rigor of basic training, he was accepted by virtually everyone in his company. "I mean, everybody thought . . . I wouldn't have to work, and I would be given special treatment and this and that," Elvis later told reporters. "But when they looked around and saw I was on K.P. and I was pulling guard and everything, just like they were, well they figured well, he's just like us."[22] His comrades were the first to discover that Presley's induction had been more than a publicity stunt; Elvis was in the Army for real.

Taking advantage of an Army regulation that allowed soldiers with "dependents" to live off base after basic training, Parker arranged for Elvis to live with Vernon and Gladys, and toward the end of June the Presleys, Elvis's grandmother Minnie, and Lamar Fike moved into a three-bedroom trailer home near Fort Hood. Finding the space too cramped, they soon rented a large house, which they intended to occupy until Elvis was assigned overseas. As Elvis fulfilled his obligations and learned the rudiments of tank gunnery and other military skills, the family entertained many visitors on weekends, including Elvis's current steady, Anita Wood. Having his family and friends nearby was a comfort, and most of the other soldiers were understanding. Elvis even invited some of his fellow GIs over to the house to join the group.

In early August, when Presley was deep in the throes of advanced training, Gladys became very sick, and she and Vernon returned to Memphis to see her doctor. Her health had been deteriorating for months, and over the summer she had lost her appetite and begun to sink into depression, a condition exacerbated by the prospect of her son going overseas. By the time she saw her physician, it was too late. She was hospitalized, but her precise ailment—probably a liver condition—remained undiagnosed, and she grew worse over the next few days. When Elvis was informed of his mother's ill health, he almost deserted in order to be by her side. After numerous phone calls from Gladys's doctor to the base commander and officials in Washington, Presley was granted an emergency leave and flew to Memphis. Seeing him improved her condition temporarily, and, along with Vernon, they spent much of the next day together. But early the next morning, August 14, Elvis was awakened by a phone call from his father informing him that Gladys had died. Elvis rushed to the hospital, where he and his father cried inconsolably and Elvis caressed his deceased mother's body until the undertaker took her away.

And they continued crying, right through the funeral and through the ceremony at which they put Gladys's coffin in its grave—despite the presence of reporters. With Elvis and Vernon virtually incapacitated by grief, Colonel Parker handled all the funeral arrangements, vetoing Elvis's suggestion that there be a public viewing of the body for his legion of fans but providing plenty of access for the press, whose coverage of the events, as Parker may well have anticipated, was very sympathetic. Many of Elvis's relatives and friends attended the services, but Presley could do little more than cry, occasionally collapsing in a heap. At the cemetery he became almost hysterical, crying aloud, "Goodbye, darling, goodbye. I love you so much. You know how much I lived my whole life for you." As he was led into his car for the ride back to Graceland, he wailed, "Oh God, everything I have is gone."[23] For the next few days he remained prone to crying fits, and when he returned to Fort Hood on August 24, he left strict orders that his mother's room be left exactly as it had been on the day she died.

Gladys's death was arguably the most important event in Elvis's life. Though he gradually cheered up, he had lost the person with whom he had always felt most comfortable. Gladys had offered him unconditional love, serving as an anchor during his dizzying ascent to stardom. She had viewed his success with a measure of skepticism and had been the one most likely to recognize the pitfalls of being rich and famous. She had also helped keep Elvis and Vernon committed to the family when other things might have pulled them away. Without her, Elvis and Vernon's relationship changed. Though Vernon continued to manage Elvis's finances, he never again had much influence over his son—nor did Minnie, whose importance to the family increased after Gladys's death but who could not provide the same kind of emotional security that Gladys had. In the wake of his mother's death, Presley became more and more dependent on his male friends for companionship, and though Vernon and other relatives remained a presence, Elvis's life became decidedly less family-oriented—at least until the mid-1960s, when another woman would try to provide the domestic influence that had been missing from Presley's life since 1958.[24]

In September, Elvis was assigned to another armored division stationed in Germany, and he and his father began preparing for Vernon, Minnie, and two of Elvis's friends, Lamar Fike and Red West, to move abroad as well. After traveling by troop train, Presley arrived at the Army terminal in Brooklyn on September 22, where hundreds of fans had gathered, and held a news conference, handling questions with his usual aplomb and good humor. When asked what he would do if rock and roll died out before his return, he jokingly replied, "I'll starve to death, sir." In response to a question about whether he planned to take advantage of any of the educational opportunities available to servicemen, he noted, "It doesn't hurt for anybody to have a profession to turn to in case something did happen to the entertainment business, or something happen to me." And when queried about the role talent had played in his success, he downplayed his abilities and displayed the customary modesty that was so disarming. "I've been very lucky . . . I mean the people were looking for something different . . . I came along just in time."[25] When the press conference was over, Presley walked up the gangplank of the transport ship eight times to accommodate all the photographers present, and once on board he gave a final interview, in which he expressed hope that his fans would not forget him. Then he was off. To enable devoted fans to savor the moment, Parker and RCA had the press conference and last interview taped and made into an EP, *Elvis Sails*, which sold sixty thousand copies.

Presley arrived in Germany on October 1 and was met at the port by another throng of fans and reporters. But almost immediately he and the other soldiers in his division were ferried by train to Friedberg, about two hundred miles away. Upon arrival, he held another press conference and made himself available to reporters while he underwent processing. But then, as at Fort Hood, he was declared off-limits to the press, and his life as a soldier really began. Within a few days, his father, grandmother, and two friends had arrived. Along with Elvis, who again had been given permission to live off base, they settled into a nearby hotel. They soon moved to a more secluded one in Bad Nauheim, farther from the base. After repeatedly annoying the hotel's rich, predominantly elderly guests with water fights and other horseplay, Presley and his dependents moved into a five-bedroom house nearby, where they would live for the duration of their stay in Germany.[26]

Elvis's life in Germany was governed by the sort of routine he hadn't experienced since his days as a truck driver for Crown Electric. As usual, Vernon attended to finances and maintained regular contact with Colonel Parker, while Minnie, whom Elvis called "Dodger," prepared her grandson's favorite meals and tried her best to be a source of emotional support. Presley was driven to the base every morning by taxi, often returning for lunch. Most evenings he spent at home, with Lamar, Red, and the new friends he had met in the service, listening to records or playing music. One of these new friends, Charlie Hodge, was also a professional musician, and two others, Rex Mansfield and Joe Esposito, were soon accepted into the group. On the weekends they played touch football, and when Elvis and the other soldiers were given leave, they traveled as a group to Munich and Paris, where they cavorted with strippers and enjoyed more decadent forms of recreation.[27]

Despite being very close to Anita Wood, with whom he corresponded regularly and even discussed the possibility of marriage, Elvis dated a number of women while in Germany, including Elisabeth Stefaniak, the German stepdaughter of an American soldier, who moved into the house in Bad Nauheim as Elvis's "secretary." Besides handling the heavy volume of fan mail, a duty she shared with Red and Lamar, Elisabeth regularly slept with Elvis. So did several other young women whom Elvis brought home. This upset Elisabeth, who soon realized that Presley had no intention of being monogamous.

But in September 1959 Elvis met a girl with whom he was instantly smitten, and it was clear that Anita now had a serious rival. The new girl's name was Priscilla Beaulieu. She was the daughter of an Air Force captain who had just moved with his family to Germany. Only fourteen, but blessed with wholesome good looks and uncommon maturity, Priscilla was soon a regular at Presley's house, often staying late into the night sequestered with Elvis in his bedroom. Having impressed her parents with his manners and professions of honorable intentions, Presley drew Priscilla into his world and began sizing up her potential as a new number-one steady. Priscilla was initially disturbed by the house's strange atmosphere, in which Elvis was very much the leader and his friends played overeager supporting roles. Yet she was soon enraptured, finding Elvis sensitive and affectionate, particularly when they were alone together and he could be himself and express his feelings. He talked for hours about his mother and the anguish he felt now that she was gone, and he revealed his worries about his career and the sincerity of some of the friends and relatives who clamored for his attention. "My heart went out to Elvis," Beaulieu confided in her memoir of their relationship. "He was a world-famous entertainer, a great star, and yet a terribly lonely man."[28] True to his word, Elvis refrained from having intercourse with her, even when she begged him on the eve of his return to the United States. Theirs, he insisted, was a special relationship, and because of that she needed to remain "pure." Of course, he held himself to a different standard, and without her knowledge he continued his usual sexual activities.

By day, Presley attended to his soldierly duties, serving as the driver for a sergeant, developing his skills in reconnaissance, and going with his troop on maneuvers near the Czech border, an ordeal that further endeared him to his peers and superiors. It was while on maneuvers that Elvis was introduced to amphetamines, which many soldiers used to stay awake for extended periods. Almost right away, however, Presley began using them during the weekends, convincing his friends to take them as well, arguing that they were harmless and commonly used by people trying to stay thin. "I honestly believed every word that Elvis said and gladly received my little bottle of amphetamines from his supply," Rex Mansfield said.[29] That supply was considerable. Presley received shipments in quart-size bottles from a source that remained a mystery to Mansfield, paying for them with "large bills" that belied his efforts to live like an ordinary soldier. Elvis's use of uppers didn't just keep him going. They began affecting his behavior, producing mood swings that made him imperious, capricious, and vindictive.

But the drugs alone were not to blame for Presley's altered behavior. Without Gladys as a steadying influence, Elvis's ego was unchecked, and at times he assumed the entitled airs of a big shot, a tendency his friends were in a poor position to counteract. On a certain level, Elvis understood what was happening. As he complained to Priscilla, his friends were partly drawn to him because he was a celebrity. And it was hard not to succumb to the temptation to pull rank, and hard not to regard being the center of attention as his birthright. During their football games, for example, the guys routinely let Elvis play quarterback and would later present him with a "most valuable player" trophy. Such a rapport began to seem natural, the way things were supposed to be.

Presley could be equally capricious with girlfriends, as Stefaniak in particular discovered. Though he was generous and sensitive and she enjoyed much of their time together, he was prone to angry, jealous fits. He insisted, for instance, that Elisabeth date no one else, even though he was deeply involved with Priscilla and regularly slept with other women, too. Even Priscilla learned to watch what she said, particularly when they were around the guys. As Priscilla eventually recognized, Presley was determined to maintain a macho image in front of his friends. Unfortunately, this often required downplaying the very side of his personality that she and his other girlfriends found most appealing.

Presley was also affected by unexpected family trouble. Within weeks of arriving in Bad Nauheim, Vernon became friendly with Dee Stanley, the wife of an American sergeant, and by the end of the year they were having a torrid affair. For Elvis, this was unseemly and an insult to his mother's memory. He was especially voluble about the affair when alone with Priscilla, expressing hope that it would end when Vernon and he returned to Memphis. When Dee took her three sons back to the United States in the summer of 1959, leaving her husband in Germany, Vernon went back as well, claiming to be attending to business. When he returned to Germany after a two-month absence, Dee followed a few days later, this time without her children, whom she had

TOP: Tupelo, Mississippi, Elvis's birthplace, was widely lauded as one of the New South's most "progressive" communities, largely because of its textile mills and other industries that had emerged from the region's traditional agricultural economy.

ABOVE: Elvis and his parents, Gladys and Vernon Presley, were very close, and during the late 1930s and early 1940s the bond between Elvis and his mother became even stronger when circumstances compelled Vernon to spend considerable time away from home.

LEFT: Churches such as the one pictured here were ubiquitous in the South during Elvis's childhood. They brought the generations together and, through music as well as prayer, forged vibrant communities of the faithful.

The prevalence of seasonal labor and the exigencies of wartime mobilization caused many working-class Southerners, including Vernon Presley, to move around a lot during the early 1940s, a process that encouraged interaction across the color line, as this photograph suggests.

Memphis, Tennessee, the city to which Elvis and his parents moved in 1948, was an important cultural crossroads where rural people, black and white, were introduced to city ways—and where population growth, new economic opportunities, and the emergence of an urban-based consumer culture made it possible for white teenagers like Elvis to come into even more frequent contact with African-Americans and their music.

Having signed with Sun Records, Elvis began to give concerts throughout the South, perfecting his stage persona and performing style. He soon became a regional sensation and was signed by RCA, one of the nation's major record labels, making it possible for him to achieve national stardom.

Though he was already a major recording star, Elvis's fame increased markedly when he appeared on Ed Sullivan's popular CBS variety show in 1956. Television performances not only enlarged his fan base, they also added fuel to the controversy ignited by his national exposure and made him a target of moralists throughout the country.

Most of Elvis's early movies were built around his real-life image as a young rock and roller and provided him with numerous opportunities to sing and dance. This publicity still from *Jailhouse Rock* (1957) displays Elvis's dynamism as a performer and captures one of the most memorable song-and-dance routines of his career.

TOP: Having Elvis serve in the Army as an ordinary private was a calculated risk that Elvis's manager, Tom Parker, persuaded his young client to take. Much to Elvis's and Parker's relief, it paid off, disarming most of Elvis's critics and positioning him for mainstream success during the 1960s. Shortly after Elvis began his service, Gladys Presley died, a blow from which he never recovered.

RIGHT: Central to Parker's strategy of making Elvis a topflight mainstream entertainer was altering Elvis's movie persona and casting him in films—such as *Blue Hawaii* (1961), a smash hit he made for Paramount—in which he appeared less dangerous and exuded a more wholesome sex appeal.

Elvis's 1968 television special rekindled his career and created a new groundswell of critical and public interest in him. In its wake, he resumed performing in front of live audiences and began to reestablish the rapport with fans that he had enjoyed during the mid-1950s.

Elvis's satellite-broadcast concert from Hawaii in January 1973 marked the high point of his career as a performer. With a repertoire that included virtually all the music he loved, he defied the trend toward musical specialization that influenced the vast majority of musical entertainers during this period and staked his claim as the consummate American artist.

placed in a boarding school. Eventually, she would secure a divorce so that she and Vernon could marry on July 3, 1960. Elvis didn't attend the ceremony, and the day after it made a point of visiting his mother's grave.

At Parker's urging, Presley rebuffed all efforts to get him to sing in public while in Germany, even for charity. The Colonel was adamant that performances of any kind would dilute Elvis's star power and undermine his own efforts to improve the terms of Presley's contracts with RCA and the Hollywood studios. Elvis made some public appearances, though, and even entertained fans who had won contests organized by his European fan clubs. Elvis listened to as many records as he could get hold of and kept close track of developments in the music industry at home. He even bought a reel-to-reel tape recorder, and with Parker's blessing he worked assiduously on his vocal technique with Charlie Hodge, hoping to improve his range and become a more effective ballad singer. Improvement stoked Presley's ambition to move in a new musical direction. By early 1960, as he prepared to return to civilian life and his career, he had decided to add emotive, inspirational ballads to his musical repertoire. Long a fan of R&B balladeers like Roy Hamilton, he had shied away from such material before, recognizing his shortcomings as a singer. But he now felt he could tackle it; the only question was how his fans would respond.

Throughout Presley's service in Germany, Parker assuaged his fears with a shower of letters and telegrams, informing him about the latest deals he was working on and the ways in which he was keeping Elvis's name in the news. Their tone reveals Parker's shrewdness in recognizing the kind of support and inside dope that his client needed to keep his spirits up. They allowed Elvis to feel like an accomplice in the Colonel's snow jobs. Presley had to be pleased with the acumen of his manager, who was waging a brilliant campaign to keep Elvis in the spotlight and allow him to emerge from the Army as a mainstream entertainer.

The first prong of Parker's strategy involved RCA. From the start, RCA's Steve Sholes had demanded a large output of recordings from Presley, and Parker had worked hard to place strict contractual limits on the number of releases his client was obliged to provide, fearing

RCA's plan would saturate the market. When Elvis was preparing to go into the Army, Sholes was frantic about recording as many songs as possible before his induction, and after Presley left for Germany, he kept badgering the Colonel for Elvis to record some material from abroad. Parker was adamantly against it, and he convinced Presley that it was in his best interests for RCA to make do with the recordings they already had in the can. Without much new product, RCA was compelled to reissue previously released material, often in the form of greatest-hits packages. Virtually all these records sold well, keeping Presley on the charts and vindicating Parker's conservative approach. Parker also forced RCA to accept new terms that increased Elvis's royalty payments and allowed him to use movie recordings to fulfill his contractual obligation of two LPs and eight singles a year. This would lessen the pressure on Presley to record in between making movies and foster a new level of synchrony between singles and soundtracks.

At the same time, Parker was busy renegotiating Presley's contracts with various movie studios, playing them off against one another in order to ensure the highest profits for his client. Convinced that Elvis was not a flash in the pan, Hal Wallis agreed to sharply increase Presley's salary for his next picture, to $175,000 plus a share of the profits. Meanwhile, 20th Century–Fox executives, not wanting to miss the boat, exercised their option to make two pictures with Elvis when he returned. At the very least, Presley could anticipate three new movie projects, paying him half a million dollars, during his first year out of the service, and MGM, also eager for his services, hadn't even entered the fray yet.

But Parker's most impressive gambit was ensuring that Elvis's name was in the news and on the minds of his fans. His office maintained close contact with the fan clubs, keeping them abreast of news about their idol, including the customary "private notes" from him about his experiences in the Army. He helped to promote the rerelease of Elvis's movies and kindled public interest in the Paramount film that Presley would soon be making. He sent telegrams and messages on Elvis's behalf to a wide assortment of show-business people, small courtesies that improved their opinion of Elvis and placed him more firmly within the mainstream entertainment community. Presley's new stature within the industry was confirmed when Frank Sinatra requested that Elvis appear on one of his television specials after his return. The fee the Colonel negotiated, $125,000, was more than Sinatra himself would be receiving as host of the show. As the day of Elvis's return drew near, Parker put his publicity mill into high gear, flooding the trade press and newspapers with items about Presley and arranging for interviews, press conferences, and public appearances.[30]

By early 1960 it was clear that the Army had not derailed Elvis's career. It had enhanced it, opening up new professional horizons. Parker had been right. Just as he had promised back in 1958, Elvis was coming home to "big movie deals" and the respect of the public, which he had earned by fulfilling his obligations as an ordinary soldier. Presley's improved image had made the Sinatra booking possible, and it was responsible for Hollywood's heightened interest. Once a polarizing figure who had embodied the "threat" of rock and roll, Elvis had joined the entertainment establishment, the very goal he had wished for in 1954, well before he ever met Tom Parker. The Colonel had seen that Elvis had the raw materials to achieve this goal, and he had devised a game plan that the two of them had executed brilliantly, capitalizing on the controversy Elvis had helped incite, then skillfully steering him away from it. With Gladys out of the picture, no one in Elvis's circle was suspicious of the Colonel, and Elvis, taken with Parker's ability to keep him on top, grew more dependent on him. Elvis came to see Parker as a kind of talisman who had made his success possible—and without whom he couldn't remain a star.

On March 2, 1960, with a tearful Priscilla waving goodbye at the airport, Presley boarded a military transport plane and left Germany, arriving at McGuire Air Force Base in New Jersey the following morning.[31] The next day Senator Estes Kefauver, a reformer well known for his animus toward youth culture, read a tribute to Presley into the *Congressional Record*, extolling him for his willingness to serve as "just another G.I. Joe." Elvis was back, and he was bigger and more popular than ever.

CHAPTER 5

Matinee Idol

THE SMALL BUILDING in back of Graceland was packed with reporters and photographers jockeying for a better angle to see the man of the hour, Sergeant Elvis Presley, newly discharged from the Army and poised to continue the career he had put on hold in 1958. It was March 7, 1960, and Presley had just arrived after a long train journey from New Jersey. Now it was time to meet the press. Seated behind the desk his father used to handle his business affairs, Elvis fielded a flurry of questions about his career plans, his military service, and his feelings on being home at last. His manner was casual, and he laughed and joked as he answered. But he also exuded a maturity that was widely noted. Asked what advice he had for other young American men facing the prospect of military service, he replied, "Play it straight . . . and . . . do your best." Resisting military discipline was fruitless and counterproductive: "If you're going to try to be an individual or try to be different, you're gonna go through two years of . . . misery."[1]

Echoing public remarks he had made before his induction, Elvis's advice acquired a new salience after the resumption of his career, when he moved in directions that profoundly altered the public's perception of him. Thanks to his military service, and Colonel Parker's careful handling of the publicity surrounding it, Elvis's public image had already become more wholesome. And even before Presley's discharge, Parker had sought to capitalize on the softening of adult attitudes toward his client, negotiating new deals with Hollywood studios and ensuring that Elvis's guest spot on the Frank Sinatra special became the pivotal event of the program, which was recast as a "Welcome Home, Elvis" celebration. This spadework paid off handsomely. After his return to civilian life, Presley achieved the mainstream success as a movie star he had always craved. But with success came new constraints and an unanticipated sense of disappointment. Rather than liberating him to fulfill his ambitions as a serious actor, becoming a movie star ensnared him in a web of commitments that made attaining that goal virtually impossible.

Two weeks after his homecoming, Presley and four of his buddies—his cousin Gene Smith, Lamar Fike, Cliff Gleaves, and Joe Esposito—traveled to Miami to film the Sinatra special. Between rehearsals with his band, which now included the vocal group the Jordanaires but not the bassist Bill Black, Elvis tried to develop a rapport with Sinatra and his show-business sidekicks, the already legendary Rat Pack. Sinatra, forced to celebrate the homecoming of a figure he had once denounced, did his best to make Elvis feel welcome. They taped the show on March 26. Presley performed two new songs he had recorded in Nashville just the week before; by the time the program aired in May, one of them, "Stuck on You," had reached the top of the charts. Yet it was Elvis's duet with Sinatra that most excited the show's huge audience and the press, with Elvis and the "Chairman of the Board," both dressed in impeccably tailored tuxedos, performing each other's songs. While Sinatra's rendition of "Love Me Tender" was perfunctory and a bit awkward, Presley's handling of "Witchcraft," a sophisticated Tin Pan Alley gem, was exemplary, demonstrating his ability to play on Sinatra's turf. Before the Army, Elvis had provided some tantalizing hints of his potential range, but here was conclusive proof. Much to Colonel Parker's delight, Presley had not just met the challenge posed by the Sinatra show; he had once again surpassed expectations.

The result was the same when Elvis returned to the recording studio. Eager for new product, Steve Sholes had scheduled a session in

Nashville right before Presley's trip to Miami, with the same musicians who had played with Elvis at his last session in June 1958. Working all night, they recorded six new songs, enabling RCA to press and ship a million copies of Presley's new single, "Stuck on You," within days of the session. In early April, Elvis went back into the studio and recorded an additional twelve songs, enough material for a new album, *Elvis Is Back!*

THESE SESSIONS gave Elvis an opportunity to record an even wider variety of songs. The most notable change was the inclusion of an operatic ballad that enabled him to make use of the vocal skills he had developed in Germany. Released as a single in July, "It's Now or Never" was a rewritten version of an Italian folk song that had once been a hit for Enrico Caruso. Elvis's version, with new lyrics commissioned by Freddy Bienstock, an executive with Hill and Range, was lushly romantic and emotive. It became a huge hit and gave Presley his second No. 1 single in a row. Elvis's next single, released in November but also recorded at the April session, was also a ballad, "Are You Lonesome Tonight?" It was another remake—the original had been popular in the 1920s—and it included a corny recitation that was clearly out of step with the times. But it was a favorite of Parker's wife and well suited to Elvis's new vocal style, and the Colonel was certain it would be a hit. Parker had never interfered in Elvis's recording or choice of material, but sensing how important this was to his manager, Elvis put his entire soul into the recording, giving the final product an ardent sincerity that captivated listeners. It was soon Presley's third consecutive No. 1 song. He followed up with another Italian-flavored tune, "Surrender," which was released in early 1961 and became the fifth straight Presley single to reach the top of the charts. It was an astonishing run, equal to the success he had enjoyed in the mid-1950s, and a testament to his fans' willingness to accept his change in musical direction.

Yet hit singles were but the tip of the iceberg, and any review of his post-Army recordings that focuses on singles alone underestimates his growth as a vocalist. The Nashville sessions in the spring of 1960 were among the most fruitful of his career and resulted in works that rank with his most original and accomplished recordings of the 1950s; subsequent sessions in October and the following spring were also productive, though not to the same degree. Inspired by the long hiatus from recording, Presley demonstrated his mastery of ballads, country-inflected pop, jaunty pop rock, and nasty blues-influenced rockers. The blues songs—particularly "A Mess of Blues" and Lowell Fulson's "Reconsider Baby," long one of Elvis's favorites—were riveting, with the crack studio musicians providing the perfect accompaniment for Presley's raunchy vocals. Even otherwise innocuous pop-rock tunes had an edge that lifted them above the bland pop songs that had come to dominate the charts since the late 1950s. "Such a Night," for example, recorded in 1960 but released as a single in 1964, exuded an uncommon vigor and panache. Had it been released right away, and not four years later at the height of Beatlemania, it would certainly have been a much bigger hit. But it was the ballads that really distinguished Elvis's post-Army recordings from his previous material. Displaying his new vocal chops and an uncanny ability to *feel* the material, Presley excelled on songs that were expressly written to suit his new musical orientation.

Elvis continued in the same vein at recording sessions held in October 1960, in March, June, and October of 1961, and in March 1962. Besides "Surrender," the October 1960 sessions yielded a stellar gospel album, *His Hand in Mine*, a project Presley had been looking forward to for several years. It did surprisingly well on the charts, reaching No. 13. The three sessions in 1961 produced hit singles—"I Feel So Bad," "His Latest Flame," and "Good Luck Charm," the latter reaching No. 1—and a number of truly distinguished songs that appeared on albums. Quite a few of the gems were written by songwriters affiliated with Hill and Range, who had become adept at crafting songs that offered Elvis opportunities to develop as a vocalist. Don Robertson specialized in romantic ballads, many of them country inflected, while Doc Pomus and Mort Shuman, who also wrote songs for groups like the Drifters, were the most reliable source for R&B-based material. In short, Presley's musical accomplishments went beyond the string of hits that habitually appear on greatest-hits albums, and belie the conventional belief that his post-Army recordings were uniformly mediocre. "Only Roy Orbison, Ray Charles, Jackie Wilson and a few Motown artists can challenge Elvis for both quality and quantity of music in this period," the critic Dave Marsh has argued, "and only Charles can touch his diversity."[2]

Despite this success, by early 1962 Colonel Parker had decided that Presley should cut back on non-soundtrack recording lest the market become flooded, and Elvis, absorbed in the grind of making three movies per year, reluctantly agreed. Elvis wouldn't return to the studio to record non-movie-related songs until May 1963. When the fruits of this session were not up to his standards, he became discouraged, and after an even more dispiriting session in early 1964 he didn't return to the studio to record non-movie material until 1966. There was, as always, an impeccable logic to Parker's reasoning, and it is hard to fault Elvis for being persuaded by it. The soundtrack to *G.I. Blues*, the first picture he made after his release from the Army, had shot to the top of the album charts, and the soundtrack to *Blue Hawaii*, released in the fall of 1961, had done even better, yielding one of his most popular singles, "Can't Help Falling in Love." Why not concentrate on the soundtracks, particularly since the Colonel had gotten RCA to accept them as a suitable means of fulfilling Elvis's contractual obligation? It was so simple, so economical. As Parker reminded Elvis, a hit single like "Can't Help Falling in Love" not only boosted sales of the soundtrack; it also encouraged people to go to theaters to see the movie—and put RCA in the business of promoting Elvis's movies while promoting his records.

But with their eyes fixed on the bottom line, neither Elvis nor Parker foresaw the growing sense of disillusionment Elvis would experience when the field in which he had achieved both financial *and* artistic success was closed off to experimentation. Making music was Presley's forte. And while he had improved as an actor, singing and playing music—whether in the recording studio or onstage—was the one thing he felt entirely comfortable doing. His command over the process gave him self-confidence, which he had used to succeed on television and in the movies. It was the wellspring from which everything else had come.

Recording only for soundtracks deprived him of the autonomy and sense of possibility that had previously characterized his sessions. The soundtracks required songs that fit the plots of films and that Elvis had to perform in situations that were often hokey and sometimes patently absurd. As a result, the quantity and variety of material submitted by Hill and Range declined, and songwriters who wrote for Elvis were encouraged to compose trite and formulaic songs. The soundtrack for *Girls! Girls! Girls!*, for example, a film released in late 1962, included a great single, Otis Blackwell's "Return to Sender," which reached No. 2, but also such forgettable tripe as "Song of the Shrimp." Given these constraints, fewer songwriters wanted to write for Elvis, particularly since doing so required sharing the publishing rights—and the royalties— with Presley and his manager. It is not surprising that Elvis became increasingly frustrated. Though he did his best with the poor-quality material that filled most of the soundtracks, recording soon became a lackluster routine, a matter of going through the motions. By the mid-1960s, he was generally recording soundtrack material in one or two takes—a far cry from the dedicated professionalism he had displayed in the 1950s and at his first sessions after the Army.

A similar interest in limiting the quantity of Presley "product" led Parker to restrict his public appearances and live performances. Before Presley's discharge, Parker was besieged with offers from concert promoters and television producers, but in typical fashion he dismissed most out of hand and agreed only to the Sinatra booking, which was designed to stimulate public interest in Presley's upcoming films. And after Elvis's return to the United States, the demands of recording and making three movies within eight months limited the time for concert tours. Yet even in 1961, after Presley's career had settled into a comfortable rhythm that might have accommodated regular tours, Parker continued to rebuff promoters and network executives.[3]

The only exceptions were benefits. In December 1960, Parker

arranged for Presley to perform two shows at Ellis Auditorium in Memphis, with all the proceeds going to assorted Memphis charities and the Elvis Presley Youth Center in Tupelo. The concerts, held on February 25, 1961, were a smashing success. Elvis looked as if he had never taken a break from performing, captivating the audience and impressing reporters. The shows raised over fifty thousand dollars and revealed that Presley could still mesmerize a crowd. The second benefit was a little over a month later in Honolulu, where Elvis had gone to make *Blue Hawaii*. The proceeds from this concert helped to pay for a memorial to the servicemen who died on the USS *Arizona* during the attack on Pearl Harbor. Accompanied by the same musicians he had grown used to working with in Nashville and Los Angeles, where he recorded his soundtracks, Elvis delivered one of his most electrifying performances. Feeding off the energy of the band and the ecstatic approval of the audience, he displayed a degree of self-assurance he never came close to showing before a movie camera. Triumphal moments like these, however, were increasingly rare in the early to mid-1960s as making motion pictures became Elvis's principal occupation.

Parker and Elvis alike had concluded that Presley's future lay in movies, for both financial and artistic reasons. As much as Elvis loved music and performing, he returned from Germany committed to developing his skills as a dramatic actor, and the string of commitments Parker had lined up for him, including two film projects with 20th Century–Fox, were meant to move him in this direction—without forsaking his original fan base or his potential for expanding it to include more adults. This required a shift in his roles and on-screen persona. Elvis's pre-Army movies, with the exception of the costume drama *Love Me Tender*, had underscored his real-life association with the music business and the controversy over rock and roll and youth culture. Even *King Creole*, the last film he made before his induction—and by all measures his best—required him to play a character who was "troubled" in typically youthful ways and whose job as a nightclub singer made the musical numbers integral to the plot. Presley's first movie project after the Army, however, eschewed this pattern and established a new one that would redefine the nature of an "Elvis picture" for the duration of his career as a movie star.

Produced by Hal Wallis for Paramount, *G.I. Blues* was a musical comedy with eleven songs, chronicling the amorous escapades of an American serviceman stationed in Germany. For the first time, Elvis's character was not merely decent, as in previous pictures, but wholesome and utterly lacking in depth. Indeed, the lighthearted plot provided few opportunities to challenge him as an actor. The final product was cute and a whopping success at the box office, yet it was a forgettable piece of moviemaking, and most of the songs on the soundtrack were mediocre, especially compared with the material Elvis had just recorded in Nashville. When Elvis complained to Wallis and the Colonel about some of the songs and the more ridiculous scenes, they insisted that a foray into wholesome, mainstream "family entertainment" was a good foundation for more serious roles to come. Privately, Wallis had doubts about Presley's potential to blossom into a serious actor and regarded low-risk vehicles like *G.I. Blues* as perfect for him. Parker, who was disdainful of artistic pretensions, may have been skeptical, too. Meanwhile, the success of *G.I. Blues* allowed Parker to play hardball with the other studios and initiate a new round of negotiations that resulted in even more lucrative movie deals that would keep Elvis busy through the mid-1960s. By the end of 1964, though several movie stars earned considerably more per picture, Elvis's regimen of three highly profitable pictures per year made him the best-paid actor in the industry. Earning at least $500,000 per film plus a share of the profits, he had become one of Hollywood's most bankable stars.

If *G.I. Blues* was a lightweight star vehicle, Elvis's next film, *Flaming Star*, presented him with a more substantial challenge. It was a Western in which Elvis played a misunderstood "half-breed," the kind of serious dramatic role for which he hankered. The part had originally been written for Marlon Brando, and the film's director, Don Siegel, was upset when, after Brando turned it down, the role went to the inexperienced Presley. The film included only two songs and marked a return to the brand of ensemble acting seen in *Love Me Tender*. Unfortunately,

Siegel never liked or respected Presley. And Elvis, recognizing this, grew more insecure and behaved in ways that only confirmed Siegel's low estimate of him. After a brief period of enthusiasm and hard work, Presley withdrew his energies, and in the final cut he appears stiff and uncomfortable. To make matters worse, *Flaming Star* did not meet expectations when it was released in December 1960. While *G.I. Blues* reached No. 2 on *Variety's* box-office survey and wound up as the fourteenth-highest-grossing picture of the year, *Flaming Star* only reached No. 12 the week of its release and was gone from the list a week later.

Presley's next movie also had potential—at least at first. But Parker and studio executives had second thoughts and persuaded Elvis to accept changes that made it more of an Elvis picture. Based on a critically acclaimed novel, and with a screenplay by Clifford Odets, *Wild in the Country* offered Presley a chance to return to familiar terrain, playing a sensitive, troubled young man. Another reason for optimism was that the film's director, Philip Dunne, was determined to make a serious and substantive movie, and was confident he could help Elvis reach a new level. Pressure from studio executives and the Colonel, however, forced Dunne to include four songs and some preposterous scenes with musical interludes. Dunne liked Elvis and sought to bring out the best in his star, but he was hampered by these external constraints and by Elvis's growing sense that forces were conspiring against him. While filming a particularly inane musical scene, Presley muttered to a co-star, "God, this is so embarrassing. Nobody would ever do this in real life. Why are they making me do this?"[4] As the film's star, he might have pulled rank and demanded a more serious script. Yet he never did. Long accustomed to deferring to authority figures, and still smarting from critical barbs that questioned his intelligence, Presley passively accepted every decision like a dutiful employee. Uncommitted to the project, he gave a flat performance. Fatally compromised by these conflicting agendas, *Wild in the Country* was a relative flop at the box office. Its fate confirmed Parker's belief that it was best for Elvis to stick to films like *G.I. Blues* rather than experiment with projects that might cause his popularity—and the Colonel's leverage in contract negotiations—to wane.

Presley's two forays into "serious" moviemaking, rather than extending his range, only served to increase his sense of insecurity and revealed the risks of moving away from the tried and true. Lacking the self-assurance he felt when recording or performing, Elvis turned for support to his friends, who always accompanied him to the set and offered him a ready group of playmates between takes and during lunch, occasions when he might have studied his lines or concentrated his mental energies on scenes to come. This cavalier attitude, which Elvis hadn't displayed when making movies in the 1950s, convinced many studio personnel that he was little more than a charismatic matinee idol whose films provided them with a measure of financial security at a time when the industry was moving in new artistic directions and grappling with sharply escalating production costs.[5] It wasn't simply Presley's preference for touch football and karate demonstrations, however, that made people in Hollywood believe he wasn't interested in developing as an actor. In front of the camera, Elvis was stiff and jumpy, often delivering his lines at a breakneck speed that elicited chuckles on the set, even among his friends. He seemed incapable of rising to the next level—or even to the modest heights he had scaled in *Jailhouse Rock* and *King Creole*.

SOME OF THIS can be attributed to the persistent insecurity he felt in Hollywood, where he thought people were making fun of him behind his back. Yet it was also a result of his increased use of amphetamines. Making use of an array of "friendly" pharmacists and phony prescriptions, which he obtained by poring over the *Physicians' Desk Reference* and passing himself off as an expert on prescription drugs, Elvis took uppers as regularly as most people take vitamins, and most of his friends took them, too, in order to keep up. As their amphetamine intake escalated, however, they were forced to take copious quantities of sleeping pills and more potent tranquilizers to settle down and get some rest before the next day's activities. Elvis rationalized his behavior by telling himself these were legal substances, not illegal ones like marijuana, cocaine, or heroin, a not-uncommon line of reasoning in the late 1950s and early 1960s, when large numbers of middle-class Americans consumed—and, like Elvis, abused—prescription medications. Like alcohol, nicotine, and caffeine, mood-altering prescription drugs were viewed by many citizens as an acceptable feature of the postwar American way of life, supplements that gave people an extra edge or enabled them to bear the strain of the workaday world and daily living.[6] Of course, the vast majority of Americans took these drugs under the care of a physician. But Elvis, exploiting his stature as a celebrity and his vast knowledge of the *PDR*, escaped such monitoring, consuming these legal drugs in increasingly dangerous quantities. In the early 1960s, however, few people thought twice about Presley's behavior on the set. If he seemed unusually hyperactive and distracted, it was ascribed to immaturity, nerves, or the presence of his friends and their habitual hijinks.

The reservations Parker had begun to feel about Elvis's halting efforts to move into more serious roles were amplified in November 1961, when *Blue Hawaii* opened and instantly became a box-office smash, peaking at No. 2 on the *Variety* survey. *Blue Hawaii* was a Hal Wallis production that returned Elvis to the realm of musical comedy. Wallis hated the movies Presley had made for Fox and was determined to make a film that better suited his star's talents. The movie's director, Norman Taurog, had worked with Elvis on *G.I. Blues*, and while filming *Blue Hawaii*, Taurog encouraged Presley to loosen up and enjoy the experience. He was even tolerant of Elvis's entourage, and the rapport he developed with Presley made him a natural to direct subsequent Elvis pictures. Partly filmed on location, the movie was a fast-paced, lightweight piece of fluff, with Elvis playing the young heir to a pineapple fortune who eschews the privileges of his class to work as a tour guide, an occupation that provides him with many opportunities for romance and high-spirited fun. Presley's performance was competent, and though many of the film's fourteen songs were banal, he sang them with an air of confident nonchalance. The most vivid quality Elvis conveys is charisma. On-screen he is handsome and charming, with a wholesome sex appeal. As the box-office receipts confirmed, this guise was very attractive to his fans, many of whom were getting older and were happy to see their idol in movies that showcased his maturity and more conventionally adult good looks. Indeed, playing such roles required little effort. Usually written with him expressly in mind, they fit like a tailored suit and asked only that he be "Elvis Presley."

Blue Hawaii was in many ways the seminal Elvis picture. His previous films were varied and fit no consistent pattern. And the movies he made immediately after returning from Germany displayed the greatest variety. One could easily imagine this Elvis, with the right support and training, moving into serious Westerns or even the contemporary adult roles popularized by actors like Paul Newman and Warren Beatty. But the relative failure of his serious pictures at the box office—and "failure" is indeed a relative concept in this case, since it was only by Parker's standards, which Elvis came to share, that *Flaming Star* and *Wild in the Country* could be construed as failures—increased the pressure on Elvis to retreat. When *Blue Hawaii* proved such a success, and so much easier to make, putting him at little risk of ridicule, Presley resigned himself and stopped badgering his manager to get him better roles. Measuring success in terms of box-office receipts and mainstream popularity, Presley and Parker were ill equipped to recognize or appreciate the new artistic currents that were already flowing through Hollywood in the early 1960s and would soon spark an unprecedented creative renaissance for actors and producers alike.[7] It wasn't the confines of the Hollywood studio system, then, that kept Elvis tethered to the formula established by *Blue Hawaii*. The studio system was already crumbling, making it possible for all kinds of new films to be made—and for actors to enjoy a new degree of artistic freedom. In the end, what led Presley to continue to make Elvis pictures was his own intrinsic conservatism.

Most of Elvis's subsequent films followed the *Blue Hawaii* formula, whether they were made at Paramount by Wallis or at other studios. They were often set in an exotic locale like Las Vegas, Acapulco, or Florida, and required Elvis to play characters with exciting, even dangerous occupations—pilot, race-car driver, rodeo rider, prizefighter. They always included plenty of attractive women who competed for Elvis's attention or otherwise added to the colorful setting. More often than not, Elvis encountered rivals, and there was usually some kind of confrontation with another man that Elvis had to win before he got the girl at the end. Besides romance, Elvis pictures included plenty of action. There were regular fight scenes, often featuring members of Presley's entourage as extras, which gave Elvis a chance to display his mastery of karate. In much the same manner as always being selected to play quarterback, Elvis always won the fights, emerging unscathed, with his hair still perfectly coiffed. And, of course, there were the songs, mostly forgettable material that Presley recorded in workmanlike fashion. Elvis was always the center of attention, something Colonel Parker ensured by closely supervising production every step of the way. When, for example, Parker thought the director of *Viva Las Vegas* was favoring Elvis's dynamic co-star, Ann-Margret, he protested to MGM executives and succeeded in reducing her prominence in the film.[8]

Making these movies was tedious and at times frustrating. Though successful and vital in making him a truly international star, his "travelogues," as he derisively referred to these films, rarely challenged him and sometimes embarrassed him. Ironically, one of the few projects that did inspire his interest was *Viva Las Vegas*, a film he made for MGM in the summer of 1963. Entranced by the talented and vivacious Ann-Margret, with whom he had a passionate offscreen affair, Presley infused the scenes in which he appeared with his co-star with an energy and commitment he hadn't displayed since *King Creole*. The musical numbers, sparked by the friendly rivalry between the two stars, were also far above the norm, even if some of the songs were pedestrian. The climax of the film, a casino-sponsored talent show in which Elvis and Ann-Margret compete for first prize, is one of the best musical interludes Presley ever filmed, and it is clear throughout the picture that for the first time in several years, Elvis is enjoying himself.

In hindsight, the lesson of *Viva Las Vegas* is that Elvis needed to be challenged, and that the spur of competition might have revived his interest in moviemaking and helped him develop as an actor, even if his forte had remained musicals. Yet Parker was loath to allow anyone to share the spotlight with his boy, and his dogged efforts to keep Elvis the focal point of the film convinced him that they should avoid situations where another performer could steal the show or use an Elvis picture to promote her own career. Presley, increasingly insecure in Hollywood, was inclined to agree.

Accordingly, in the wake of *Viva Las Vegas* his movie projects became even more formulaic as he struggled to summon up the energy to fulfill contractual obligations the Colonel had negotiated—and Elvis had blithely agreed to—years before. In one respect, things got even worse. After *Viva Las Vegas* went way over budget, a development that Parker blamed on feckless executives at MGM, the Colonel signed a deal with Sam Katzman, an MGM producer who had a reputation for making movies at minimal cost. Katzman, heralded in Hollywood as the "King of the Quickies," made Elvis's next picture, *Kissin' Cousins*, and *Harum Scarum* in 1965, implementing a new regimen that Parker made the template for all subsequent film projects. By cutting shooting time in half, to less than three weeks, eliminating expensive location footage, and skimping on scripts and the kinds of production values that Hal Wallis had regarded as de rigueur, Katzman dramatically lowered the cost of making an Elvis picture. These economies were important. With box-office receipts decent but hardly at the level of *G.I. Blues* and *Blue Hawaii*, they ensured that Presley's films would continue to make a healthy profit.

But Katzman's new regimen also caused the quality of Presley's movies to decline. Scripts became absurd, the songs mostly dismal, and the look of the films shoddy—at a time when many studios were investing huge sums in lavish musicals, costume dramas, and serious pictures like *Bonnie and Clyde* and *The Graduate*. Even Parker was appalled by the final cut of *Harum Scarum* and half-jokingly suggested to MGM brass that a talking camel be added as a narrator.

Surprisingly, the movies continued to draw a sizable hard core of Elvis fans. And because of the new economies imposed, they made money for the studios and their star. Given the deals Parker had been able to negotiate in the early 1960s, when Presley's star power was at its peak, Elvis's income from motion pictures actually increased as the quality—and box-office receipts—of his films declined. In 1962, for example, a year that began with *Blue Hawaii* still in theaters and saw the release of three other pictures, including *Girls! Girls! Girls!*, another Hal Wallis production set in Hawaii, Elvis made over $900,000 from motion pictures. By contrast, in 1967, when three dreadful Elvis films were released, his income from movies was $2.7 million. This windfall was easy money, and as it kept rolling in, Elvis kept making movies, accepting some scripts without even reading them, let alone demanding changes to improve them. The money and the lifestyle it enabled him to lead compensated, at least in part, for the humiliation of having his name associated with such forgettable projects as *Tickle Me* (1965), *Paradise, Hawaiian Style* (1966), and *Easy Come, Easy Go* (1967), a film whose title aptly summarizes Presley's experience with moviemaking in the 1960s.

But it was still galling. And on occasion Presley would complain to his friends about his predicament—locked into making three formulaic movies per year, under a regimen that made it impossible to produce a decent picture or provide him with a chance to expand his range as an actor, his greatest unfulfilled ambition. He was especially upset when he was reminded that the revenues his films generated helped to finance some of the serious pictures being produced by Wallis and others. "In order to do the artistic pictures," Wallis explained to a reporter in an article that enraged Elvis, "it is necessary to do the commercially successful Presley pictures."[9] Elvis had been relegated to the role of cash cow.

This was not what Presley or his manager had envisioned in 1960 when Elvis returned from Germany. And though most of the time Elvis did his job without complaining and kept his frustration and disillusionment to himself, in the mid-1960s he and his manager began to quarrel. It wasn't just the poor quality of the films that led Presley to question the wisdom of the man who had taken him to the very apex of show-business success. By 1965 his movies were attracting smaller and smaller audiences, the soundtracks weren't making the album charts, and his singles were being outsold by new music that had taken over Top 40 radio and captivated a new generation of young people—the ebullient sounds of Motown and the girl groups, the California pop rock of the Beach Boys, and the innovative R&B-influenced music of the Beatles and other "British Invasion" bands. From Elvis's perspective, Parker seemed out of touch. Their confrontations became increasingly heated. When angry, Presley and the Colonel would sequester themselves in a room and scream at each other, then emerge and sulk, sometimes not speaking for a week or more afterward. But in the end they always reconciled, usually when Elvis began to envision the prospect of continuing his career without the man who had done so much for him over the years. The bond between them was too strong, and despite his anger and frustration Elvis was comfortable having someone else handle all the business decisions. "If he followed the Colonel's advice more often than he should have," Elvis's friend Joe Esposito concluded, "it was because he preferred that someone else take responsibility in case a decision turned out to be wrong."[10] As tempting as it is to blame Parker for Elvis's fate in Hollywood, Presley was ultimately responsible. Unlike other aspiring actors, he was simply unwilling to do the work required to make a meaningful attempt to attain his goal, and his cavalier attitude toward the business end of his career gave the Colonel more influence and authority than any manager ought to have over a client.

Nor was Parker as obtuse as Presley liked to believe. By 1966 the Colonel was equally concerned about the decline in box-office revenues and Elvis's waning fortunes on the music charts. His first response, however, was to tie himself even more firmly to his only client, sitting Elvis down and officially formalizing a "partnership agreement" that recognized Parker's enormous stake in Presley's career and compensated him accordingly. Under the new agreement, which took effect on January 1, 1967, Parker continued to receive his usual 25 percent management fee on all contracts and the payments that derived from them. But any profits that Elvis earned over and above this, including those on various "side deals," would now be split fifty-fifty. This was unprecedented, and has inspired many writers to accuse Parker of being an avaricious parasite.[11] Yet as Peter Guralnick has argued, Parker had good reasons for renegotiating the terms of their partnership. Committed to a single client whose popularity was seemingly in decline and who worked in fields that were undergoing sweeping, unpredictable changes, Parker was seeking some insurance that the time and energy he spent promoting Elvis would be adequately compensated. Given the challenges that lay ahead, who could blame him? Certainly not Elvis, who signed the agreement well aware of its implications. Though he and Parker might have differences of opinion, he could never doubt his manager's commitment to him. As Esposito noted, "The bottom line is that Elvis would never have been as popular as he was without the Colonel's brilliant management. Nor would the Colonel have had so much success with anyone else."[12]

There was another reason for Parker's concern. From the beginning of his career, Elvis had always worked hard and met or exceeded expectations. He could always be counted on to do his job, even when it was not entirely to his liking. This meant not only showing up and doing his best when making movies or recording music, but also avoiding scandal and projecting a wholesome image to the press and the public at large. But as the quality of his film projects declined, he began displaying new and disturbing traits. The Colonel had always let Elvis handle the music and the movies, while he had concentrated on business. This arrangement had worked very well in the 1950s and in the immediate wake of Presley's discharge from the Army, when he was brimming with enthusiasm. By the mid-1960s, however, when Elvis's lack of commitment to his movie projects became palpable, Parker found himself in the awkward position of having to make excuses for his client. Elvis wasn't doing his job, and the more Parker thought about it, the more he concluded that the problem was not just the poor quality of the material but the whole tenor of Presley's private life.

Though Parker might not have recognized it, the seeds of Elvis's decline were planted in the early 1960s, well before any problems were visible. By the summer of 1961 Elvis's life had settled into a rhythm. Three times a year he would travel to Los Angeles, accompanied by his entourage, to make movies and record soundtracks. By early 1964, Elvis had stopped recording in Nashville, and Hollywood had become his primary place of work, with Memphis the place he returned to between movie projects, often in a customized motor home at the head of a caravan of automobiles carrying the rest of the guys. To make his visits to Los Angeles more comfortable, Presley rented a large house in the exclusive Bel Air district of Beverly Hills. Some of his friends moved in, with the others living in rented apartments paid for by Elvis.

Presley's entourage in the early 1960s included some of the same men who had been with him before the Army, but it was larger than before. Joe Esposito had assumed the role of "foreman," and newcomers like Marty Lacker, Jerry Schilling, and Sonny West—Red West's cousin—had joined the group. Beyond the inner circle were a number of other men whose involvement with Elvis was short-lived or intermittent. Presley's friends accompanied him nearly everywhere, and they were companions, not bodyguards. Never one to be happy alone, Elvis had traveled with friends from the outset of his career, and now that he was successful, he found it comforting to be constantly in their company.[13]

When in Los Angeles, fueled by ever-increasing quantities of amphetamines, Elvis and the guys led lives of bacchanalian excess. With their steady girlfriends and wives back in Memphis, they hosted wild parties at Presley's home in Bel Air, to which they invited a bevy of attractive women, including many of the prettiest groupies who regularly congregated at the front gate of the house in the evening, eager for a chance to meet Elvis. Movie people attended these parties, too, usually co-stars with whom Elvis had become friendly, but they were in the minority. Influenced by the movie colony's freewheeling ways, Elvis began serving liquor at his parties, and for a couple of years he and the guys drank more than previously. But he remained opposed to the use of marijuana and "hard drugs," and guests who indulged in them had to do so out of his sight. With women vastly outnumbering men, once Elvis had made his choice for the evening, the guys were left to pounce on the also-rans. In keeping with the frat-house atmosphere, Elvis even had a two-way mirror installed in the cabana, enabling him and his buddies to watch female visitors get in and out of their swimsuits.

Parties were not their only recreation. Presley and his friends, outfitted in custom-made uniforms, also played touch football games in local parks, usually against teams composed of young actors such as Gary Crosby, Pat Boone, Robert Conrad, and Ricky Nelson. As in Germany, Elvis always played quarterback, and his team was augmented by new friends like Max Baer, Jr., the hulking star of the popular television program *The Beverly Hillbillies.* Much to the consternation of their neighbors, they bought motorcycles and zoomed through the canyons of Beverly Hills and out on Sunset to the beach. They avidly practiced karate, offering demonstrations to party guests and people they met at the studios. And they took regular road trips to Las Vegas, where they caught the shows and partied with strippers and showgirls, staying up for days at a time. Decked out in matching black mohair suits and carrying identical briefcases, they exuded a masculine cool that captured the fancy of the press and led to their depiction as the "Memphis Mafia," Elvis's answer to Sinatra's Rat Pack.

Things were only slightly more subdued in Memphis. With Gladys no longer present to provide a motherly influence, and with Vernon and his new wife living in another house around the corner, only Elvis's grandmother Minnie remained at Graceland. But she kept mostly to her room, encouraging Elvis to do as he pleased. The atmosphere at Graceland changed markedly, becoming, in Alan Fortas's recollection, "more like a whorehouse."[14] Of course, Elvis still had his steadies, like Anita Wood, whom he continued to see after his discharge from the Army, but this didn't stop him—or the rest of the guys—from consorting with many of the women who gathered at Graceland's gates and were invited inside. He also continued renting movie theaters, roller rinks, and the local amusement park, where he and the guys, usually with dates, would go after hours. But most of the time they fraternized at Graceland, which Elvis had redecorated to reflect his new guise as a swanky playboy, and sang gospel songs, listened to music, watched football, practiced karate, drove custom-made go-karts, or played with the elaborate stock-car track that Elvis had installed in one of the large rooms that had been added to the house. Life with Elvis was a perpetual adolescence.

Relations between Elvis and his entourage were complex. Ostensibly, they were his buddies and Elvis was just one of the guys. Mostly Southerners like himself, they were a particularly reassuring presence in Hollywood. "Elvis didn't like Hollywood. He didn't like the people. He didn't like the phoniness," Marty Lacker noted. "Although he became more polished as the years went on . . . he was still a country boy at heart, with simple tastes. He didn't want to go to parties. He didn't want to go out and be seen."[15] Being with Elvis allowed the guys, none of whom was especially handsome, to meet and have sex with scores of beautiful women and gain admission to a world far removed from their usually humble origins. The guys also performed various tasks for Elvis, running errands, taking care of his fleet of cars and motorcycles, making arrangements with the owners of establishments Presley wanted to rent, setting up after-hours shopping expeditions, and ensuring that Graceland and Elvis's home in Bel Air were well provisioned. For several years in the late 1950s and early 1960s, Presley didn't pay them salaries; he only covered their living expenses, which caused several of them considerable hardship, since being with Elvis was more than a full-time job and made it difficult to earn money on the side. When this was gently pointed out to him, he put a number of them on the payroll and formalized their responsibilities.

Their dependence not only complicated their friendship and encouraged them to act like sycophants; it also inspired jealousy and backbiting within the group as the guys competed for Elvis's favor. Many of the guys came to resent Chicago-born Joe Esposito. His role as the group's foreman in charge of expenses, and his penchant for trying to create an inner circle around Elvis, generated a lot of hostility and encouraged some of his rivals to conspire against him. Lamar Fike, a longtime butt of Presley's jokes, was mercilessly teased by the others simply because Elvis derived pleasure from it. Most of the time Fike took the teasing in stride, but when it got especially cruel, his feelings were hurt and he began to despise his tormentors. To make matters worse, by the mid-1960s, as Presley's intake of drugs escalated, he became more capricious, making it harder to stay on his good side without resorting to explicit brownnosing that looked bad in the eyes of everyone else. His temper flared when he didn't get his way, and he often fired members of the group for the slightest mistake or a remark that was not to his liking. These outbursts were invariably followed by bouts of generosity. A remorseful Elvis, unable to say he was sorry, would send word that he wanted the fired man back, offering gifts that might include an automobile or down payment on a house. Members of the group, even their wives and girlfriends, learned to watch their tongue as well as their behavior. As virtually all of them came to recognize, there were rules that everyone had to follow. The entourage had to display the proper deference to Elvis, the "boss." "The sad thing is, as good a time as we had back then," said Lacker, "I think there were always doubts in Elvis's mind about why we were there."[16] These doubts, which plague most celebrities, were exacerbated in Presley's case by the cumulative effect of the drugs, and led him to make extravagant demands on the guys in order to prove their loyalty.

Relations between Elvis and his entourage were further complicated because Vernon, who continued to manage Elvis's personal finances, deeply resented the substantial expenses the entourage incurred. Poorly educated and deeply wary of outsiders, Vernon was in over his head as his son's personal financial manager, and as Elvis began spending more time and money in Los Angeles, the costs of maintaining residences in Memphis and on the West Coast made Vernon increasingly anxious, even as Elvis's income grew. When Elvis's entourage became larger, and Elvis began to spend more and more money on extracurricular activities, Vernon grew convinced that most of the Memphis Mafia were leeches—a fear seemingly confirmed when Elvis formally put them on the payroll.

Things went from bad to worse in 1966, when Elvis, taken with horseback riding, began buying horses for himself, his family, and the guys. In February 1967, finding the grounds at Graceland too small for his new hobby, Elvis bought a 160-acre ranch in northern Mississippi, ten miles from Graceland. He named it the Circle G and proceeded, in only a few months, to purchase hundreds of thousands of dollars' worth of horses, cattle, pickup trucks, trailer homes, and assorted equipment. Envisioned by Elvis as a kind of faux-Western commune, where he and the guys, and their wives, girlfriends, and children, would live in pastoral bliss, the ranch became his abiding interest—and the cause of many a sleepless night for Vernon. With Presley's movies doing less business at the box office, and his musical career in the doldrums, Vernon was terrified that Elvis's reckless spending would drive them into bankruptcy. Fortunately for Vernon, by midsummer Elvis had lost interest in the ranch, and Vernon began to sell the cattle, trailers, and trucks bought at the height of his son's enthusiasm.

Colonel Parker began to share Vernon's worries. Parker himself liked to live in high style, and for a number of years he had been quite tolerant of Elvis's excesses. Keeping out of Elvis's private life, after all, was a cardinal principle of their relationship. Unlike Vernon, who feared fate could take away Elvis's success just as quickly as it had bestowed it, Parker was confident of Elvis's ability to remain at the top, and he saw Elvis's spending as a just reward. Parker was also more understanding than Vernon about the entourage. Recognizing Elvis's insecurity in Hollywood, the Colonel saw the benefits of having Elvis surrounded by people with whom he was comfortable. More important, it worked to Parker's advantage, limiting Presley's contact with other entertainment people, who might give him ideas and possibly undermine the Colonel's influence. Beginning in 1964, however, when it was clear that Elvis was distracted and merely going through the motions on movie sets, Parker became concerned. He began using some of the guys—Joe Esposito in particular—to get information that might explain the changes in Elvis's appearance and attitude.

The problems with Elvis's appearance were clear enough. Since his discharge from the Army, he had gained weight. As early as 1961, on the eve of the making of *Blue Hawaii*, Wallis had complained to Parker that Elvis needed to maintain his youthful physique. During the next few years, these complaints from producers became more insistent. To get in shape for his movies, Elvis went on various crash diets. But after finishing production, he invariably returned to his old ways, including the high-fat foods he loved to consume in large quantities. By the mid-1960s he had already begun a pattern of preproduction dieting and postproduction bingeing that would contribute to serious health problems in later years. Presley's changed attitude was less explicable to Parker, who prided himself on always doing his job and expected the same of Elvis. Bored, disillusioned, and absorbed in the hijinks that were central to his relationship with the guys, Presley was no longer the reliable trouper he had been in previous years, and the movie people, to Parker's dismay, were starting to complain. Clearly, Elvis's mind was no longer on his work. Yet Parker's ability to straighten him out was suddenly undermined by a new development. In the spring of 1964 Elvis began what Parker disdainfully viewed as a "religious kick."

It began when Presley met Larry Geller, a Hollywood hairdresser who was sent to Elvis's home as a fill-in for his regular stylist. As Geller worked on his hair, Elvis abruptly asked, "What are you into?" Geller, a serious devotee of the New Age spiritualism that had already begun to attract followers in Southern California, told Elvis about his interests and the many books that had inspired him to think about the meaning of life. Elvis was fascinated, and they continued talking for hours, with Elvis peppering Geller with questions. "I've always known that there had to be a purpose for my life," he earnestly told Geller. "I've always felt an unseen hand behind me, guiding my life. I mean, there *has* to be a purpose . . . there's got to be a reason . . . why I was chosen to be Elvis Presley."[17]

After their first meeting, Elvis induced Geller to quit his salon job and come to work for him full-time, and their discussions continued as Larry became part of the entourage and a regular visitor at Elvis's house. Geller began bringing over dozens of books like *The Impersonal Life* and *Autobiography of a Yogi*, which Elvis read with great interest. "He devoured the books like a person studying for a college final,"

Geller recalled. "It was never enough for him to read a book; he had to absorb it, think about it, question it, link its thoughts and ideas with all he had read before and things he had heard people say."[18] Geller encouraged Elvis to visit the Self-Realization Fellowship, a New Age retreat in nearby Pacific Palisades. Presley found the experience deeply rewarding, and he immediately struck up a friendship with the retreat's guru, Sri Daya Mata. Impressed with Elvis's sincerity, the guru was also struck by his eagerness to find "shortcuts" to enlightenment, a version of the same impatience that had derailed his growth as an actor. Elvis's new interest prompted him to build a meditation garden at Graceland, and after a religious experience in the Arizona desert, on a drive from Memphis to Los Angeles, he even considered quitting show business to become a monk.

Occurring at the very moment when Sam Katzman was initiating his regimen at the studio and draining Elvis's picture projects of every pretense of artistry, Presley's new interest in spiritualism was enormously satisfying, enabling him to achieve an inner peace he hadn't felt since his mother's death. But it upset the routines of his daily life, particularly in Los Angeles, and dismayed members of his entourage, who quickly came to resent and despise Larry Geller. With Elvis absorbed in his studies and long philosophical conversations with Geller, there were no more parties, and the adolescent fun and games came to a virtual end. Even worse, as Presley got more and more into spiritualism, he badgered the guys to read the same books and join him in his quest for enlightenment. When they showed no interest, Elvis was hurt and withdrew, forming a closer bond with Geller. In the spring of 1965, after Presley began visiting Daya Mata at the Self-Realization Fellowship's retreat, the guys shared with Colonel Parker their fear that Geller was brainwashing Elvis. Parker distrusted Geller from the outset and treated him with a mixture of contempt and cynical chumminess. He was certain Geller was just another manipulator trying to get an angle on his boy. For Parker, what made Geller particularly dangerous was the way in which his influence reinforced the waning of Elvis's interest in show business. It was galling to the Colonel to see Presley's energies rekindled and then directed away from his work. Something had to be done. But with neither Vernon, the guys, nor Parker enjoying much influence over Elvis, there didn't seem to be many options.

Parker found an unlikely ally in Priscilla Beaulieu, the girl Elvis had met and become close to in Germany. Presley and Beaulieu had kept in touch after his return to the United States in March 1960, and though he had resumed dating Anita Wood and having affairs with some of his co-stars and assorted Hollywood starlets, he remained tantalized by the prospect of transforming the impressionable young teenager into his ideal woman. She was equally smitten with him, and she badgered her parents into letting her visit Elvis in Los Angeles in June 1962, after lengthy negotiations between her father and Presley in which Elvis promised that the sixteen-year-old would be properly chaperoned. Her visit was a wonderful experience, since she and Elvis, completely unchaperoned, picked up where they had left off in Germany. After Priscilla returned home, the Beaulieus reluctantly agreed to let her spend the Christmas holidays in Memphis. During this visit she and Elvis began hatching plans that would enable her to move there without her parents and finish high school as Vernon and Dee Presley's ward. Amazingly, after extensive negotiations in which Elvis implied he would eventually marry Priscilla, her parents consented to let her move in with Vernon and Dee. In March 1963, immediately after her father went back to Germany believing that his daughter would be residing with her new guardians, Priscilla moved into Graceland and began life as Elvis's first live-in steady, a development Presley and Beaulieu concealed from her parents and Parker kept from the press.

Priscilla's appeal to Elvis lay in her youth and willingness to do as he pleased. Unlike the starlets he dated or even Anita Wood, whom Elvis had gradually stopped seeing, Priscilla was completely committed to him. "I wasn't interested in a career, in Hollywood, or in anything else that would draw my attention away from him," she later wrote.[19] This meant a lot to Elvis and was the deciding factor that led him to end his relationship with Ann-Margret, whom he met only a few months after Priscilla moved into Graceland. In the end, though he and Ann-

Margret were quite compatible, she was an equal with a career as important as his—and not, like Priscilla, someone utterly dependent on him. As in Germany, Elvis refused to have sexual intercourse with Priscilla, insisting, to her dismay, that he was waiting for the "right" time. They found many other ways of satisfying each other, and when Elvis was in Memphis between movies, he and Priscilla were very close, creating their own private world from which even the guys were partially excluded. But Elvis had a policy of not allowing girlfriends or wives to join the entourage in Los Angeles, and when Priscilla read of his alleged romances in the gossip columns, she became distraught and began asserting herself more. At her insistence, she and the wives and girlfriends began to be allowed to visit Los Angeles, and in 1966 she persuaded Presley to rent a new house where they could have more privacy and, she hoped, lead a more "normal" life.

Priscilla's resolve to forge a closer relationship with Elvis was soon resented by many of the guys. She openly favored some of them, like Joe Esposito and Jerry Schilling, and encouraged these favorites to include their wives in a more intimate brand of socializing that excluded the rest of the entourage. She also became close to Colonel Parker, and as Parker came to trust her and regard her as a positive influence on Elvis, he began to pressure Presley to make good on his promise to marry her. Unwilling to commit, Elvis held off for several months, but as the press got wind of things and began to write about his relationship with Priscilla, his "live-in Lolita," and Parker reminded him of what the fallout from a scandal might be, he succumbed and proposed to her in December 1966. This development strengthened Priscilla's hand even as it exacerbated tensions between the in-group and others in the entourage. But whatever their feelings for Priscilla, by this time the guys had come to realize that all of them—even Priscilla and the Colonel— had a common enemy: Larry Geller.

Elvis tried very hard to arouse Priscilla's interest in his spiritual studies. Eager to please, she struggled to get through the books he bought for her and listened patiently as he explained his philosophy of life. His efforts failed. She never caught the spark and was soon turned

off by the whole business, particularly when Elvis decided that his
quest for enlightenment required forsaking sex and other pleasures he
had indulged in for years. Frustrated, Priscilla, like the others, came to
see Geller as a threat. As she later explained to Peter Guralnick, it
wasn't just that Geller took Elvis away from them. Immersed in his
books and long conversations with Geller, Elvis became "passive"—he
lost the energetic spark that had been the essence of his personality.[20]
She tried valiantly to get him involved in other things, buying him his
first slot-car set and encouraging the interest in horses and ranching
that culminated in his purchase of the Circle G. Thanks to these efforts, Elvis was able to strike a balance between his spiritual studies
and his relationship with Priscilla and the guys. But it remained a
source of tension, especially when Elvis came to realize that she had
lost interest in sharing this aspect of his life. By the fall of 1966,
Priscilla had come to the same conclusion as Parker: that Geller's influence on Elvis was pernicious. Their power to wean him away from
the "swami" was limited, however, and Elvis became enraged when
Priscilla or the guys criticized Geller or acted in ways that ostracized
him from the group.

In March 1967 an opportunity to drive a wedge between the two finally presented itself. While in Los Angeles to begin filming *Clambake*,
Presley, woozy from his now-substantial regular dose of sleeping pills,
slipped in the bathroom and hit his head, sustaining a concussion and
forcing a delay in shooting. Absorbed with the ranch and woefully out of
shape, he had already gotten Parker to push back the shooting date
twice, and his manager had grown tired of making excuses for him.
Parker had also heard an earful from Vernon, who was exasperated by
Elvis's spending on the Circle G. The concussion was the last straw. In
a closed-door meeting, Parker admonished Elvis for his irresponsibility.
He prohibited him from reading spiritual books, and then called in the
guys and announced that big changes were in the offing. Embarrassed,
Elvis sat silently as his manager laid down the law. Near the end of his
peroration Parker turned to Geller and declared that conversations with
Elvis about religion were banned; later he instructed Joe Esposito to pre-

vent Geller and Elvis from spending any time together alone. In the end, some jobs were reshuffled and a few of the guys had their salaries cut, and Geller, taking the hint, faded out of the picture. A few months later Priscilla persuaded Elvis to burn a large box of the books Parker had banned, a ritual that allowed the couple to "kiss the past goodbye."[21]

In the wake of the Colonel's coup, a chastened Presley dutifully completed *Clambake* and, despite some last-minute jitters, married Priscilla on May 1, 1967, in Las Vegas. Parker made all the arrangements, carefully concealing his plans from the press. To ensure secrecy—and underscore his new authority—he invited only a small number of Elvis's friends to the event, and at the last minute he informed all but Joe Esposito and Marty Lacker that due to a lack of space in the suite where the ceremony would take place, they could only attend the reception. This indignity angered several of the guys; Red West was so mad that Elvis had not stood up to the Colonel that he abruptly quit and remained estranged from Presley for the next two years. Several of Elvis's other longtime friends were surprised and disappointed when they learned about the wedding from the newspapers, and though they were invited to the large reception hosted by Elvis and Priscilla in Memphis at the end of May, the bitterness persisted. Gradually, the core that had coalesced around Presley in the late 1950s and early 1960s began to disintegrate as most of the charter members of the Memphis Mafia struck out on their own, often taking advantage of show-business connections opened up by their proximity to Elvis.[22]

Having succeeded at last in getting Elvis to marry her, Priscilla was elated. She looked forward to something like a normal married life. Parker and Vernon were content as well. Both of them hoped that marriage would provide Elvis with a stabilizing influence and help him get his career back on track. Moreover, they recognized Priscilla as an ally in their effort to reduce the number of flunkies and hangers-on who were perpetually drawn to Elvis. For a while, Presley did seem to settle down, particularly when Priscilla became pregnant shortly after the wedding. Ironically, the pregnancy was disappointing for Priscilla, who had hoped that she and Elvis would remain childless for several years, when they might travel and enjoy a romantic life without the constant presence of the guys. But Elvis was overjoyed when she told him the news, and in many ways during her pregnancy they became closer than ever, enjoying a lusty sex life that continued almost until the day she gave birth to their daughter, Lisa Marie, on February 1, 1968.

The joys of marriage and fatherhood, however, proved fleeting. Soon Elvis was overwhelmed by the demands of his career. Nor was he entirely over the "religious kick" sparked by his friendship with Larry Geller. Though he stopped talking about it, spirituality remained on his mind, a powerful yearning that had been building in him since the beginning of his career, when he had been plucked from obscurity and transformed into "Elvis Presley." It was a yearning that had become more insistent since his mother's death, and since his return from the Army and his immersion in moviemaking. Unlike so many of his other enthusiasms, this was no temporary obsession. It was a response to his dashed ambitions and discontent, and it pointed him toward a role that was miles away from the bland matinee idol he had become in the 1960s.

CHAPTER 6

The King of Rock and Roll

IN AUGUST 1965, while Elvis was busy making movies and still immersed in his spiritual studies with Larry Geller, he entertained some unusual guests. The Beatles were touring the United States and staying in Los Angeles, and they were eager to meet the man who had so powerfully influenced them. They arrived at Presley's Bel Air home with high hopes of not merely paying homage but really connecting with Elvis. And Priscilla and Elvis's extended entourage were giddy with anticipation, going out of their way to be hospitable. At first, however, Elvis was indifferent to their presence, continuing to watch TV after their arrival. Eventually, he picked up a bass guitar and began playing along with a song on the jukebox, and before long John Lennon and Paul McCartney had picked up guitars and joined him.

By the time the Beatles left, everyone, including Elvis, had loosened up, and Lennon invited Presley to visit them before they returned to England, an offer Elvis never took them up on. In the end, however, the meeting was not what the Beatles had hoped for. As Lennon later confided to Jerry Schilling, it had been an honor to meet Elvis. Yet they could not miss the signs of his isolation and disaffection, could not help but conclude that making Elvis pictures had transformed Presley, as one of their press agents later put it, into a "boring old fart."[1]

The Beatles' visit could not have come at a worse time for Elvis. Since early 1964 the British combo had dominated the pop charts and broken sales records previously held by Presley. They had starred in an innovative, wildly successful film, Richard Lester's *Hard Day's Night*; their second movie, *Help!*, had just been released and was already a sensation. They had also begun to record material that diverged from the simple, R&B-influenced pop that had first won over British and American audiences. Their new music—singles like "I Feel Fine," "Ticket to Ride," and "Help!"—was original and extremely popular, enabling the band to win over an enormously wide range of listeners, including young adults raised on Elvis, Chuck Berry, Little Richard, and Buddy Holly who had been bored by much of the pop rock of the early 1960s.[2] Even more remarkable, their music had begun to elicit the respect and admiration of some highbrow critics and adult music fans who normally looked down on rock and pop. Susan Sontag, for example, spied in the commercial success of the Beatles a sign that a "new sensibility" had emerged in the advanced industrial West, a "new, more open way of looking at the world" that was "defiantly pluralistic" and accessible to the vast majority.[3]

As for Elvis, 1965 marked the beginning of the new Katzman-inspired regimen at the movie studios. Box-office revenues from his most recent films were down from previous years. *Paradise, Hawaiian Style*, the movie he was working on when the Beatles visited, was the third film he had made since the beginning of the year, and the extent of his film commitments left him little time for anything else. Presley's goal of securing meaty, dramatic roles seemed further away than ever as he went from one mediocre project to another. All he had to show for them was the money his manager had been able to extract from the studios. By the summer of 1965 he had lost most of the confidence he had felt after his return from the Army. And his performances in front of the camera had deteriorated, reinforcing his passivity with directors and producers.

Presley's position in the music business was no more secure. Aside from "Crying in the Chapel," an unexpected hit recorded in 1960 but not released until Easter 1965, sales of his singles had declined since the early 1960s. Typically, they sold fewer than 500,000 copies and rarely appeared in the top ten. Often material recorded several years before, or songs from movie soundtracks, his records lacked the verve and ebullience of many songs on the pop singles charts. Big hits in the summer of 1965, for example, included "Ticket to Ride," the Four Tops' infectious "I Can't Help Myself," the Byrds' folk-rock rendition of Bob Dylan's "Mr. Tambourine Man," and "Satisfaction" by the Rolling Stones. Elvis's contribution that summer was a ballad, "I'm Yours," culled from a session held in June 1961, a decent song at the time of its recording but a relic by 1965. Nor were the soundtracks as successful as before. *Girl Happy*, released in the spring of 1965, reached the top ten, but its follow-up, the soundtrack of *Tickle Me*, was a failure, selling only 100,000 copies. An August release, *Elvis for Everyone*, which included several non-movie songs, fared better, reaching No. 10 on the album charts and selling 250,000 copies. But like Presley's singles, the songs on this album were dated, and appeared even more so by the end of the year, after the commercial success of Dylan's *Highway 61 Revisited* and the Beatles' *Rubber Soul*, complex, sophisticated albums that inaugurated a new era in popular music. By early 1966 the audience for Elvis's records had been reduced to an aging cohort of hard-core fans, most of them female, who had been drawn to him in his heyday and would buy virtually anything that Parker and RCA decided to release.

But Elvis's decline as a musical artist wasn't just reflected on the charts or on radio playlists, where Motown, the music of the British Invasion, and folk-rock groups like the Byrds and the Lovin' Spoonful were more likely to achieve heavy rotation. It took the form of growing irrelevance, a sense on the part of many music fans, including some who had grown up listening to him, that his day had passed. These feelings were especially common among teenagers, the first wave of the baby boom. Children during Presley's rise to fame in the mid-1950s, they began following the music scene after his discharge from the Army in 1960, when he eschewed rock and roll and devoted most of his energies to moviemaking. They might have fond memories of Elvis rocking out on Milton Berle's or Ed Sullivan's show, and appreciate his contributions to the birth of rock and roll. But for many fifteen- to twenty-year-olds, Elvis was history.[4]

By the mid-1960s, thanks in large part to the Beatles, Dylan, the Rolling Stones, and California's Beach Boys, rock-and-roll music had begun to change. Emboldened by new studio technologies and a growing sense that attitudes and tastes once confined to intellectuals and artists had spread to substantial numbers of middle-class youth, rock musicians began producing music that was more sophisticated, both lyrically and musically, than the rock and roll that Presley and the genre's other trailblazers had produced. Pitched to listeners who were increasingly aware of themselves as a generational cohort, this new music quickly garnered a large audience and inspired musicians to experiment even further. Recognition that much of their audience would follow along led musicians to venture in a variety of directions, resulting in an outpouring of highly original rock and pop—from the surreal, bluesy folk rock of *Blonde on Blonde*–era Dylan and the pop wizardry of *Sgt. Pepper's Lonely Hearts Club Band* and the Beach Boys' *Pet Sounds* to the psychedelic-inspired rock of Jimi Hendrix, Jefferson Airplane, and the Doors.[5]

By 1967 many musicians identified themselves as "artists" in ways that echoed the modernist commitments that poets, novelists, painters, and photographers had expressed in the early twentieth century but that would have been incomprehensible to Presley, Chuck Berry, Little Richard, Buddy Holly, and Jerry Lee Lewis. Committed to writing their own songs and displaying their abilities through complex, often pretentious lyrical wordplay or instrumental virtuosity, they rejected many of the pop-rock conventions established in the late 1950s and early 1960s. Because they defined their own work in opposition to the pop mainstream, their inroads onto the pop charts seemed all the more like acts of defiant subversion. The surprising commercial success of much of this music encouraged record companies to sign artists working in the same vein. More important, it led many musicians and fans to believe that the record business—and perhaps all of Western civilization—was in the throes of a major artistic renaissance, a trend being spearheaded by a new vanguard: affluent youth. The rock and roll developed by Elvis and his comrades had morphed into rock, a more varied set of styles that perfectly captured the heady spirit of the late 1960s. In such a milieu, Presley's records didn't just sound dated; they sounded like they came from another century.[6]

In ways perhaps even he didn't recognize, Elvis was disturbed by these changes in the music business. Nothing demonstrated this more than the Beatles' success. At first it was simple chagrin at seeing benchmarks he had established surpassed and hearing commentators liken Beatlemania to the mass hysteria he had sparked in the 1950s. Yet over time his jealousy toward them deepened, particularly when their music changed and, in their wake, other musicians began to experiment and achieve success with music that departed from pop conventions. "Elvis was very threatened by the Beatles," noted his cousin Billy Smith, "but he tried to hide it."[7] He resented their artistic freedom and their eagerness to take risks. Ironically, the Beatles had learned much from Elvis's pioneering example. They had seen what could come with success, and they were better prepared to deal with the restraints and commercial pressures imposed by managers, record companies, and fans. They also had the luxury of appealing to more sophisticated and knowledgeable fans who would happily follow them as they moved beyond the simple, catchy music that made their reputations—fans who would soon come to expect artistic growth from rock musicians.[8]

But as much as part of Presley might have yearned for such freedom, another side of him looked on it with contempt. He was, after all, a child of the working-class South, where music was central to the forging of communities and linked young and old—and, if Presley and Sam Phillips had had their way, black and white. He had grown up enamored of the pop conventions he had encountered in the movies and on network radio. For Elvis, these pop conventions were the ticket to acceptance and inclusion, the basis for the forging of a *national* community that might transcend class, race, and region. He could never comprehend the desire to move beyond them, much less the belief, derived from the modernism that now influenced rock musicians, that they limited artistic creativity. Elvis loved virtually every kind of music, and he couldn't imagine making the kinds of value judgments and critical distinctions that were becoming common among musicians and many fans. The concept of authenticity, which had arisen in many fields in response to the commercialism of the culture industries and provided fans and musicians alike with a yardstick for measuring quality and who had sold out, was utterly mystifying to him. He was equally bewildered by the cavalier attitude that artists like Dylan and the Beatles sometimes displayed toward their fans. He was appalled, for example, by Dylan's decision to "go electric," which caused a great row among folk music fans and, for Elvis, was evidence of Dylan's disrespect for the people who had made him a success.

By training and disposition, Elvis was an entertainer, not an artist. And though he harbored ambitions that were inspired by yearnings for self-expression and personal fulfillment—to make his mark in an original way—they were filtered through a catholic and capacious sensibility that measured success through public acceptance and his ability to please. To experiment in the manner of Dylan or the Beatles was simply not in his nature.

Despite his discomfort with many of the rock artists of the era, Presley was intrigued by some of their music. He was particularly fond of the new folk music of Peter, Paul and Mary and the singer Odetta, and he became a fan of Simon and Garfunkel as well. It was through pop-oriented folksingers that Elvis first came to appreciate the songs of Dylan, whose abrasive voice he disliked. By the time of the Beatles' visit there was a lot of new music on the jukeboxes at Graceland and at the house in Bel Air, and it was as common for Elvis and Charlie Hodge, the only real musician among the entourage, to fool around playing the new stuff as it was for them to sing gospel songs, pop ballads, or R&B. By early 1966, as Presley listened to and absorbed the new music—as well as old favorites like Hank Williams, Judy Garland, Mario Lanza, and Ray Charles—he had become interested in reentering the studio to try his hand at some non-soundtrack material.

Colonel Parker agreed. Eager to recoup ground lost to the Beatles and others, and well aware that the new Katzman-conceived economies of moviemaking would never provide Elvis with a sense of satisfaction, Parker was confident that Presley could reverse his declining fortunes by producing records unrelated to his films. Returning to the field where he had first achieved stardom, the Colonel figured, was just the challenge Elvis needed. After all, it was a lack of interest in his work that had led Elvis to become distracted—and susceptible to the mysticism of Larry Geller. As Parker knew from experience, Elvis had always been prone to enthusiasms, but only in recent years, as his films became trite and formulaic and his recordings exclusively restricted to soundtracks, had he let them affect his work.

A Nashville recording session was scheduled for May 1966, but Elvis began preparing for it well before. He previewed material sent to him by representatives from Hill and Range and, to their chagrin, announced his intention to record songs the publisher didn't hold an interest in. Presley, Hodge, and Red West, who had begun to write songs and work as a talent scout, went over a wide range of material, including some gospel numbers that Presley and RCA were hoping to record and release as an album. When they arrived at the studio, they discovered that the veteran producer Chet Atkins had hired a new man no older than Elvis to preside over the session.

This proved fortuitous. Felton Jarvis had been an Elvis fan since 1955, and he and Presley hit it off from the start. After discussing the merits of some of the records Felton had produced for other artists, including Fats Domino, Elvis revealed his displeasure with his RCA recordings since his discharge from the Army. The problem, he confided to Jarvis, was with the mix. The final product never sounded like it did when they finished in the studio. His voice always overpowered the accompanying musicians, and the result was bland and uninspiring. Jarvis agreed, and they resolved to inject some new energy and instrumental punch into the session, giving Presley's music some of the vitality that characterized the music of the British Invasion. Like Sam Phillips, Jarvis had an uncanny ability to set the proper mood and cajole

Elvis to put all his energy into a recording. Even more important, he was willing to be Elvis's advocate with RCA officials in New York to ensure that his records retained the sound that he and Presley had conjured in the studio.

The first sessions with Jarvis were tremendously fruitful. Moving seamlessly between gospel, R&B, and countrified pop, Elvis worked harder than he had in years, with Felton encouraging him to record whatever he felt like, regardless of whether it might be suitable for release. "He started taking it serious again," Billy Smith recalled, contrasting the session with the desultory performances Presley had given when recording soundtracks.[9] As in the early 1960s, he took songs through take after take, and with Felton in his corner he was confident the mix wouldn't be adulterated by engineers in New York. Not coincidentally, Presley did the best on the gospel tunes, which eventually appeared on *How Great Thou Art* in 1967. Energized by the presence of the Imperials, an all-star gospel quartet led by Jake Hess, a longtime idol, he poured his heart into the recordings. Some of the secular songs he recorded were just as strong. Perhaps most surprising were his raunchy R&B performances, material Elvis hadn't recorded since the early 1960s. These songs were unsuitable for release as singles, yet they demonstrated clearly what Presley was still capable of. Elvis also recorded a heartfelt version of Bob Dylan's "Tomorrow Is a Long Time," as well as several ballads. One of the best, "Love Letters," was the first single to come out of the Jarvis-led sessions. Issued in July 1966, it was more suited to the country charts than the pop charts, and it reached no higher than No. 19 on the latter. "Indescribably Blue," another ballad, was an even greater commercial disappointment, reaching only No. 33 after its release in January 1967. Its poor showing coincided with Elvis's head injury in his bathroom and the bad feelings that followed Colonel Parker's efforts to exert some control over his client's private life.

More promising were the songs recorded at a September 1967 session, when a chastened, now-married Elvis returned to Nashville determined to cover Jerry Reed's "Guitar Man." To get the right sound,

Jarvis summoned Reed himself to the studio, and the result was a collaboration that produced several first-rate R&B-inspired songs. Unfortunately, a dispute between Reed and Freddy Bienstock, a Hill and Range rep, over the publishing rights to "Guitar Man" eventually derailed the session, and the singles released from it didn't do as well as everyone had hoped. Only "U.S. Male" made it into the top thirty. Artistically, however, they were a triumph, displaying the "hotter" sound that Presley and Jarvis had been seeking, and situating Elvis among a wide array of performers—including Dylan, the Band, the Byrds, and Creedence Clearwater Revival—who were exploring the terrain between rock, blues, and a more roots-oriented country music. But in early 1968, as his new singles struggled to get airplay, few music fans paid attention, and Elvis's audience remained largely confined to the diehards who could be counted on to buy his every release. For younger fans in particular, he was still a historical figure, defined by his movies and the forgettable pabulum that filled their soundtracks.

Colonel Parker had his own plan to revive Elvis's sagging fortunes. In October 1967 he began negotiations with NBC for Presley to appear in a television special. When they were completed, in early January 1968, Parker had a clear picture in his mind of the form the special would take. He envisioned a Christmas show, with Elvis singing holiday songs, that would build on Presley's mainstream appeal and the relative success of the recently released gospel album, *How Great Thou Art*, which would soon receive a Grammy for Best Sacred Performance. But Elvis was far from pleased when he learned of Parker's plan. It confirmed his sense that his manager was woefully out of touch with the times.

Fortunately for Presley, Bob Finkel, the producer assigned to the show, was renowned for his understanding of contemporary tastes, and NBC, which had just begun airing the innovative comedy show *Rowan and Martin's Laugh-In*, was interested in more original programming. Finkel thought the special should be varied and unorthodox, and provide Elvis with an opportunity to reach out to younger viewers who might regard him as a has-been. He pressed his case with Parker, NBC executives, and the program's sponsor, the Singer sewing-machine company, and eventually got them to agree. Recognizing his short-comings as an interpreter of the new zeitgeist, Parker only stipulated that the show conclude with a Christmas song.

To give the special the right feel, Finkel hired a young director, Steve Binder, who had already made a name for himself for "mod" programming, directing the acclaimed concert film *The T.A.M.I. Show*, which featured performances by the Rolling Stones, James Brown, Chuck Berry, and the Supremes. Choosing Binder was inspired. Though he wasn't an Elvis fan, Binder knew how to marry the medium of television with the new music of the 1960s. And his method of producing was spontaneous and intuitive, which was also Presley's preferred way of working. The two men got along immediately. Even more than Finkel, Binder was convinced that the special was Presley's opportunity to display to the public what the *real* Elvis was like. The special would showcase an Elvis freed at last from the trappings of Hollywood stardom—the musician and entertainer who had mesmerized audiences in the 1950s and inspired younger artists like the Beatles. Binder persuaded Elvis that the special was his last, best chance to restore his reputation as an active, engaged musical performer. Through the medium of television, which had served him so well in the 1950s, Presley could return to his roots *and* reinvent himself for a new era.

Though his vision of the program was totally different from Parker's, Binder, with Elvis's support, forced the Colonel to accept it. His script called for Elvis to perform in a series of linked skits that would evoke his career and use his recently recorded "Guitar Man" as a unifying musical motif. In a stroke of genius, he also decided to include an informal, sitdown jam session that would be taped before a live audience. Set on a small stage that resembled a boxing ring, with adoring female fans sitting at arm's length from Elvis and a few other musicians strumming acoustic guitars, this portion of the show would enable Elvis to display the humor and conviviality that Binder saw when he interacted with his friends. It would also provide a contrast to the more stylized production numbers and the conventional stand-up segment, in which Elvis, accompanied by a full orchestra, would perform an updated medley of some of his old hits. To give the sit-down segment an additional charge and to encourage Elvis to reminisce between songs, Binder flew Scotty Moore and D. J. Fontana in from Nashville to accompany him. They would join Charlie Hodge and Alan Fortas on the small stage, a setting designed to get Elvis's musical juices flowing.

A week before the show was scheduled to be taped, Binder achieved his greatest coup. Surprised by Elvis's authentic feeling for black music and the outrage he expressed over the recent assassinations of Martin Luther King, Jr., and Robert F. Kennedy, Binder convinced him to replace the show's original scripted ending, Presley singing "I'll Be Home for Christmas," with a new song written expressly for the special. "If I Can Dream" was a powerful "message song" typical of the socially aware pop music of the late 1960s. Yet it was quite unorthodox for Elvis, and Binder had to have the song's composer play it several times before Presley agreed to include it. As Binder later explained to Peter Guralnick, "I wanted to let the world know that here was a guy who was not prejudiced, who was raised in the heart of prejudice, but who was really above all that."[10] Once Elvis made his decision, he became totally committed to the number, delivering a hair-raising vocal performance in the studio for the show's soundtrack.

This dedication extended to the show as a whole. Presley became engrossed in preparing for the special, moving into his dressing room at the NBC studios in Burbank during the last week of rehearsals before taping began at the end of June. Tan and thinner than he had been since his discharge from the Army, he worked tirelessly, just as he had when he first started making movies. He and Binder became co-conspirators, and as Binder waxed eloquent about the impact the project could have on his career, Presley became a believer. The depth of his commitment convinced Parker not to object to the new ending or to many of Binder's other suggestions, a remarkable change given that the Colonel was no fan of the emerging popular culture and had never been keen on anyone seeking to influence his boy. He must have realized that this was perhaps their last chance to reverse the slow, seemingly inexorable slide of the past few years. And so he reverted to his old ways, allowing Elvis complete control of the music, confident that the magic his client had produced in the past could be revived.[11]

His confidence was not misplaced. Elvis did a terrific job in the recording studio preparing the soundtrack for the production numbers, and after exhaustive rehearsals the complicated "Guitar Man" sequence was taped. Despite a last-minute attack of stage fright, when Elvis realized it had been seven years since he had performed in front of a live audience, the concert segments were an even more exhilarating triumph. Dressed in a specially designed black leather jumpsuit, Elvis tore through the material with a swagger and air of commitment he hadn't shown in years. Feeding off the good feelings of the other musicians, just as Binder had hoped, he joked, relaxed, even forgot the lyrics to songs. Yet the casual, improvisational air of the performance only added to its intensity, and when it aired in December, this made it all the more impressive to younger viewers, including the first generation of rock critics like Guralnick, Jon Landau, Greil Marcus, and Dave Marsh.

"There is something magical about watching a man who has lost himself find his way back home," Landau wrote in a review of the special. "He sang with the kind of power people no longer expect from rock 'n' roll singers. He moved his body with a lack of pretension and effort that must have made Jim Morrison green with envy. And while most of the songs were ten or twelve years old, he performed them as freshly as though they were written yesterday."[12] Even the production numbers were riveting by the standards of the day, and the closing number was astonishing, one of the most impassioned vocal performances in the history of television. "It was the finest music of his life," insisted Greil Marcus a few years later in a widely read retrospective essay on Presley's career.[13] Elvis knew it, too. After the first live segment, as the wardrobe people struggled to free him from his perspiration-soaked leather suit, he was ecstatic with relief and renewed optimism. He announced to the Colonel, "I want to tour again. I want to go out and work with a live audience."[14]

Singer Presents Elvis was even more successful than its producers had expected. Edited down to the requisite sixty-minute format and hyped by Parker's usual array of promotional techniques, it aired on December 3, 1968, and was seen by 42 percent of the viewing public, becoming the most-watched television program of the season. And while some of the reviews were mixed, others were positively rhapsodic in their praise of Elvis. Reviews in the youth-oriented rock press were especially good, encouraging younger fans to see Presley in a new light. Meanwhile, sales of the single "If I Can Dream" increased sharply as the song rose to No. 12 and nearly reached million-seller status. Sales of the program's soundtrack were also brisk. It reached No. 8 on the album charts and sold 500,000 copies during its initial run. These were the best numbers Elvis had posted in several years, and they were now accompanied by a new level of critical respect and a groundswell of interest, stoked by the Colonel, in Presley's imminent return to live performing.

Within days of the Singer broadcast, Colonel Parker was inundated with offers from television producers, and he could easily have lined up appearances that would have fully restored Presley to the public visibility he had enjoyed in the 1950s. Yet Parker, true to form, had something more grandiose in mind—an engagement in Las Vegas, scene of Elvis's only previous live-performance flop and now the show-business mecca that the Colonel had shrewdly sensed it would become back in 1956. Instructing his contacts at William Morris to turn down the TV offers, he began negotiations with executives from the International Hotel, which would open in the summer of 1969 and include a luxurious, state-of-the-art two-thousand-seat showroom, the largest in Vegas. By Christmas, Parker and hotel representatives had reached an agreement. Elvis would play the standard two shows a night, seven nights a week, for four weeks, for a sum of $400,000. This was the kind of salary that only the biggest headliners—Sinatra, Dean Martin, Barbra Streisand—typically received, and it came with perks that made it particularly attractive to Presley and the Colonel: complimentary suites and, more important, provisions for recording a live album and producing a television special or documentary film. And if Elvis proved himself, as Parker was certain he would, it was a deal that could be improved upon, just as Presley's RCA and movie contracts had been regularly upgraded, enabling Elvis to become the biggest headliner in Las Vegas.

In the wake of Parker's successful deal with the International, Elvis returned to the studio in January 1969 with the intention of recording an album and two new singles. Rather than travel to the RCA studios in Nashville, however, he and Jarvis decided to hold the session in Memphis at American Studios, a small facility that had become a hit-making factory for artists such as Wilson Pickett and Dusty Springfield. Several members of the entourage had connections with American and its owner, Chips Moman. Moman employed a talented group of studio musicians and songwriters and specialized in producing soul- and R&B-influenced pop best epitomized by the Box Tops' 1967 hit, "The Letter."

Over the next two weeks, Elvis recorded seventeen songs, and with input from Moman and the studio band he developed a new soulful style that was suitable for a variety of songs and drew on all the sources that had long influenced him. Displaying a level of commitment that was eye-opening to Moman and the session men, Elvis sang his heart out, while Jarvis wisely took a backseat and let Moman run the show. The session's highlights included searing gospel-laced ballads like "Long Black Limousine" and "Without Love," blues-inflected reworkings of country hits such as "I'll Hold You in My Heart," and a self-conscious protest song written by Mac Davis, "In the Ghetto," which Elvis, once again, had to be persuaded to record but then plunged into with abandon. The final song he recorded, "Suspicious Minds," was the one Moman was the most confident about. When it was completed, and Elvis and Moman were interviewed by a local reporter at the end of the session, they were justifiably upbeat. Elvis predicted that several songs they had recorded were likely to be hits. "Maybe some of your biggest," Moman added.[15]

Still energized by the January session, and relieved by the resolution of a publishing dispute between Freddy Bienstock and Moman, who adamantly refused to relinquish the rights to "Suspicious Minds," Elvis returned to American in mid-February for another week of recording. Drawing again from R&B, contemporary country, and "blue-eyed soul," he recorded an additional fourteen songs, Moman's victory over Bienstock having paved the way for Presley to record a much wider range of music. They were every bit the equal of the songs recorded in January, providing Jarvis and RCA with more than enough material for the album they had gone into the studio to record. Among the best songs were Eddie Rabbitt's "Kentucky Rain," an inspired cover of Jerry Butler's soul hit "Only the Strong Survive," and another bluesy rendition of a country song, "After Loving You." A truly remarkable, gut-wrenching blues tune, "Stranger in My Own Home Town," in which Elvis and the session men really cut loose, was the pièce de résistance. On this number Presley finally produced the raucous, funky sound he had been trying to achieve since the late 1950s, when he first quarreled with Colonel Parker and RCA officials about the appropriate balance between his vocals and the instrumental backing. By the end of the session, Jarvis had begun to resent Moman's control over the proceedings, and because of the resulting tension Presley never recorded at American again, despite the success of the experiment.

The American sessions remain an important milestone in Presley's career, the culmination of his development as a vocalist and recording artist. One reason for the high quality of the material was the contribution of Moman and his wonderful session men. Having been worked on by talented musicians and a producer who had a superb mastery of the technologies of recording and overdubbing, the songs were produced in a way that none of Elvis's previous material had been. As Dave Marsh commented, "Rather than simply being layered on, the strings, horns and backing voices [were] fully integrated into the arrangements." Yet it was Elvis's vocals that ensured the songs didn't sound too refined or sterile. They were pop records, to be sure, but with a "sense of aggression" derived from rock and a "groove . . . inevitably born of the blues."[16] Musically complex and unabashedly adult in theme, they not only encapsulated all the influences apparent in Presley's previous music but also went beyond them, resulting in a music that was greater than the sum of its parts. The apogee was "Suspicious Minds," Elvis's most accomplished single and perhaps the most stirring recording of his entire career. Though a good deal of the single's power stemmed from Jarvis's addition of an unorthodox fade-out and coda, which sought to mimic Presley's live rendition of the song, its majesty was just as plain in the original, undubbed master recorded by Moman on the last night of the January session. Even without the signature strings, horns, and background voices accompanying him, Elvis's voice exuded a breathtaking depth and maturity. It was the sound of a man who had at last found material and a setting worthy of his talents, and made the most of it.

Chips Moman's confidence in the recordings was entirely justified. The first single from the session, "In the Ghetto," was a smash hit when released in April 1969. It dominated AM and FM radio playlists, rose to No. 3 on the pop charts, and sold 1.2 million copies, the most since "Can't Help Falling in Love" in 1961. "Suspicious Minds," released in August, did even better, becoming Presley's first No. 1 single since "Good Luck Charm" in 1962 and creating a groundswell of interest in Elvis that sparked sales of his next single, the sentimental ballad "Don't Cry Daddy," when it appeared in stores in November. With sales of 1.2 million and a chart position of No. 6, "Don't Cry Daddy" was yet another commercial success, Presley's third top-ten single of the year. And though the first release of 1970, "Kentucky Rain," failed to reach the top ten and sold only 600,000 copies, half as many as its predecessor, it was lauded by critics and concluded Presley's most successful run since his release from the Army.

Elvis also enjoyed renewed success on the album charts—an even more remarkable achievement considering the prominent role LPs had come to play in the industry. Since the release of the Beatles' *Sgt. Pepper's Lonely Hearts Club Band* in the summer of 1967, the album had become the key showcase for artistically ambitious rock musicians, allowing them to display their talents as songwriters and instrumentalists and make social, philosophical, and in some cases political statements. Rather than comprising a hit single or two and assorted "filler," albums like *Sgt. Pepper*, the Rolling Stones' *Beggar's Banquet*, the Band's *Music from Big Pink*, and the Who's *Tommy* were ambitious works full of first-rate material, often put together with great care in order to tell a coherent story or evoke a particular mood. Thanks to the trend toward free-form radio programming, which enabled disc jockeys to play a greater diversity of music, including cuts never intended for the singles market, the audience for albums increased markedly. Even more important, many music fans began to view albums as the centerpiece of their record collection.

Presley's first real success in this new climate came with the soundtrack of the Singer special, which rose to No. 8 on the album charts and sold over 500,000 copies. Its follow-up, *From Elvis in Memphis*, the first album of material culled from the sessions at American, was not quite as successful, reaching only No. 13. But it received glowing accolades from critics, including a rave review in *Rolling Stone*, a new magazine aimed at "hip" young people that had begun to specialize in thoughtful, sophisticated rock music criticism. "The new album is great," wrote *Rolling Stone*'s critic, a young Peter Guralnick, "flatly and unequivocally the equal of anything he has ever done."[17] Such reviews not only boosted sales, particularly among younger music fans; they also encouraged rock aficionados to view Elvis as relevant, and in some cases drew a direct line between his new music and the pathbreaking material he had recorded for Sun. By underscoring the connections between contemporary rock and pop and the R&B and rockabilly of the 1950s, critics like Guralnick, Greil Marcus, and Dave Marsh helped to construct a new rock music canon in which Elvis occupied a central place, akin to the one literary critics accorded to Shakespeare. Elvis had been proclaimed the "King of Rock and Roll" since the late 1950s, but now his title was more than a marketing slogan. As younger fans duly learned, it was a position he had *earned*.

But Presley had no interest in merely pleasing critics. The American sessions had opened up his musical horizons, and when he returned to the studio in June 1970—this time to RCA's facility in Nashville, with

Felton Jarvis once again in command—he was determined to record the same wide range of songs he had gotten on tape the year before. Working with another group of accomplished Nashville players that Felton had organized, Elvis recorded thirty-five songs over the course of a week. As before, they included gospel, blues, country, and pop, but Presley was especially drawn to ballads and, toward the end of the session, older country tunes. He recorded so many of the latter that RCA released an entire album of them, *Elvis Country*, in January 1971.

The material recorded in Nashville was generally well received by critics, yet it failed to achieve the sales of the songs produced at American. "You Don't Have to Say You Love Me," a cover of Dusty Springfield's hit, performed the best, reaching No. 11 in the fall of 1970. None of the other singles from the session, however, reached the top twenty, and by early 1972 Presley had faded once again from the pop charts. One reason for this was his choice of material. The syrupy ballads to which he was increasingly drawn were unappealing to many younger fans and critics who were eager for more of the complex, hard-edged tunes he had made at American. It was no coincidence that when he made a brief reappearance in the top five in the summer of 1972, it was with a high-energy rocker, "Burning Love," a song Jarvis had to plead with him to record.

But if Elvis's new direction disappointed some people, particularly the element of his audience interested in rock, it increased his popularity among country fans and strengthened their impression of him as a "country" artist, even though his covers of country standards were more pop-oriented than the typical fare produced in Nashville and Elvis himself would never have accepted such a narrow definition of his musical ambitions. Many country fans in the late 1960s and early 1970s had grown up listening to early rock and roll, and as they grew older, they proved receptive to changes in country music that brought it closer to rock and mainstream pop. Indeed, by the time Elvis began appearing on the country charts, the distance between country and rock and pop had decreased, country music was gaining new fans who had once listened to rock, and several artists—Glen Campbell, John Denver, and Linda Ronstadt—were beginning to enjoy success by straddling the line between the genres. Alienated by much contemporary rock, especially hard rock and the psychedelic-inspired experimentation that produced "progressive" rock, many country fans had no problem embracing Elvis or seeing their own music as intimately related to his rock and roll of the 1950s. From their perspective, it was the hippies, druggies, and radicals who had perverted the music and taken it away from its roots. This was a dramatic revision of earlier views, expressed by country purists in the 1950s and early 1960s, which had held rock and roll in contempt, largely because of its promiscuous mingling of black and white influences.[18]

By the summer of 1969, as Elvis reemerged on the record charts, he was hard at work preparing for the Las Vegas engagement that Parker had booked back in December. Presley, excited about returning to performing, approached the Vegas shows with the same determination and eagerness he had exhibited before the Singer special—but also with a new degree of confidence. For Elvis, the gig provided an even better opportunity to present himself as he wished the public at large to see him. Rather than merely reprising his old hits—or eschewing them in favor of the new adult material he had developed at American, the course most musicians who fancied themselves "artists" would have taken—he resolved to incorporate all the different kinds of music that had shaped his life. This was a greater risk than it might appear, for by the end of the 1960s the popular music audience had begun to fragment into diverse "taste cultures," and increasing numbers of musicians were seeking to appeal to these more specific markets by narrowing the range of music they played.[19] Even crossover artists like Campbell and Denver, who sought to appeal to two or more markets, played songs that were essentially cut from the same musical cloth. But not Elvis. Defying the commercial logic of the era, he combined pop, soul, country, gospel, rock, and blues into a repertoire that, as Guralnick has noted, embodied "the *full spectrum* of American music."[20]

First, however, he had to hire vocalists and musicians who could play the diverse styles that would make up his show. After consulting with many different candidates, including Scotty Moore, D. J. Fontana, and some of the session men who had worked with him in Nashville and at American, Presley held auditions and made his selections. None of them had ever played with Presley before, but the band's leader, James Burton, was someone Elvis had respected since the 1950s, when he played guitar in Ricky Nelson's band. Burton, a well-known L.A. session man, helped Elvis pick the rest of the musicians. It was by far the most accomplished band that had ever backed Elvis, and from the first rehearsals he impressed the musicians with his determination to put on a good show.

For nearly two weeks they rehearsed, first in Los Angeles, then in Las Vegas, until they perfected the sound—and mastered the repertoire—that Presley was determined to achieve. To give the music a fuller sound, he added two vocal groups to accompany him: a white male gospel quartet, the Imperials, who had worked with him on *His Hand in Mine*; and a black female quartet, the Sweet Inspirations, who had recently backed Aretha Franklin. Displaying the perfectionism that he first showed at his recording sessions in the 1950s, Presley was explicit about what he wanted, instructing each group to alter their voices in order to give the songs the right dash of gospel and soul. Yet he also let them experiment as they saw fit, and he gladly incorporated their contributions when he found them to his liking.

While Elvis and his extended band rehearsed, Colonel Parker went to work on publicity and promotion. Though advance sales had been huge, with over three-quarters of the showroom's seats sold by early July, Parker pulled out all the stops. He had billboards and posters placed all over Las Vegas and arranged for RCA to provide thousands of glossy photos, catalogs, calendars, and souvenir booklets for sale at special Elvis booths in the lobby and throughout the hotel. He flooded the airwaves and newspapers with ads trumpeting the show and brilliantly orchestrated a run of interviews and feature stories in the press that appeared in the weeks before the opening. And he meticulously compiled the opening-night guest list, ensuring that it included not only his cronies but also important show-business and movie people and influential New York critics. As a testament to their importance, the latter were flown out to Vegas on a private jet.

When opening night arrived, on July 31, the showroom was packed with celebrities and VIPs, including the actor Cary Grant and musicians such as Fats Domino and Phil Ochs. Sam Phillips was there, too, at Elvis's special invitation. Just as in Los Angeles the year before, Elvis experienced a bout of stage fright moments before the show. "He just had no idea of how he was going to be received," Joe Esposito recalled. "He was pacing back and forth, back and forth; you could see the sweat just pouring out of him before he went on stage."[21] But when he came out, he exhibited no signs of it as he launched into a rocking version of "Blue Suede Shoes," and the audience—full of jaded show-business types—leaped to their feet. The energy never let up. Throughout the entire hour-long set Elvis brought the crowd to a state of near delirium as he performed hits old and new with a sustained brilliance unknown in Vegas and achieved only by the most inspired rock and jazz performers. Even more remarkable was his physical agility. As he sang, he grooved with the band, fell to his knees, slid across the stage; at points, he even performed spontaneous somersaults and flips, to the amazement of his intimates, many of whom had not known him during his heyday as a live performer. The showstopper was "Suspicious Minds," which would soon be released as a single and quickly became his new signature tune, as "Hound Dog" had been in the 1950s. Between songs he told self-deprecating jokes and regaled the audience with a highly personal account of his rise to stardom. He concluded it with a confession: though Hollywood had been good to him, "I really missed the people. I really missed contact with a live audience. And I just wanted to tell you how good it is to be back."[22]

The energy and dedication displayed on that first night continued for the duration of the engagement. As the days passed, Presley became even more relaxed and high-spirited. During the final week RCA began recording the shows to provide material for a projected live album, which would allow Elvis to fulfill his contractual obligation to the company and, in Parker's reasoning, provide fans who could not make it to Vegas with a taste of the experience. Reviews of the engagement were rapturous, inspiring accolades from the alternative press and organs like *The Village Voice* as well as from mainstream newspapers and the trade press. Elvis and the Colonel could not have envisioned a more perfect outcome. After the opening-night show, Parker came backstage and, with tears in his eyes, embraced Elvis, a remarkable gesture for both of them. Capitalizing on the euphoria of the moment, Parker met with a hotel executive and quickly finalized plans for a subsequent engagement and terms that would enable Elvis to appear regularly at the International. According to the new contract, Presley would play two engagements per year for the next five years, receiving $500,000 for each four-week gig. The contract included provisions that virtually guaranteed Elvis would remain the highest-paid headliner; if Streisand or Sinatra or anyone else got a better deal, Presley's compensation would be increased to match or exceed it.

During the early 1970s, as Elvis returned to Las Vegas for his twice-yearly engagements, his shows became legendary and continued to set attendance records. Building on the material he debuted in 1969, he developed a unique repertoire that relied increasingly on covers of contemporary pop-rock and country hits—songs like Simon and Garfunkel's "Bridge Over Troubled Water," Marty Robbins's "You Gave Me a Mountain," and "The Impossible Dream," an inspirational ballad from the musical *Man of La Mancha*. A high point was his cover of Mickey Newbury's "An American Trilogy," a medley of "Dixie," "Battle Hymn of the Republic," and "All My Trials," an African-American spiritual. No other song so nicely reflected Presley's complex musical and national inheritance. His concerts became, as Greil Marcus has observed, a kind of unifying ritual, as if Elvis, through his charisma and commitment, could bind the nation's wounds and heal the divisions that had racked America since the mid-1960s.[23] Presley continued to perform many of his old songs, and his set still included blues and up-tempo rockers like "Tiger Man" and Tony Joe White's "Polk Salad Annie." The latter often ran as long as ten minutes and, like "Suspicious Minds," included karate-inspired choreography. But Elvis's tastes tended toward the sentimental and inspirational, and over time this kind of material came to dominate the show, which always ended with "Can't Help Falling in Love" and his hasty exit from the theater.

Presley's Vegas show was visual as well as musical. He gave careful consideration to his wardrobe and came to rely on elaborate costumes designed by Bill Belew, a well-known Hollywood costumer who had outfitted him for the Singer special. Belew's creations included high collars, capes, and wide, jewel-encrusted belts. Adorned with rhinestones, they made Elvis appear almost supernatural, a cross between a superhero and a show-business shaman. These garish, outlandish costumes were perfect expressions of Elvis's peculiar sensibilities, which were distinctly Southern, working-class, and evangelical, yet also infused with New Age spiritualism and a penchant for excess derived from the "populuxe" aesthetic of postwar consumer culture.

Yet Presley's costumes were only one facet of the show's visual spectacle. A series of poses and gestures soon became Elvis trademarks. Influenced by his interest in karate and a persistent belief that he was the instrument of some divinely ordained plan to bring happiness, through music, to the public, Elvis would strut and gyrate across the stage like a Vegas sun god, stopping periodically to distribute kisses or scarves or sweat-drenched handkerchiefs to women in the first few rows. This bestowal of gifts also became a ritual. When Elvis broke into certain songs, women, as if on cue, would line up near the front to receive his offerings. In August 1971 Elvis added another feature that gave the show an even more spectacular aura—a new opening in which he appeared onstage to the accompaniment of Richard Strauss's *Also sprach Zarathustra*, known to fans as the theme from the film *2001: A Space Odyssey*. Some of these touches drew on established Las Vegas conventions. Others, however, were new and redefined the nature of a Vegas floor show. After Elvis, many other entertainers developed more opulent and extravagant shows, often employing new technologies of light and sound to create spectacular effects that became a hallmark of Vegas-style entertainment.

The changes in Presley's Vegas show dismayed some critics. They also disillusioned many younger fans who had come to like some of his new music. For rock devotees in particular, Las Vegas epitomized glitz and mainstream show-business values, and Presley's capitulation to its reigning ethos was demoralizing. It was as if, having made music of transcendent importance, Elvis was content to throw his talent away. This might have been true if he had perceived his career in these terms, but the fact is he didn't. From the beginning, he sought widespread ac-ceptance, eagerly embracing music and production values that would help him reach this goal. The evolution of his Vegas act was perfectly in keeping with this philosophy.

Indeed, as attendance figures confirmed, Presley's increasingly bom-bastic Vegas act pleased the vast majority of his fans, including new ones who were drawn to him for the first time during those years and who continue to revere Elvis's Vegas incarnation. Unlike rock critics or the hip readers of *Rolling Stone* and *The Village Voice*, who identified, to one degree or another, with the counterculture and defined "good" music according to the modernist yardstick of authenticity, many of the fans Presley attracted in the early 1970s were alienated by the social, politi-cal, and cultural movements of the 1960s and regarded themselves as conservatives. They appreciated Elvis's religiosity, his continued interest in country and gospel music, and his invocation of patriotic and spiritual themes in songs like "An American Trilogy" and "How Great Thou Art." Often working-class evangelicals, they were unembarrassed by the sen-timentality and ritualistic bombast of Presley's concerts, which derived in part from the Southern evangelical tradition.

And they were deeply grateful to Elvis for the solicitude he dis-played toward his fans. Many had lived through dramatic changes dur-ing the postwar economic boom, when widespread affluence had lifted countless poor and working-class people into the ranks of the comfort-able middle class. In a sense, Elvis's success epitomized their own. Yet they applauded his interest in honoring his roots and the traditions that had influenced him. The distance many had traveled from their often humble origins left them nostalgic and sentimental, emotions expressly evoked by Elvis's show, with its combination of oldies, blues, country and gospel standards, and contemporary pop hits. These new fans, who were virtually all white and included substantial numbers of people who had been children during Presley's heyday in the 1950s, were an important addition to his audience. And it was his ability to attract them, while still appealing to his older fans, that enabled him to remain Vegas's most popular headliner.

Elvis's success in Las Vegas in the summer of 1969 inspired Parker to resume the touring that Presley had largely given up when he began concentrating on his movie career. Two weeks after his client's triumphant opening, Parker completed a deal for Elvis to perform several shows at Houston's Astrodome in early 1970. Occurring after Presley's second Vegas engagement, these concerts provided a test of whether he could still draw an audience outside Las Vegas. Despite poor acoustics, which made it impossible for Elvis to hear himself or his band, virtually the same group that backed him in Vegas, the Astrodome shows were well received by fans and critics alike. And they attracted huge crowds, including a record-setting 43,614 for one of the evening performances.

In the wake of this achievement, the Colonel arranged for a "pilot" tour in September 1970 to determine the feasibility of more extensive touring. Working with professional concert promoters, who introduced Elvis to the wonders of an up-to-date sound system, Presley and his band and background singers played concerts in Phoenix, St. Louis, Detroit, Miami, Tampa, and Mobile. The results were encouraging. First, it was clear that the elaborate show Elvis had created in Las Vegas could be taken on the road. And the revenue generated revealed that touring could be an excellent source of income, despite the substantial expenses involved in moving such a large group of musicians and singers from city to city. As Presley and Parker both came to realize, they could earn more from a weeklong tour than from a monthlong Vegas engagement. More important, as the Vegas experience became routine, touring enabled Elvis to reconnect with his audience—his *real* audience, not the fortunate few able to get tickets to his shows in Las Vegas. In November 1970 Elvis toured the West Coast, and the following year he made an even more extensive tour of the Midwest and Northeast, appearing in Boston, Philadelphia, and Baltimore. And in June 1972, after a spring tour of cities in the Midwest and South, Presley gave three concerts at New York's Madison Square Garden.

The Garden shows marked the apogee of his career as a performer. He had not played New York City since his television appearances in the 1950s, mostly because Parker wanted to protect him from the cynical New York media. But times had changed, and the Colonel was confident that Elvis would receive better treatment from the press. The prospect of playing at the fabled Garden inspired Presley, sparking the energy he habitually showed when preparing for a new challenge. He wowed reporters at a preconcert press conference, displaying his characteristic humor. When asked about his image and the criticism he had received in the early years, he replied mordantly, "It's very hard to live up to an image," eliciting howls of laughter.[24] The concerts themselves were spectacular, prompting accolades from some of the very newspapers that Elvis and Parker had once feared. Likening Presley to the legendary prizefighter Joe Louis and the Yankee great Joe DiMaggio, a writer for *The New York Times* proclaimed him "a champion, the only one in his class."[25] Drawing eighty thousand fans to four sold-out shows, a Garden record, Elvis affirmed he was the number-one musical attraction in the country. Within days RCA began selling a live album recorded at one of the performances, which reached No. 11 on the album charts and sold over 500,000 copies, his biggest-selling LP in nine years.

After Presley's triumphant return to performing, Parker arranged for several documentaries about Elvis to be filmed. The first, *Elvis: That's the Way It Is*, followed Presley as he prepared for his August 1970 Vegas engagement. It was produced by MGM and released at the end of the year. A more ambitious documentary, *Elvis on Tour*, was produced in 1972. Made by a team of filmmakers who specialized in the new genre of rock documentaries, it focused on Presley's spring tour prior to the Madison Square Garden shows and included some revealing interview segments in which Elvis spoke candidly about his disappointment making movies. "I had thought that they would . . . give me a chance to show some kind of acting ability or do a very interesting story," he noted ruefully, "but it did not change . . . and so I became very discouraged. They couldn't have paid me no amount of money in the world to make me feel self-satisfaction inside."[26] Both documentaries were successful at the box office and were effective at conveying the special features that distinguished Presley's live act from conventional rock concerts. In particular, *Elvis on Tour* offered a glimpse of the powerful bonds that linked Presley to his fans and gave his shows the flavor of a religious revival.

Parker's greatest coup was the *Aloha from Hawaii* special. Since the early 1960s the Colonel had been intrigued by the prospect of having a live performance piped into theaters for a simultaneous closed-circuit broadcast, but the technical and logistical problems involved were overwhelming. By the early 1970s, however, closed-circuit broadcasting had become common for big-time sporting events like championship prizefights, and Parker brought the idea to two young concert promoters who had a reputation for innovation. When he was unable to secure terms sufficiently to his liking, he approached NBC and RCA and negotiated a deal for a different kind of show: a concert to be held in Hawaii that would be beamed via satellite to a worldwide audience of 1.5 billion viewers. NBC would pay Elvis $900,000 for his services. This was the sort of event Parker lived for—the biggest, most grandiose scheme in the history of show business and another milestone for Presley and his canny manager.

Elvis himself was thrilled with the plan, and he prepared for it with his customary zeal. He pored over his repertoire to come up with a list of appropriate songs and had Bill Belew design a new costume for the occasion, a jewel-encrusted jumpsuit and cape emblazoned with American eagles. Concerned about his weight, which had begun to attract critical notice, he went on a crash diet. By the time he arrived in Honolulu on January 9, 1973, he had dropped twenty-five pounds and looked great. Presley loved the stage and set designed for the show, which allowed him to walk out on a runway into the audience. After extensive preparations and a dress rehearsal in front of a live audience, which was taped as insurance against potential technical glitches during the satellite broadcast, Elvis took the stage shortly after midnight on January 14 and delivered a characteristically spirited performance, at one point hurling his ten-thousand-dollar cape into the crowd. The show was broadcast live to the Far East and in Japan garnered the highest ratings of any program in that nation's history. A few hours later it was rebroadcast to European viewers. Americans did not get to see it until April 4, but when it was finally shown, it drew a huge audience, 57 percent of the viewing public, and confirmed Presley's reputation as the world's preeminent superstar.

By building on the critical and commercial success of the 1968 Singer special, Elvis had not only moved out of the movie business and restored his visibility as a musical performer; he had reached a new level of popularity as well. Though no longer the media sensation he had been in the 1950s, Presley now attracted an audience much more diverse than in the past. It included people of many different ages, including the children of fans who had followed him since the era of "Hound Dog," as well as young adults who had only discovered him since his comeback.

For some, Elvis embodied rock and roll: a sexy, charismatic rebel whose music oozed vitality and good spirits. And while they might have been disappointed by the prominence of ballads and inspirational songs in his live act, they attended his shows all the same, knowing they were witness to a piece of rock history and could say that they had seen Elvis, the King of Rock and Roll. Yet for other fans, Presley's stature in the pantheon of rock was irrelevant. They loved Elvis the traditionalist and patriot, the Elvis who openly, unabashedly acknowledged his roots and the cultural traditions that had inspired him since his youth—the same traditions that influenced many of his fans, even while, like Elvis, they enjoyed the bounty of the postwar American way of life.

His audience also included people from outside the United States, from Europe, Latin America, and Asia. Thanks to the worldwide distri-

bution of American records and movies, Presley was able to build a devoted following in countries he had never heard of, much less visited,
and in the eyes of many of these fans he stood for something altogether
different—the abundance, freedom, and wide-open spaces of America,
a land of opportunity where even a poor boy from the sticks could become successful and admired.

Ironically, it was this particular version of Elvis, culled from his
movies and hit songs, forged outside the United States by people who
fantasized about living the American Dream, that Elvis himself may
have most identified with. For it was the only version that was truly inclusive, that refused to acknowledge the divisions that had emerged
like fault lines throughout the United States during the 1960s, that expressed the yearnings and hopefulness that Presley had felt when he
moved to Memphis, encountered an astounding variety of opportunities, and from these raw materials developed the ambition and musical
vision that enabled him to become one of the most important musical
artists of the twentieth century.

Despite Presley's efforts to deny the reality of social conflict and bring
Americans together, one group was now conspicuously absent from his
concert audiences and record-buying public: African-Americans. This
was perhaps the supreme irony of his comeback and re-coronation as the
King of Rock and Roll.

During the 1950s and early 1960s blacks had been among his most
avid fans. Recognizing Elvis's sincere affection for gospel, soul, and R&B,
and his willingness to acknowledge his debt to the African-American musicians who had influenced him, black Americans had a higher regard for
Presley than for any other white performer of the era. But when civil
rights activists encountered white resistance and developed a heightened
degree of race consciousness, many blacks were discouraged from pa-
tronizing white artists, and Black Power ideologues began assailing
whites for "stealing" from blacks. Elvis became a principal target of these
assaults, and his African-American audience gradually melted away. This
contributed to the myth that Presley had never appealed to blacks and

made it easier for younger blacks to ignore the important role he had played in fostering white appreciation for African-American music.[27]

There is no question that in the early years of rock and roll, some whites cynically appropriated black culture for commercial purposes and deprived African-American artists of recognition and royalties. But Elvis Presley was not among them. And to identify him as one of the main culprits was bad history, a misperception of the facts.

CHAPTER 7

Living Legend

IN JANUARY 1971 Presley's stature as a mainstream entertainment icon was affirmed when he was named by the national chapter of the Junior Chamber of Commerce as one of the nation's ten "outstanding young men of the year." The Jaycees had been handing out these awards to men under thirty-five since 1939. Over the years the organization had bestowed them on such distinguished Americans as Nelson Rockefeller, the composer Leonard Bernstein, and the consumer advocate Ralph Nader. Elvis had been nominated by Bill Morris, a former Memphis sheriff and longtime friend, and he was thrilled, particularly when he learned that the awards ceremony would take place in his hometown of Memphis.

He spent hours working on his acceptance speech, often stopping to show Priscilla what he had written and soliciting her advice. Its sincerity and simple eloquence surprised her; it revealed a side of him that, with the guys around all the time, she rarely saw. He was mature and reflective at the prayer breakfast and press conference that opened the festivities, answering difficult questions about the influence of popular music on young people in a manner that underscored his respectability and surely pleased the event's sponsors. "I don't go along with music advocating drugs and desecration of the flag," he announced. "I think an entertainer is for entertaining and to make people happy."[1] And he was equally impressive at the cocktail party and dinner he held for the other winners and Jaycee officials. Brimming with pride, he played the part of courteous host and happily showed off Graceland.

At the awards ceremony, held later that evening at Ellis Auditorium, he beamed as his name was read and his many accomplishments cited. Lauded for his philanthropy, "strength of character," and "loyalty to his friends," he then rose from the table to receive his award and deliver his meticulously prepared speech. It was pure Elvis. "When I was a child, ladies and gentlemen, I was a dreamer," he confessed to the crowd. "I read comic books, and I was the hero of the comic book. I saw movies, and I was the hero in the movie. So every dream that I ever dreamed has come true a hundred times."[2]

What might have been on his mind as he stood at the podium and recited these words? The shotgun shack in East Tupelo? The period of fear and uncertainty when his father was in prison and he and his mother had been forced to move in with relatives? The awe and bewilderment he had felt when they first moved to Memphis? The panic he had experienced when facing the audience at the Overton Park Shell or when Dewey Phillips was going to play his first record on the radio? The long, grueling drives through the South he and Scotty and Bill had made in 1954, when virtually no one had heard of Elvis Presley and Sam Phillips was having problems convincing radio stations to play his records? The dread he had felt when he put his career on hold and entered the Army, and then, on the eve of his assignment to Germany, his mother passed away, depriving him of the only person who had ever truly understood him? Or the frustration he had endured making movies in the 1960s, while the Beatles and other artists were eclipsing him on the music charts? The speech wasn't hyperbole: Elvis's life had been like the plot of a comic book or movie. One of Hal Wallis's scriptwriters couldn't have written it better.

Behind the scenes, however, things were not so idyllic. The triumphs of the past two years had not banished all his problems, and his return to performing had created new ones that would prove even more vexing. Elvis's difficulties were not yet apparent to casual observers, so it was easy for reporters covering the ceremony to emphasize the positive—and for Elvis himself to revel in his accomplishments. At least for the moment, he could forget about his deteriorating marriage and health, his fears for his safety, his concerns about the loyalty of his friends, or the boredom he had begun to feel in the recording studio and onstage, which encouraged him to dissipate and spend money at a rate that shocked even Colonel Parker. From 1969 to early 1973 these developments were interspersed with achievements and milestones, culminating in the *Aloha from Hawaii* special, and this led Presley and his intimates to downplay their seriousness. Yet soon enough they became impossible to ignore.

One source of discord stemmed directly from his comeback. Preparations for the Singer special in 1968 had consumed virtually all his time and energy during the first few months after Lisa Marie's birth, and though he and Priscilla had reconnected after the special's completion, their relationship was never the same. For reasons that were deeply perplexing to Priscilla, Elvis refused to have sex with her after their daughter was born—despite her best efforts to woo him. He had told her years before that he could never make love to a woman he knew had given birth, but she had assumed this squeamishness would not apply to his wife, the mother of his own child. Things became even more difficult when he returned to performing. They spent less and less time together, and when she came out to see him in Vegas in August 1969, there were so many other people around—including other women—that she found it hard to get, let alone keep, his attention. She even took up karate, hoping that a shared interest might revitalize their relationship. But aside from occasional moments of platonic intimacy, he remained aloof and uninterested.

Justifiably suspicious of his fidelity, Priscilla became disillusioned with their marriage and began spending more time with Lisa Marie in L.A. She had an affair with her dance instructor, and soon began a more serious romance with Mike Stone, a karate champion she had met through Elvis. Though she continued to serve as Elvis's escort for events like the Jaycees awards ceremony, appeared regularly at opening-night performances in Vegas, and spent a few months a year at Grace-land, where they shared a bedroom and tried to be a family, by the end of 1971 their relationship had become a regular topic of speculation in the gossip columns.

The gossip resulted as much from his behavior as from hers. Elvis's return to performing restored his credentials as a sex symbol and brought him into contact with scores of women eager to have sex with him. By the summer of 1970 Presley had returned to the wild, woman-izing life he and the guys had enjoyed in the early 1960s. Like before, he had favorite girlfriends, and he often had them flown to Vegas or Memphis to keep him company when Priscilla was in Los Angeles. He made a token effort to hide these relationships from Priscilla, but his blatant womanizing in Las Vegas inspired gossip items in newspapers around the country. And when he was queried about all the "fun" he was having without Priscilla, his response raised eyebrows: "That's what a bad marriage does for you!"[3] As far as Elvis was concerned, his marriage was open and he could have sex with whomever he wanted.

Yet like a classic chauvinist, he still expected Priscilla to be faithful and raise Lisa Marie, and so he was shocked in December 1971 when Priscilla arrived in Memphis for the Christmas holidays and told him she wanted a divorce. One of the principal reasons Elvis had been at-tracted to Priscilla was his confidence that she would submissively ac-cept the double standard that had always governed his relationships with women. "Elvis wanted to have his cake and eat it too," she con-cluded in her memoir.[4] But Priscilla was smart and ambitious; by ig-noring her, he inadvertently encouraged her to become independent. Determined to achieve the happiness she had hoped to find with Elvis, she resolved to seek a divorce. Two months later, in late February 1972, she went further, telling Presley about her relationship with Mike Stone. Already stunned by her Christmastime announcement that she was leaving him, Elvis went over the edge when he heard about Stone. He became enraged, and for the next few weeks he brooded over her betrayal, conveniently overlooking the role his own infidelity might have played in her decision.

Stone remained a sore spot. The following year, when four over-zealous male fans jumped onstage during a concert and Elvis mistakenly took them to be thugs intent on beating him up, he became convinced that Stone was behind the "attack." In a drug-induced fit of paranoia, he went so far as to instruct Red West to investigate having Stone killed. Fortunately, Presley came to his senses and squelched the plan, but his obsession with Stone and Priscilla became a regular subject of conversation with the guys and contributed to the bad moods that afflicted him after his divorce was finalized in October 1973.

His friends found it easy to attribute Elvis's melancholia to the breakup of his marriage. His downbeat state of mind was especially apparent when he returned to the recording studio in March 1972. Mournful ballads like "Separate Ways," a song Red West had written about a couple's marital problems, clearly interested him the most. Finally, after persistent prodding from Felton Jarvis, Presley recorded "Burning Love." But Elvis recorded the song only as a favor to his producer, and the success it enjoyed on the charts, reaching No. 2, his best performance since "Suspicious Minds," had no effect on his musical preferences. At subsequent sessions he remained drawn to lugubrious ballads that stood little chance of achieving the same degree of success. His somber mood was also evident during concerts—not only in his choice of songs but also in his between-song monologues, during which he often alluded to his marriage and insisted that he and Priscilla remained "close friends."

But blaming the divorce for his downbeat state of mind was too easy, enabling his friends and family to overlook another contributing factor, his continued abuse of prescription drugs. Presley had never stopped taking amphetamines and sleeping pills, even during his rigorous preparations for the Singer special and his first Vegas engagement. These new challenges, however, encouraged him to limit his intake. Indeed, whenever some new endeavor, like the Madison Square Garden show or the Hawaii special, appeared on the horizon, he was able to focus, curtail his usage, and prevent the drugs from affecting his work. These periodic demonstrations of self-control impressed his intimates and made them less inclined to question his drug use. "We'd all seen him suddenly stop drugs," explained Joe Esposito, "so there was always hope that one day he would clean up for good."[5] Unfortunately, because of business decisions that Presley himself had a hand in making, challenges that inspired periods of sobriety did not arise often enough, and when the Vegas shows and his concert tours became routine, his drug intake increased. With few incentives to push himself, Elvis was soon bored and ripe for distraction. According to Jerry Schilling, "That's when he began to have a lot of time to just start getting into other things."[6]

To make matters worse, Presley enjoyed even greater access to drugs in Las Vegas and Los Angeles than he did in Memphis. In Vegas and L.A., physicians were used to catering to the whims of big stars, particularly when, like Elvis, they had vast knowledge of prescription drugs and could fake symptoms in order to obtain what they wanted. This made it very difficult for Elvis's regular doctor in Memphis, George Nichopoulos, to track Presley's intake or limit the drugs' harmful side effects. By 1973, thanks to regular "acupuncture" treatments in L.A., Presley had become addicted to Demerol, a dangerous synthetic opiate, and regularly consumed large quantities of potent sleeping pills and downers like Percodan and Dilaudid. In the mid-1970s he even began using cocaine, not least because it offset the effects of the other drugs and added a charge to his usual "booster shot" of vitamins and amphetamines. Elvis continued to rationalize his drug use. "I need it," he insisted to a girlfriend who had the temerity to question his massive daily dose of pills. And as his drug use increased, he became angry and defensive when Vernon or members of his entourage brought up the subject.

Presley's drug abuse not only raised the risk of addiction and overdose but also contributed to the deterioration of his mental health, making it that much more dangerous and debilitating. Several Elvis biographers have argued that Gladys Presley suffered from depression throughout her life and that her son may have inherited a predisposition to it. If this is true, Elvis might have succumbed to depression regardless of his career or lifestyle—even if he had married Dixie Locke, had children with her, and become an electrician. And he might have coped with his condition as so many other people who never get treatment do, by consuming large quantities of alcohol or anything else he could get his hands on. But Elvis's celebrity opened up a new world to him and allowed him to pursue more exotic diversions. From his perspective, the beauty of prescription drugs, at least at first, was that they enabled him to alter his moods, perhaps in response to cues from his brain that demanded compensation for other imbalances, without having to drink alcohol, a substance he associated with the "rough" working class that he and his parents had risen above. And prescription drugs, by his rationale, were emphatically not illegal drugs, which by the 1960s he associated with subversives and rabble-rousers. Legal or not, the drugs increased Presley's susceptibility to depression and made it much harder for him to escape its grip.

His drug abuse caused other health problems as well. Over time, his intake of downers led to severe intestinal problems, liver damage, and bloating. As these ailments became debilitating, he was forced to cancel performances and enter the hospital for treatment. Far more serious, however, were the combined effects of the drugs, which encouraged him to take larger and larger doses, risking an overdose. The inevitable first occurred in October 1973, when Elvis was rushed to a Memphis hospital in a semi-comatose state. After extensive tests revealed his addiction to Demerol, his doctors began treating him with methadone, the classic treatment for heroin addicts. For a couple of months afterward, Presley remained relatively sober, with Nichopoulos carefully monitoring his intake of barbiturates, which the doctor conceded the hyperactive Elvis needed in order to sleep after shows. Yet by the fall of 1974 Elvis had reverted to his old ways, using his many contacts and physician friends to evade Nichopoulos's watchful eye. In the end, it was hard for people to say no to Elvis Presley, and he exploited that fact to the hilt.

Fortunately for Elvis, a few months after he split with Priscilla, he met a woman who temporarily lifted his spirits and was willing to provide him with the kind of attention he had always craved. Linda Thompson, a Memphis beauty queen, was only twenty-two when she and Presley first met in June 1972. But she possessed qualities that made her an ideal companion for him. Intelligent, high-spirited, and entranced by Elvis's attention, Thompson happily adapted her own life to his and soon became his most consistent steady. She nursed him back to health after his near overdose in 1973, and in her presence he felt more secure than he had in years. "She spent four years basically taking care of Elvis—and I mean taking care of him," Marty Lacker recalled. "She was like a mother, a sister, a wife, a lover, and a nurse. She understood that he saw other girls when she wasn't around. But from the last part of '72, when Linda started, to '75, he didn't fool around that much on the road. Because she was with him all the time."[7] Having grown up in a sheltered middle-class family, Thompson knew virtually nothing about drugs, and Elvis had little trouble assuaging her concerns about his reliance on them. But as his dependence increased, she became more worried, and, despairing at her inability to get him to stop, she gradually eased her way out of his life. She left him for good in November 1976, a development that most of his friends now regard as an important turning point.

By this time Elvis had found a new steady, Ginger Alden, an immature, self-centered nineteen-year-old. Alden was far less compliant and accommodating than Thompson. She played hard-to-get and used her relationship with Elvis to bring her family members into his inner circle, where they appeared most interested in the financial benefits of such proximity. This angered many of Presley's friends and made her unpopular with them. But all their insinuations about Ginger being a gold digger fell on deaf ears. Elvis remained smitten, and in January 1977, less than three months after they had met, he proposed, she accepted, and they began to contemplate a life together. Much to Elvis's dismay, their engagement had little effect on Ginger's independence. She continued to demand time alone and refused on several occasions to accompany him on tour. Her fickleness sent him into frequent emotional tailspins, an irony immediately apparent to longtime friends like Joe Esposito. A world-class womanizer with scores of females at his beck and call was being tied up in knots by a mere twenty-year-old—all in an effort to demonstrate that at forty-two, he was still virile enough to have a young girlfriend. Yet by the mid-1970s, as most of Presley's friends knew, his relationships involved very little sex. Reduced to near impotence by the drugs, he was mostly interested in security and companionship, qualities a young woman like Alden, perhaps justifiably, was reluctant to provide.

During the 1970s Elvis also began to fear for his safety. He was shocked by the rash of assassinations and kidnappings in the United States and Western Europe during the late 1960s and early 1970s, and he began to worry that he, too, might be a target. Presley's fears were seemingly confirmed in August 1970, when Joe Esposito received word from an anonymous caller that Elvis would be killed during a performance in Las Vegas. Though nothing came of the threat, it led Presley to gradually transform the entourage into a gun-toting, karate-powered security detail. Elvis himself began to carry guns and dole out firearms to friends and relatives as gifts. It was also at this time that he became close friends with John O'Grady, a tough-talking former narcotics agent who was hired by Elvis's lawyer to investigate the threats. O'Grady regaled Presley with accounts of his derring-do and encouraged him to identify with the police in particular and the forces of law and order more generally. Fearful for his life and disturbed by the rising tide of anti-Americanism that seemed to be sweeping the country, Elvis developed a powerful sense of identification with the "establishment," inspiring him to collect police badges and fraternize with law-enforcement officials.

His interest in police work, especially undercover work of the sort O'Grady had engaged in, soon became a fixation, and in the fall of 1970 he grew obsessed with acquiring an official badge from the Federal Bureau of Narcotics and Dangerous Drugs. This ironic quest soon led him to Washington, D.C., where, through the efforts of California's Senator

George Murphy, whom he just happened to encounter while traveling on the same plane, he was able to meet with President Nixon and get the coveted badge.

The meeting with Nixon remains one of the most surreal moments in recent American history, as Elvis, decked out in a flamboyant crushed-velvet Edwardian suit and wearing the huge gold belt that the International Hotel had awarded him in recognition of his record-setting engagement, embraced the president. The two men then posed for photographs with Jerry Schilling and Sonny West, Elvis's escorts for the trip. The absurdity of the occasion—Presley seeking official credentials from the federal agency responsible for the government's war on drugs while medicated to a degree that would certainly have flattened an ordinary person—was lost on Elvis. And the determination he displayed in achieving his objective was thoroughly genuine. When Presley heard that Senator Murphy was on the same Washington-bound flight, he wrote a plaintive note to the president and asked Murphy to deliver it. This gave him another option when his first request for a badge was turned down by the head of the BNDD. Circumventing the federal bureaucracy, Elvis went straight to the top.

Even more interesting are the points Presley stressed in his note to the president. After expressing his admiration for Nixon and the nation, Elvis informed the president that he had a measure of influence over the counterculture and the New Left. "The Drug Culture, the Hippie Elements, the SDS, Black Panthers, etc. do *not* consider me as their enemy or as they call it The Establishment." He then suggested he could wean young people away from these anti-American influences and "help the country out" through his role as an entertainer. "I wish not to be given a title or an appointed position," he explained. "I can and will do more good if I were made a Federal agent at Large." Elvis reiterated these points during their Oval Office meeting, insisting that he wanted to "restore some respect for the flag" and repay America for the opportunities he had been granted. Claiming to have studied "communist brainwashing techniques" and the "drug culture" for over ten years, he presented himself as an ideal candidate for such undercover work.

All he needed was the badge.[8] Moved by Elvis's sincerity and the weird-ness of the situation, Nixon instructed an aide to get Presley his badge. The King left the White House in a jubilant mood, having proven once again that he could get anything he wanted. Now armed with his badge, he was reassured not merely of his star power but of the validity of his belief that it could be used for good, to defend America against its en-emies and detractors.

Elvis's appeal to Nixon may well have been disingenuous. Friends have argued that he would have said or done anything to get the badge. But there can be no doubt that Elvis held at least some of these views, which may first have arisen when the success of the Beatles began to un-dermine his sense of self-importance. In fact, he pointedly mentioned the Beatles in his meeting with Nixon, suggesting that the British group was fomenting anti-Americanism, and he drew connections between the drug culture, the hippies, and the New Left that were quite similar to those Nixon and conservatives in both major parties had been mak-ing for several years. More significant than Presley's newly awakened conservatism, however, was his belief that he had influence over Amer-ica's dissident elements and could somehow bring everyone together again. For in offering his services to the president, he did not empha-size his ability to root out and arrest subversives. Instead, he high-lighted his ability to be accepted and to convert, to steer the young people of America away from "bad influences." This was not the spirit of a law-enforcement agent; it was the spirit of a crusading evangelist, a man who could not fathom why young people would rebel against a society that had been so good to him—and could be good to them, too, if they played by the rules, as he was certain he had. Because he was born an outsider, Presley's gratitude for his success easily grew into conservatism when he was confronted by the spectacle of the late 1960s, when social and political movements once devoted to working within the system turned against it, and when the disaffection caused by civil rights struggles and the Vietnam War caused these currents of political dissent to seep into other areas of American society, including the attitudes of many of the young.[9]

Elvis's fears for his safety led to the return of some of the guys who had left in the late 1960s. But the entourage remained a hothouse of jealousy and backstabbing, and for this Presley himself was mostly to blame. At first, when the Vegas engagements and concert tours fell into place, it was like old times. Joe Esposito resumed his role as foreman, while Red West, Sonny West, Lamar Fike, Jerry Schilling, and Charlie Hodge were all assigned specific jobs. In appreciation of their loyalty, Elvis gave each of them a gold lightning-bolt-shaped pendant displaying the letters TCB. "Takin' care of business—in a flash" became the group's motto and briefly inspired a new level of esprit de corps. Very quickly, however, Elvis resumed his capricious favoritism, and most members of the entourage resumed the brownnosing that such treatment inspired.

Predictably, Presley came to believe that many of his friends—even some of the old guard who had been with him since the 1950s—were only interested in the money and perks that came from being a member of the entourage. With his judgment clouded by drugs, this suspicion soon grew into a firm conviction, encouraging him to treat them even more capriciously. "In the early seventies, and up to the end, Elvis got really mean," Lamar Fike later reported.[10] Presley grew boastful and belittling, always reminding them who was boss. Much of this was attributable to the drugs he was ingesting, which made his behavior unpredictable. But, according to Fike and other close friends, his cruelty was also a result of dissatisfaction and the same boredom that had afflicted him in Hollywood. Some of the old guard, like Fike and Jerry Schilling, became exasperated and left to seek careers outside Elvis's orbit. They were replaced with younger men, including Dee Presley's sons, who were more employees than friends and reinforced Elvis's worries about loyalty.

Relations between Elvis and the entourage were also strained by the new emphasis on providing security. Using his law-enforcement connections, Presley was able to get permission for himself and members of his "security detail" to carry concealed weapons, which he often brandished in his hotel suite to impress visitors or intimidate members of the entourage. Unfortunately, in his frequently drug-addled state, he was not especially careful about handling his weapons, and on several occasions guns were discharged and bystanders were nearly killed or wounded. Presley was hardly restrained by these accidents, and in subsequent years he would fire his guns at will, often at television sets and chandeliers. On one occasion he elicited howls of laughter when he shot up a hotel toilet.

Though the guys were more careful with their firearms, they also routinely got into trouble. Encouraged by Presley's macho posturing and his paranoid belief that some criminal element was out to get him, Red West and a couple of the other guys beat up people seeking admission to Elvis's suite, inspiring lawsuits and bad publicity. The lawsuits angered Elvis and Vernon, who later used them as an excuse to fire Red and Sonny West. Yet Elvis directly encouraged the Wests' behavior. After all, it was he who had insisted they learn karate, and who regularly displayed his prowess in spontaneous exhibitions in which he always prevailed—even though some members of the entourage were far more skilled than he was. And it was Elvis who persuaded his clique that they were besieged by would-be attackers or assertive interlopers. What better way to prove their loyalty and show off *their* skills than by beating up some drunk who was trying to get close to Elvis, trying to gain admission to their own privileged world? By acting like the biggest badass, Elvis egged them on.

Maintaining an entourage was expensive, as Vernon could readily attest. But Elvis spent as much or more on himself, continuing his pattern of profligacy begun in the 1960s. Now earning well over five million dollars a year, he felt no compunction about buying anything, and by the mid-1970s he had acquired a fleet of expensive cars and motorcycles; an arsenal of weapons, including many rare collector's items; and closets and drawers full of clothes and jewelry. He continued to redecorate Graceland, adding the latest creature comforts and transforming a large room off the kitchen into a Polynesian-themed den that came to be known as the Jungle Room. These makeovers effaced much of Priscilla's decorative influence and made Graceland, more than ever,

an expression of Elvis's peculiar tastes. By far his most extravagant purchases were airplanes, which he began to acquire in 1975, largely because other top-rank entertainers were acquiring them, too. But while
most stars were content with small Learjets, Elvis did them one better,
buying a decommissioned airliner from Delta that he had renovated
into a flying mansion and christened the *Lisa Marie*. He purchased, or
attempted to purchase, several smaller jets as well, and even bought
one for Colonel Parker, who tactfully refused the gift. Like his automobiles, Elvis's planes became a source of pride, and he used them to fly
to distant cities at the slightest whim, often to impress a new girlfriend.

Much of Presley's spending in these years was also sparked by an ex-
cessive and foolhardy generosity. Always one to share his wealth, Elvis
now became impetuously generous toward his family, friends, and business acquaintances—sometimes even perfect strangers. He bought them
custom-made rings, necklaces, bracelets, and pendants. His jewelry
purchases became so frequent and extravagant that his favorite Memphis jewelers were happy to fly to Las Vegas or wherever he was to take
an order or make a special delivery. He presented guns as gifts to
friends and acquaintances; he even tried to give a rare Colt revolver to
President Nixon. He continued to buy the guys expensive cars and new
homes or give them money to start new business ventures, often after
having treated them badly. Auto dealerships relished his visits, because
he frequently bought several cars at a time. During one shopping spree
at a Memphis car showroom in July 1975, he spent $140,000 on four-
teen Cadillacs to give away as gifts, including one for a woman who just
happened to be window-shopping when Elvis arrived. Presley's penchant for giving away cars was so widely reported that a Denver news-
caster made an on-the-air pitch for one. When Elvis heard of the stunt,
he promptly bought the stunned anchorman a Cadillac Seville.

Presley rationalized such spending by pointing to his increased income, which had doubled since he turned from movies to performing.
This was no consolation to Vernon, who, fearing bankruptcy, continued
to warn his son to control his spending, often enlisting Colonel Parker
and Priscilla for support. But these appeals were fruitless. Indeed, in

response to Vernon's nagging complaints, Elvis bought him a new Mercedes. The next day, when Vernon and Priscilla made their most concerted attempt to confront him about his spending, Elvis blew up and left town without telling them where he was going, an adventure that culminated in his bizarre meeting with President Nixon. As Elvis's drug use and sense of self-importance increased, Vernon found it more and more difficult to admonish his son. Nor could he rely on Parker. A compulsive gambler, the Colonel was deeply in debt to Vegas casinos and in no position to moralize about thrift. Vernon lost his most reliable ally when Priscilla and Elvis separated. With Priscilla's place taken by more compliant girlfriends, Presley was surrounded by people dependent on his largesse. Lacking real leverage over him, how could they possibly restrain his spending? What did they stand to gain by doing so?

There is no doubt that Presley derived pleasure from his spending and his ability to buy people things they could never have afforded themselves. A fan of the television program *The Millionaire*, in which a mysterious wealthy "angel" gave away million-dollar fortunes to deserving ordinary citizens, Elvis intended his lavish gifts to have a similar effect. His spending was also influenced by his background and a persistent belief that his wealth was ephemeral and might vanish just as quickly as it had appeared. Rather than sock his money away, the typical bourgeois response to a windfall, Elvis, like many Americans who had experienced poverty and suddenly struck it rich, was determined to enjoy and share his good fortune. The problem arose when spending became Presley's way of compensating for his faltering professional life, and when his already powerful self-indulgent inclinations were reinforced by drugs and his penchant for using money and gifts to control the entourage. As Elvis's behavior became compulsive and pathological, threatening the family's financial security, Vernon began to worry.

There were, in fact, good reasons for Vernon—and Elvis, had he been sober—to be concerned. By any yardstick, Presley's consumption was irresponsible, and by the mid-1970s he was spending considerably more than he was taking in. More important, by spending so recklessly, and establishing a lifestyle in which ready cash was vital to his self-image,

Elvis needlessly narrowed his career options and bound himself more tightly to business strategies that were designed to make quick money but offered him few opportunities to try something new. Here Parker shares much of the blame, for his gambling debts made him just as dependent on quick infusions of cash. In practical terms, this meant regular concert tours, which were far more lucrative than the Las Vegas engagements. In 1972, for example, the first year he toured extensively, Presley made $4.3 million from personal appearances, over three-quarters of it from tours in April, June, and November. The tours, of course, provided Elvis with other compensations, including close contact with his "real" fans. But they were grueling, and they often left him too exhausted to record or think about other projects, particularly when he struggled to stay reasonably straight while on tour and then indulged himself wantonly when the tour ended.

To overcome these difficulties, Felton Jarvis and RCA officials arranged for Presley to record at the Stax studios in Memphis, not far from Graceland, in July 1973. RCA was desperate for some new studio material to release as a follow-up to the *Aloha from Hawaii* soundtrack, which had reached No. 1 on the album charts, and Jarvis was confident that Elvis would respond if the sessions were held in his hometown. At the very least, RCA wanted enough material for a pop album, a gospel album, and two pop singles that stood a chance of equaling the success of the previous summer's big hit, "Burning Love."

The sessions were a disaster. Elvis didn't even show up on the first night, and when he finally appeared on the second, he was five hours late, visibly stoned, and uninspired. Several of the session men had not seen him since 1969 and were disturbed by his slurred speech, bloated appearance, and lack of interest in recording. "He just didn't seem to care," recalled one of them. "He was a totally different person."[11] The songs Freddy Bienstock of Hill and Range had brought to the session were also bad, and Elvis wouldn't even bother with most of them. Instead, he demonstrated karate moves and regaled the musicians with wild stories. The next few evenings were only marginally better, and when the sessions finally concluded after four frustrating days, Presley had completed only eight songs, none very promising. The first single from the Stax sessions, "Raised on Rock," was a commercial disap-pointment, selling only 250,000 copies and reaching No. 41 on the pop singles charts.

Presley returned to Stax in December 1973. This time the out-come was more positive. Rejuvenated and sober after the two-week spell in the hospital during which he was treated for Demerol addic-tion, Elvis completed eighteen masters in a week of recording, his most productive session in several years. Yet productivity did not equal com-mercial success, and none of the tunes recorded at Stax came even close to the sales of "Burning Love." A competent ballad, "I've Got a Thing About You Baby," sold half a million copies in the first half of 1974, but it barely cracked the Top 40 and received little airplay on pop radio stations. Its success was largely attributable to country deejays, who helped lift it into the top five on the country charts. To boost Pres-ley's fortunes on the pop charts, RCA heavily promoted his next three singles, all recorded at the more productive December sessions, and though they charted better than his previous ones, with "Promised Land," released in September 1974, reaching No. 14, sales of Elvis's records remained slack. Despite Elvis's enormous appeal as a live at-traction, the audience for his new music had shrunk to a hard core of no more than 200,000 fans.

Another shortsighted business decision may well have encouraged this trend. For over a decade RCA had been prodding Colonel Parker to allow the company more leeway to release greatest-hits packages drawn from Elvis's extensive back catalog. Parker had steadfastly refused, fear-ing that a flood of old material would undermine sales of new music. In March 1973, however, after consulting with Presley, the Colonel finally relented, and he negotiated a deal in which RCA purchased the rights to Elvis's entire catalog of pre-1973 recordings for $5.4 million. RCA now had the freedom to repackage the old material it had long coveted, and the lump-sum payment to Elvis was split fifty-fifty with the Colonel, in accordance with the new partnership agreement they had recently signed that gave Parker half the proceeds of *any* new deal pertaining to recording.

Though delighted with their acquisition, RCA was hardly giving up on Elvis. In the course of the negotiations, they also offered Presley a new seven-year contract, obliging him to provide the label with two albums and four singles per year. Devised to spur Presley into action and the source of another large infusion of cash, the new contract soon proved to be the bane of Colonel Parker's existence. As Elvis found it more and more difficult to summon the inspiration to record, the Colonel had to release all sorts of unorthodox material in order to fulfill the terms of the deal—assorted live albums, grab bags of mostly mediocre songs recorded at several different sessions, and perhaps the ultimate throwaway, *Having Fun with Elvis on Stage*, a collection of humorous monologues from Presley's live shows released in 1974. Worse still, RCA wasted no time releasing a series of greatest-hits packages. The first, *Elvis: A Legendary Performer, Volume One*, sold a very respectable 750,000 copies and confirmed Parker's original fears about the impact that reissues would have on Elvis's new music. Over the next few years, reissues consistently outsold the dwindling supply of new releases and furthered the public's impression that Elvis had become little more than an oldies act.

Presley's drug abuse and attendant health problems left him unable to record and challenge this impression. A session held in Los Angeles in March 1975 resulted in the completion of only ten masters, with the best of the lot, the spirited, R&B-flavored "T-R-O-U-B-L-E," selling only 200,000 copies. In hopes of inspiring him, Felton Jarvis had RCA send its mobile recording unit to Graceland, and in February 1976 another session was held in the recently redecorated Jungle Room. The results were again disappointing. Elvis and his band recorded twelve songs, several of them notable for their quality and Presley's level of commitment. But during much of the session Elvis was distracted or drug-addled, and when sober he wasted time showing off his collection of police badges and lecturing on the finer points of New Age mysticism. Recording at home also allowed him to escape to his bedroom for hours at a time. Here he listened to gospel records, watched television, or plotted to kill, vigilante-style, all the leading drug dealers in Memphis. Jarvis set up another session at Graceland in October 1976, but it was even less successful, producing only three songs. Again Elvis, distracted and acting odd, spent most of the time in his bedroom. At one point, he emerged armed with a submachine gun, and when a shipment of new motorcycles arrived, he abruptly halted recording and insisted on taking them for a spin around the neighborhood. On the second night, sensing he wouldn't be able to deliver, Elvis apologized to the musicians and canceled the session. In early 1977, despairing at his inability to get Presley into the studio, Jarvis began recording his concerts, hoping that live material might compensate for the lack of studio product.

As record sales declined and his new music virtually disappeared from all but country radio station playlists, Presley became more dependent than ever on touring as his principal source of income and self-esteem. In 1974, for example, he spent three weeks on the road in March, played several shows on the West Coast in May, and went out on tour again for two weeks in mid-June and in October. These tours brought in about $4 million, while his two Las Vegas engagements—in January and August, each lasting two weeks—and a weeklong May gig in Lake Tahoe generated far less, approximately $700,000. Besides income, Presley's concerts provided him with opportunities to bask in the adoration of his fans. Their devotion meant a lot to him, particularly when, under the influence of drugs and spiraling toward depression, he began to doubt the loyalty of his entourage. When, in the mid-1970s, his concerts began to receive negative reviews, many of his fans responded defensively, and this expression of support reinforced Presley's identification with them. For some of his older fans, it was like old times, with the sophisticated elite media once again casting aspersions on their hero. But even many newer fans redoubled their commitment to him. While Elvis and the entourage were "takin' care of business," his hard-core fans resolved to "take care of Elvis" by dutifully buying his records and attending his shows.[12]

This kind of devotion proved crucial in transforming Elvis's fan base into a genuine subculture. Clearly, for many of his fans, Presley was more than an entertainer, and the experience of seeing him in concert, which some of them did dozens of times, went well beyond a run-of-the-mill show-business event. As Erika Doss has suggested in her fascinating book *Elvis Culture*, Presley's concerts resembled religious rituals, and the bond that developed between Elvis and many of his fans during these shows prepared the ground for their posthumous devotion to him. Yet this devotion also had a downside, which even Presley recognized toward the end of his life. No matter how subpar his performances, his fans cheered him wildly.

His fans' loyalty became a crutch, an excuse to avoid innovation and risk taking. It became license to be as predictable and "safe" a performer as he had been a movie actor. Dependent on their continued adoration and their dollars, Elvis became afraid of alienating them. On several occasions in the early 1970s, he and his band prepared a raft of new songs for his concerts, some of them lesser hits from the 1950s and 1960s, some of them covers of soul or R&B songs that Elvis had always liked. But when, on the first night he performed them, fan response to the new songs was not up to his expectations, he abruptly went back to his usual material and the ovations he knew he could elicit from standards like "Don't Be Cruel," "Heartbreak Hotel," and "Can't Help Falling in Love." And in the 1970s, when he did introduce new songs into his repertoire, he carefully chose well-known hits by artists like Olivia Newton-John that he knew would be familiar and inoffensive. Realizing that only a fraction of his audience were buying his new records, and that the vast majority were keen on hearing his hits and ritualistic showstoppers like "Suspicious Minds," he tailored his repertoire to the majority's expectations rather than insisting that his fans accept him on his own terms.

This was, of course, the strategy he had followed since the late 1950s, the strategy of an entertainer in love with all American music but attuned to the commercial mainstream. There are different kinds of entertainers, however, and in the early 1970s little was remaining of the mainstream. The audience for most commercially produced popular culture had already begun to fragment into subcultures and smaller, more specialized markets, and with a large, devoted fan base that would happily have listened to *anything* he sang, Elvis might successfully have gone in any number of different directions. Of course, none of them would have earned him the level of success he had enjoyed in the past. But he certainly could have achieved a more modest level that would have enabled him to live comfortably and perhaps feel the kind of artistic fulfillment that had long eluded him. But Elvis's understanding of himself and his success simply precluded this. From the era of "Heartbreak Hotel," he had always aspired to be the biggest, most successful star. Anything less was failure.

A different manager might have helped Presley avoid this trap, but Elvis and Colonel Parker were too similar in outlook. Both viewed show business from essentially the same perspective, and Parker's management of Elvis's career reinforced Presley's determination to fulfill the expectations of fans and stick with the tried and true. Sharing Elvis's fixation on appealing to a mainstream that increasingly ceased to exist, Parker could never imagine allowing his client to take advantage of changes in the music and movie industries. This is not to say that Elvis and Parker always saw eye to eye; in the 1970s they quarreled more frequently than ever. But their disagreements rarely involved big strategic decisions about the direction of Elvis's career, and when these kinds of issues arose, Presley always came around to the Colonel's thinking since it so closely resembled his own.

THE MOST COMMON CAUSE for arguments was Elvis's unprofessional behavior, which became increasingly common in the early 1970s. Their biggest blowup occurred in September 1973, when, during one of his concerts, Elvis criticized the management of the Las Vegas Hilton over their treatment of a favorite employee. Elvis had always liked to inject zany, often risqué humor into his Vegas act, and Parker had sometimes found it necessary to remind him to behave himself. But during this particular engagement Presley was out of control. Adversely influenced by drugs, his behavior onstage had become erratic, and his bloated physique and listless performances had sparked negative reviews in the press. And despite warnings from Parker, he had begun to include frequent obscenities in his rambling, occasionally incoherent onstage monologues and to add X-rated lyrics to some of his familiar songs. But when he lit into the Hilton management while onstage, Parker finally blew up and stormed into Elvis's suite after the show, where the two men engaged in a heated argument. When Parker insisted he had no right to criticize publicly the hotel that was paying him to perform, Elvis retorted, "I don't need you, I can handle my own business," and fired the Colonel. Parker returned to his suite and prepared release papers enumerating the millions of dollars Elvis owed him for assorted deals and commissions the Colonel hadn't yet cashed in. When Elvis and Vernon saw how much it would cost Elvis to break with Parker, they were shocked. After two weeks of tense negotiations—conducted through intermediaries, since Elvis and the Colonel wouldn't speak to each other—Elvis finally capitulated and apologized, and the Colonel picked up where he had left off.[13]

A more serious bone of contention concerned proposals for a European tour. Beginning in the late 1950s, Elvis and Parker were approached on numerous occasions by promoters eager to arrange for Presley to perform in Europe. But the Colonel always vetoed these offers, citing logistical difficulties and the greater financial rewards that could be earned from domestic opportunities. The conventional wisdom, among fans and many Elvis scholars, is that Parker scuttled foreign tours to protect his secret identity as an illegal alien—and, some sensationally suggest, avoid criminal charges for mysterious crimes he is alleged to have committed as a young man in the Netherlands.[14] There may be some truth to the first charge, but, as Joe Esposito has noted, the Colonel could easily have delegated management of any foreign tour to one of the promoters he ordinarily worked with on Elvis's domestic tours. In the 1970s, when the offers became more frequent and potentially lucrative, Elvis's reluctance to travel abroad may have been the deciding factor. Fearing new security measures that would have made it difficult to travel with his drugs and guns, Presley may not have wanted to risk being arrested. The rumors about the Colonel, Esposito has suggested, simply provided Elvis with "a convenient excuse for not touring abroad."[15]

Perhaps the best example of Parker's shortsightedness was his decision not to accept Barbra Streisand's offer for Elvis to co-star in her remake of *A Star Is Born*. It was a great opportunity, and when Streisand and her boyfriend, Jon Peters, who was slated to produce and direct the picture, first approached Elvis in March 1975, he was very excited. For a while, Esposito recalled, it was "all that Elvis talked about," a chance to reinvent himself much as Frank Sinatra had done with *From Here to Eternity*.[16] The movie looked to be just the kind of thing that might snap Presley out of his drug-induced torpor. Yet Parker had reservations from the start, fearing that with the inexperienced Peters at the helm, the film would become a showcase for Streisand, not Elvis. His fears were confirmed when Streisand's formal offer arrived. Aside from a flat $500,000 salary, it would have granted Elvis a mere 10 percent of the profits and no cut of the publishing or recording rights. Parker's counteroffer demanded a cool million as a salary, a fifty-fifty split of the profits, approval of songs Elvis would perform, and provisions that would have enabled the Colonel to wrangle a share of the publishing. Not surprisingly, Streisand's production company never responded, and Kris Kristofferson was cast instead. Parker mollified Elvis by insisting he was a bigger star than Streisand's offer suggested; better look elsewhere for opportunities than sign on to a "cheap deal." As usual, the sticking point was not just money but control. But as even Esposito, Parker's biggest defender among the former Memphis Mafia, now concedes, turning down this opportunity was a mistake. With no new challenge on the horizon, Presley sank even deeper into depression. And with Elvis looking more and more worn out, Parker was unable to find anything more promising or lucrative.

By 1975 even Las Vegas and the tours had become a minefield of problems. After Presley's two-week hospitalization in October 1973, the Colonel was hopeful that Elvis could get back on track, and reviews of his first Vegas engagement in the wake of his release from the hospital were overwhelmingly positive. Elvis was back to his old ways by the middle of 1974, however, and at his summer engagement in Las Vegas, after a triumphal opening, his onstage behavior once again became weird and unpredictable. He devoted lots of time between songs to exhibitions of karate, and on the final night, with Priscilla and six-year-old Lisa Marie in the audience, he launched into an embarrassing, at times incoherent "explanation" for his divorce that shocked Priscilla and left much of the audience shaking their heads.

Things got even worse on his next tour, in the fall of 1974. Elvis appeared dazed and woefully out of shape, and over the course of the next year the quality of his performances deteriorated markedly. He routinely forgot lyrics and came to rely on Charlie Hodge for crib sheets. As his health problems mounted, he found it difficult to project his voice. His stage patter became increasingly bizarre, and on some nights his speech was so slurred from the drugs that he was hard to understand. Some performances ended after a mere thirty minutes, while others lasted longer only because of Elvis's monologues and strange antics. And much to Colonel Parker's dismay, on a number of occasions concerts had to be canceled, undermining the reputation for professionalism they had cultivated since the 1950s. Cancellations were also potential public-relations nightmares. After seeing Presley visibly stoned onstage, how long would fans and the press buy the official line that he had been sidelined by "throat problems," "intestinal difficulties," or "the flu"?

Presley's increasingly frequent hospitalizations were even more worrisome. He was admitted to a Memphis hospital on January 29, 1975, after Linda Thompson discovered him on the verge of an overdose. For two weeks Dr. Nichopoulos attempted to regain control over his drug intake, having discovered that Elvis's myriad connections among compliant physicians had allowed him to evade his earlier strict regimen. To prevent this from occurring again, Nichopoulos established a new routine in which nurses visited Graceland daily to dispense precise allotments of prescription drugs. And "Dr. Nick" himself accompanied Elvis on the road to ensure that his patient followed the new regimen while on tour. Among the drugs Nichopoulos and the nurses now administered were new ones Presley needed for health problems developed from years of drug abuse and an unhealthy diet. At Nichopoulos's urging, Elvis also took up racquetball, and soon had a court built at Graceland.

But the new system was no more effective than the old. Presley became adept at identifying and discarding the placebos that Nichopoulos often included in his daily allotments, and he managed to acquire precisely the kinds of drugs—highly addictive narcotic downers—that his physician was trying to keep him away from. In August 1975, at the conclusion of another dismal Vegas engagement that was canceled after only three days, Presley was back in the hospital. As physicians tried to ascertain the seriousness of Elvis's liver and lung problems, Nichopoulos turned to a more serious matter, Presley's mental state and the likelihood that his drug abuse had exacerbated a genetic predisposition to depression. Elvis recovered sufficiently for a successful Las Vegas engagement in December and a record-setting New Year's Eve concert at the Pontiac Silverdome near Detroit. But when he went on tour again, the Colonel pointedly kept him away from major media markets, sending him instead to smaller cities in the Midwest and South where any problems were less likely to be noticed by the national press. This was a smart decision, for by April 1976 Presley's condition had again deteriorated. When John O'Grady, the private investigator who had worked for Elvis in the early 1970s, saw him at a concert at the Sahara Tahoe, he was dismayed. "He was fat. He had locomotive attacks where he couldn't walk. He forgot the words to songs. I went backstage and looked at him, and I really thought he was going to die."[17]

In the end, no one could get Presley to stop taking drugs. Nichopoulos was stymied by Elvis's access to alternative sources. Linda Thompson, having done her best, gave up and drifted away. Since Gladys's death and his own affair with and marriage to Dee Stanley,

Vernon had been unable to control his son. "His daddy could try to talk to him," noted Billy Smith, "but nobody could tell him what to do."[18] Members of the entourage were in an even worse position to be assertive. Often struggling with drug problems of their own and dependent on Elvis for their livelihoods, they lived in mortal fear of being fired. Members of the old guard who tried and failed to get Presley to admit he had a problem usually responded to their failure as Thompson did, by distancing themselves from him. "You had to be there to understand why we all put up with it," Joe Esposito explained in his memoir of life with Presley. "His drug abuse was a slow, gradual process that pulled you in as well. Before you knew it, even the craziness at the end seemed almost normal."[19]

Even the Colonel was unable to exert influence over Elvis. "Parker waited too long, and said too little," insisted Marty Lacker.[20] His preferred method was to work behind the scenes, in a vain effort to intimidate the physicians and dentists who were providing Elvis with drugs, rather than confront his client and risk angering Elvis and being fired. This was the terrible, tragic downside of being the King. Elvis had no equal; with everyone close to him being in his service, no one close to him could give him the help he needed. As Lamar Fike concluded, Presley's drug abuse can't be blamed on Parker, Priscilla, Nichopoulos, or any of the other convenient scapegoats. "Elvis was the problem—his own worst enemy."[21]

As Presley's condition deteriorated and his performances became more inconsistent, he became the object of press criticism. At first, in the early 1970s, it took the form of occasional negative reviews of his Las Vegas shows, usually by pop music critics or writers for trade papers like *Variety* or *The Hollywood Reporter*. But they showered him with accolades as well, and critics like Robert Hilburn of the *Los Angeles Times* could be as effusive as any fan when Elvis delivered a strong performance. After the *Aloha from Hawaii* special, in January 1973, when Presley's weight ballooned, his behavior onstage became more erratic, and the quality of his shows began to nose-dive, reviews of his concerts became more consistently negative. As one critic noted after Presley's opening in Las Vegas in August 1973: "He's not just a little out of shape, not just a little chubbier than usual, the Living Legend is fat and ludicrously aping his former self . . . It is a tragedy, disheartening and absolutely depressing to see Elvis in such diminished stature."[22]

By 1975 even reporters and critics from provincial newspapers were compelled to question Presley's fitness for performing. To be sure, right up to his death Elvis was able to deliver some terrific performances, and when he did, the press responded with ecstatic approval, hoping they had witnessed a turnaround. But by 1976 the poor shows far outnumbered the good ones, and even sympathetic journalists like *The Houston Post's* Bob Claypool were forced to express their disappointment. After witnessing an absolutely terrible concert at a local arena, "a depressingly incoherent, amateurish mess," Claypool admonished Presley for presenting such a sorry spectacle: "The man who had given us the original myth of rock 'n' roll . . . was now, for whatever reason, taking it all back."[23] Bill Burk of *The Memphis Press-Scimitar* was even more blunt after the end of Presley's Vegas engagement in December 1976. Why, he wondered, would Elvis "subject himself to possible ridicule by going on stage so ill-prepared"? How much longer could he continue like this "before the end comes, perhaps suddenly"?[24]

By the mid-1970s Presley had also become fodder for supermarket tabloids like *Star* and *The National Enquirer*, which since the 1960s had capitalized on the breakdown of the Hollywood publicity machine and on public suspicions that many slick, mainstream magazines and newspapers were protecting celebrities. When Elvis and Priscilla broke up, the tabloids had a field day publicizing their various infidelities. The rumors of drug abuse and bizarre behavior, however, really got them going. By 1974, much to Presley's dismay, stories emphasized his weight problems and weirdness, and in November *The National Enquirer* published a cover story that greatly disturbed him. Accompanied by a lurid artist's sketch and unflattering photos, and drawing on extensive quotations from critics, fans, and various hotel employees who had seen

Presley up close during his most recent Las Vegas engagement, the story, titled "Elvis at 40—Paunchy, Depressed and Living in Fear," was devastating. Not only was it close to the truth, but, if anything, it underestimated the chaos now dominating his private life. Not surprisingly, Elvis's rants against the tabloids during his concerts only encouraged them more.[25]

Stung by negative reviews and the tabloids, and ashamed of his weight gain and increasingly evident drug abuse, Elvis became even more depressed. When not on tour, he spent most of his time secluded in his bedroom at Graceland, usually with one of his girlfriends. During these periods of seclusion, only Billy Smith, Billy's wife, Jo, Dr. Nichopoulos, and Elvis's nurses would see him. The entourage remained downstairs, though Elvis kept tabs on them by installing surveillance cameras that allowed him to monitor activities below. One reason for Elvis's reclusive behavior was a growing fear of betrayal. With most of the old guard gone, by 1975 the entourage consisted of mostly newcomers, including the Stanley brothers, whom Elvis suspected of being self-interested and potentially disloyal. Always resentful of the entourage, Vernon did nothing to allay his son's fears, and in July 1976, after consulting with Elvis, he called Red West, Sonny West, and one of the new guys, the karate expert Dave Hebler, and informed them they were fired, ostensibly for economic reasons. The men were stunned and deeply hurt, particularly since it was Vernon, not Elvis, who told them, and Elvis refused to see them or take their calls after it was done. For Red West in particular, who had known Presley since Humes High, it was a bitter pill to swallow. "I'm sure a whole lot of it had to do with the fact that Sonny and Red confronted him about the drugs," Billy Smith said. "Red, especially. And a lot of times, they intercepted stuff coming in."[26]

Inspired by a mixture of greed, resentment, and concern for Elvis, the three men began collaborating with Steve Dunleavy, a reporter for *Star*, to produce an exposé that would force Elvis to admit his drug problem and seek help. When Presley learned of their impending book, his fears of betrayal increased. If Red and Sonny were willing to stab him in the back, whom could he trust? Using John O'Grady as a go-between, Elvis offered each of them fifty thousand dollars and an "education allowance" to help them begin a new career in exchange for shelving the book project. They refused. As a last resort, Presley called Red. But, during a long conversation in which Elvis was clearly stoned, he could not bring himself to discuss the book or apologize, and Red and the others became more determined than ever to issue their wake-up call. The so-called bodyguard book was never far from Presley's mind during the first half of 1977, and as its publication date approached, he began to prepare for the worst.

If Elvis had been able to control his deportment in public, he might not have had much to fear. Yet his concert performances remained inconsistent, and at many shows his onstage antics reached new levels of weirdness. During a concert in Baltimore at the end of May, he abruptly left the stage for half an hour, leaving his band and background singers to soldier on while fans exchanged perplexed looks. Surprisingly, given the frequency of Presley's poor performances, Colonel Parker signed an agreement with CBS to produce a one-hour television special derived from footage from an upcoming tour. The tour, which began on June 17 in Springfield, Missouri, and concluded a little over a week later in Indianapolis, was better than any of them had a right to expect. Though Elvis appeared fat and at times listless, he gave several good performances that enabled the CBS film crew to put together a creditable special that would air in the fall.

By this time, however, excerpts from the bodyguard book had begun to appear in *Star* and foreign publications. As Elvis contemplated his next tour, which was slated to begin in mid-August, he became concerned about the reception he might receive. His concern mounted when *Elvis, What Happened?* was finally published at the beginning of August and immediately began attracting publicity. As they had in the past, Elvis and the Colonel responded by refusing to comment, but in private Elvis agonized over what to do if he was heckled during a concert. According to

Billy Smith, Presley's first instinct was denial. Yet as the date of the tour approached, he decided to admit he had a problem—but only if confronted by a hostile audience, "if they started booing and throwing things." Such an admission would have been a "giant step." "For the first time," noted Marty Lacker, "he was going to own up to his problems."[27]

Smith and Lacker are right. This would have been a remarkable admission, particularly since it ran against the policy of silence that Elvis and Parker had followed since the early 1960s. But it would have been important in another sense as well. By owning up to his problems and acknowledging what all but the most deluded had become painfully aware of, Presley would have finally subjected himself to the only authority he really respected and was willing to obey: his fans.

For years he had been able to count on their support regardless of his actions in his private life. Indeed, after he became a celebrity and he and the Colonel succeeded in cleaning up his public image, Elvis gradually came to feel he was exempt from most of the rules and limitations that governed other people. "He had no parameters," insisted Lamar Fike. "He moved the lines of behavior wherever he wanted them, and if he went too far, he moved them out farther."[28] But this freedom was only possible because he and Parker were able to control and manipulate his image, encouraging the public, and especially his fans, to believe he was a wholesome, down-to-earth, God-fearing, law-abiding man. So long as Elvis played along and acquitted himself responsibly during public appearances, as he had for the first fifteen or so years of their partnership, his fans had no reason to doubt the veracity of his image.

When his public behavior became noticeably erratic, however, the press began to ask questions. Soon revelations from within the Presley camp began to emerge, contradicting the version of Elvis that Presley and Parker had carefully projected through the media. As Elvis recognized, the bodyguard book was the last straw. By seeming to confirm the worst, it would shatter his image and provide the public with a very different glimpse of him. His fans would learn the truth—that the real Elvis bore little resemblance to the image he and the Colonel had been peddling since he went into the Army. But since Presley desperately wanted to retain the admiration of his fans, he had but one choice: to act like the man he claimed to be—the man that Gladys and Vernon had raised him to be—and seek treatment for his drug problem.

Sadly, Elvis never had the opportunity, for on August 16, 1977, the day he was scheduled to leave for the first gig of his new tour, in Portland, Maine, he collapsed in his bathroom at Graceland and died. He was forty-two years old. According to spokesmen at Baptist Memorial Hospital and Graceland, Elvis died of heart failure, but the actual cause of death was "polypharmacy," a fatal reaction to the combination of drugs he had been taking in enormous quantities for years. A blind lab report filed after his autopsy revealed no fewer than fourteen drugs in Elvis's system at the time of his death, nine of them in significant quantities and five at levels that, even had they been taken alone, would have approached or exceeded toxicity. In a final gesture to the public edifice Elvis and the Colonel had built, doctors at Baptist Memorial Hospital refused to make this information public, and only after two decades of lawsuits and recriminations was the truth finally revealed.[29]

Regardless of the circumstances, Elvis Presley fully deserved the accolades and tributes issued in the days and weeks after his tragic death in Memphis. For he was, quite unwittingly, a true musical pioneer, in the same league as Louis Armstrong, Bing Crosby, and the Beatles. Rock and roll would surely have appeared without Elvis, but it would not have been quite the same—would not have had the same associations and meanings, and probably would not have exerted the same kind of influence on other musicians and the vast legions of young people who were later drawn to the Rolling Stones, Bruce Springsteen, Nirvana, or Eminem. But Elvis did more than help forge a new musical idiom; he strove to weave this new idiom back into the diverse cultures from which it had sprung. In the spirit of Walt Whitman, he was committed to creating music that "contained multitudes," encompassing the richness of our tangled, complex heritage—at a time when virtually every force in the land was encouraging strife and disunion and leading people to forget about the values they shared with their fellow citizens. In the twenty-first century, with the American public fragmented into assorted niche markets, consumption communities, and zealously partisan political factions, such an aspiration now seems hopelessly dated and naive. Yet it may be the only route back to common ground—and to a complete understanding of America.

Notes

INTRODUCTION

1. Quoted in Peter Guralnick, *Careless Love: The Unmaking of Elvis Presley* (Boston: Little, Brown, 1999), p. 639.

2. Red West, Sonny West, and Dave Hebler, as told to Steve Dunleavy, *Elvis, What Happened?* (New York: Ballantine Books, 1977).

3. See in particular Greil Marcus, *Dead Elvis: A Chronicle of a Cultural Obsession* (New York: Doubleday, 1991), and Gilbert B. Rodman, *Elvis After Elvis: The Posthumous Career of a Living Legend* (New York: Routledge, 1996).

4. For more on the master narrative that shapes media representations and the public's view of celebrities, see Charles L. Ponce de Leon, *Self-Exposure: Human-Interest Journalism and the Emergence of Celebrity in America, 1890–1940* (Chapel Hill: University of North Carolina Press, 2002).

5. For a fascinating introduction to the fan subculture that has developed around Presley, see Laura Victoria Levin and John O'Hara, *Elvis & You: Your Guide to the Pleasures of Being an Elvis Fan* (New York: Perigee, 2000); and for a scholarly investigation of this subculture, see Erika Doss, *Elvis Culture: Fans, Faith, and Image* (Lawrence: University Press of Kansas, 1999).

1. FROM TUPELO TO MEMPHIS

1. Charles G. Sellers, *The Market Revolution: Jacksonian America, 1815–1846* (New York: Oxford University Press, 1991); Christine L. Heyrman, *Southern Cross: The Beginnings of the Bible Belt* (New York: Knopf, 1997).

2. Eric Foner, *Reconstruction: America's Unfinished Revolution, 1863–1877* (New York: Harper and Row, 1988); Edward L. Ayers, *The Promise of the New South: Life After Reconstruction* (New York: Oxford University Press, 1992). See also the brilliant and still-revealing classic by C. Vann Woodward, *Origins of the New South, 1877–1913* (Baton Rouge: Louisiana State University Press, 1951). Also useful for information about the new pressures faced by poor blacks and whites in the postbellum South is Jacqueline Jones, *The Dispossessed: America's Underclass from the Civil War to the Present* (New York: Basic Books, 1992).

3. Federal Writers' Project, *Mississippi: A Guide to the Magnolia State* (New York: Viking, 1938), pp. 261–66.

4. For an account of the impact of the Great Depression and New Deal on the South, see George B. Tindall, *The Emergence of the New South, 1913–1945* (Baton Rouge: Louisiana State University Press, 1967). For a more expansive account that covers developments in the postwar years and emphasizes the migration of rural people to towns and cities, see Jack Temple Kirby, *Rural Worlds Lost: The American South, 1920–1960* (Baton Rouge: Louisiana State University Press, 1987).

5. Federal Writers' Project, *Mississippi*, pp. 261–66.

6. Edward L. Ayers, *Southern Crossing: A History of the American South, 1877–1906* (New York: Oxford University Press, 1995), p. 199. See also Robert Mapes Anderson, *Vision of the Disinherited: The Making of American Pentecostalism* (New York: Oxford University Press, 1979).

7. For a penetrating analysis of the importance of respectability to Southerners, written during Presley's childhood, see W. J. Cash, *The Mind of the South* (New York: Knopf, 1941). See also John Shelton Reed, *Southern Folk, Plain and Fancy* (Athens: University of Georgia Press, 1986).

8. On wartime mobilization and its impact on the South, see Bruce J. Schulman, *From Cotton Belt to Sunbelt: Federal Policy, Economic Development, and the Transformation of the South, 1938–1980* (New York: Oxford University Press, 1991).

9. See Cash, *Mind of the South*; Greil Marcus, *Mystery Train: Images of America in Rock 'n' Roll Music* (New York: E. P. Dutton, 1975); and Peter Guralnick, *Feel Like Going Home: Portraits in Blues and Rock 'n' Roll* (New York: Vintage, 1981).

10. On the development of country music, see Colin Escott, *Lost Highway: The True Story of Country Music* (Washington, D.C.: Smithsonian Books, 2003), and Bill C. Malone, *Country Music, U.S.A.*, 2nd rev. ed. (Austin: University of Texas Press, 2002).

11. Peter Guralnick's musings on this subject are particularly insightful; see his *Last Train to Memphis: The Rise of Elvis Presley* (Boston: Little, Brown, 1994), pp. 25–29.

12. Ibid., p. 28.

13. See Ted Ownby, *American Dreams in Mississippi: Consumers, Poverty, and Culture, 1830–1998* (Chapel Hill: University of North Carolina Press, 1999).

14. See Beverly G. Bond and Janaan Sherman, *Memphis: In Black and White* (Charleston, S.C.: Arcadia, 2003).

15. Quoted in Peter Guralnick and Ernst Jorgensen, *Elvis: Day by Day* (New York: Ballantine Books, 1999), p. 8. On public housing and its role in helping working-class Americans enjoy a more comfortable standard of living, see Gail Radford, *Modern Housing for Urban America: Policy Struggles in the New Deal Era* (Chicago: University of Chicago Press, 1997).

16. Quoted in Alanna Nash, *Elvis Aaron Presley: Revelations from the Memphis Mafia* (New York: HarperCollins, 1995), p. 23.

17. Bernard Lansky interview, Aug. 14, 1992. Rock 'n' Soul Interviews, transcript, National Museum of American History.

18. See Brian Ward, *Radio and the Struggle for Civil Rights in the South* (Gainesville: University Press of Florida, 2004), and William Barlow, *Voice Over: The Making of Black Radio* (Philadelphia: Temple University Press, 1999).

19. On gospel, see James R. Goff, *Close Harmony: A History of Southern Gospel* (Chapel Hill: University of North Carolina Press, 2002).

20. See Pete Daniel, *Lost Revolutions: The South in the 1950s* (Chapel Hill: University of North Carolina Press, 2000), and Michael T. Bertrand, *Race, Rock, and Elvis* (Urbana: University of Illinois Press, 2000).

21. Quoted in Bertrand, *Race, Rock, and Elvis*, p. 188.

22. This argument is more forcefully expressed by Bertrand in ibid. See also George Lipsitz, "Land of a Thousand Dances: Youth, Minorities, and the Rise of Rock and Roll," in Lary May, ed., *Recasting America: Culture and Politics in the Age of the Cold War* (Chicago: University of Chicago Press, 1989), pp. 267–84.

23. For a good account of the impact of postwar affluence on American adolescents, including working-class teens like Elvis, see Grace Palladino, *Teenagers: An American History* (New York: Basic Books, 1996).

24. For a fascinating account of such subcultural self-expression, see Daniel, *Lost Revolutions*.

25. Quoted in Nash, *Elvis Aaron Presley*, p. 24.

26. Quoted in West et al., *Elvis, What Happened?*, p. 17.

27. Ibid., p. 95.

28. For a stimulating explanation of the ways in which Southern Evangelicalism intersected with modern secular consumer culture, see John Shelton Reed, *The Enduring South: Subcultural Persistence in a Mass Society* (Chapel Hill: University of North Carolina Press, 1986).

29. Quoted in Guralnick, *Last Train to Memphis*, p. 80.

30. On Phillips, see Guralnick, *Feel Like Going Home*, and Colin Escott and Martin Hawkins, *Good Rockin' Tonight: Sun Records and the Birth of Rock 'n' Roll* (New York: St. Martin's Press, 1992).

31. Quoted in Marcus, *Mystery Train*, p. 168.

32. For a succinct and revealing discussion of these complexities, see Daniel, *Lost Revolutions*.

33. Quoted in Guralnick, *Last Train to Memphis*, p. 64.

34. Ibid., p. 83.

2. THE HILLBILLY CAT

1. Quoted in Guralnick, *Last Train to Memphis*, p. 95.

2. Ibid., p. 96. For a more detailed discussion of these early sessions, see Escott and Hawkins, *Good Rockin' Tonight*.

3. Quoted in Guralnick, *Last Train to Memphis*, p. 100.

4. Ibid., p. 101.

5. Quoted in Memphis *Commercial Appeal*, Sept. 29, 1968.

6. Sales figures for "That's All Right" mentioned by the Memphis *Commercial Appeal* are cited in Guralnick and Jorgensen, *Elvis: Day by Day*, p. 18.

7. Quoted in Edwin Howard, "He's Made $2 Million on Disks—Without a Desk," *Memphis Press-Scimitar*, April 29, 1959.

8. "In a Spin," *Memphis Press-Scimitar*, July 28, 1954.

9. Quoted in Guralnick, *Last Train to Memphis*, p. 110.

10. Presley's hybridity is a major theme in Michael Bertrand's book *Race, Rock, and Elvis*.

11. "Spotlight," *Billboard*, Aug. 7, 1954.

12. On the Grand Ole Opry and its role in the development of country music, see Charles K. Wolfe, *A Good-Natured Riot: The Birth of the Grand Ole Opry* (Nashville: Vanderbilt University Press, 1999); Malone, *Country Music, U.S.A.*; and Richard A. Peterson, *Creating Country Music: Fabricating Authenticity* (Chicago: University of Chicago Press, 1997).

13. Quoted in Guralnick, *Last Train to Memphis*, p. 130.

14. See Tracey E. W. Laird, *Louisiana Hayride: Radio and Roots Music Along the Red River* (New York: Oxford University Press, 2004).

15. Marcus, *Mystery Train*, p. 194.

16. On rockabilly, see Craig Morrison, *Go Cat Go! Rockabilly Music and Its Makers* (Urbana: University of Illinois Press, 1996).

17. Marcus, *Mystery Train*, p. 165.

18. Dave Marsh, *Elvis* (New York: Quadrangle, 1982), p. 28.

19. Guralnick, *Last Train to Memphis*, p. 134.

20. Marcus, *Mystery Train*, pp. 186–87.

21. This subject is a prominent theme of Elaine Dundy's book *Elvis and Gladys* (New York: Macmillan, 1985).

22. Quoted in Guralnick, *Last Train to Memphis*, p. 185.

23. On Parker, see Alanna Nash, *The Colonel: The Extraordinary Story of Colonel Tom Parker and Elvis Presley* (New York: Simon and Schuster, 2003); and Dirk Vallenga and Mick Farren, *Elvis and the Colonel* (New York: HarperCollins, 1990).

24. On the emergence of a national culture in the United States, see James L. Baughman, *The Republic of Mass Culture: Journalism, Filmmaking, and Broadcasting in America Since 1941* (Baltimore: Johns Hopkins University Press, 1992). On the relationship between this national culture and various regional and ethnic subcultures, see George Lipsitz, *Time Passages: Collective Memory and American Popular Culture* (Minneapolis: University of Minnesota Press, 1990).

25. On the emergence of television, see Eric Barnow, *Tube of Plenty: The Evolution of American Television* (New York: Oxford University Press, 1975), and Cecelia Tichi, *Electronic Hearth: Creating an American Television Culture* (New York: Oxford University Press, 1991). On the development of Las Vegas as a modern pleasure capital, see Hal Rothman, *Neon Metropolis: How Las Vegas Started the Twenty-first Century* (New York: Routledge, 2002).

26. See Nash, *The Colonel*, pp. 116–18, for details about how Parker was able to become Presley's manager with Bob Neal's unwitting cooperation.

27. Quoted in Guralnick, *Last Train to Memphis*, p. 156.

3. ELVIS THE PELVIS

1. For more on these details, see Nash, *The Colonel*, pp. 118–34.

2. Baughman, *Republic of Mass Culture*.

3. See also William Boddy, *Fifties Television: The Industry and Its Critics* (Urbana: University of Illinois Press, 1992).

4. Quoted in Guralnick, *Last Train to Memphis*, p. 242.

5. These developments are recounted in several noteworthy books. See, for example, James Miller, *Flowers in the Dustbin: The Rise of Rock and Roll, 1947–1977* (New York: Simon and Schuster, 1999).

6. See Glenn C. Altschuler, *All Shook Up: How Rock 'n' Roll Changed America* (New York: Oxford University Press, 2003); David P. Szatmary, *Rockin' in Time: A Social History of Rock and Roll*, 5th ed. (New York: Prentice Hall, 2003); and Richard Aquila, *That Old-Time Rock & Roll: A Chronicle of an Era, 1954–1963* (Urbana: University of Illinois Press, 2000).

7. For a very insightful discussion of the implications of the Presleys' move to the Audubon Park area, see Karal Ann Marling, *Graceland: Going Home with Elvis* (Cambridge, Mass.: Harvard University Press, 1996).

8. Quoted in Guralnick and Jorgensen, *Elvis: Day by Day*, p. 69.

9. See Vallenga and Farren, *Elvis and the Colonel*, pp. 90–111.

10. On the development of teenpics, see Thomas Doherty, *Teenagers and Teenpics: The Juvenilization of American Movies in the 1950s* (Philadelphia: Temple University Press, 2000).

11. The source of this quotation—and the one that follows—was the screenwriter Allan Weiss, who was present at the screen test. Quoted in Guralnick, *Last Train to Memphis*, p. 260.

12. Quoted in Guralnick and Jorgensen, *Elvis: Day by Day*, p. 72.

13. New York *Daily News*, June 8, 1956.

14. *New York Times*, June 6, 1956.

15. "The Rock Is Solid," *Time*, Nov. 4, 1957, p. 48.

16. On the ways in which rock contributed to anxieties about mass culture, see Bertrand, *Race, Rock, and Elvis*.

17. See James B. Gilbert, *A Cycle of Outrage: America's Reaction to the Juvenile Delinquent in the 1950s* (New York: Oxford University Press, 1986).

18. For a good introduction to this subject, see Palladino, *Teenagers*. See also Thomas Hine, *The Rise and Fall of the American Teenager* (New York: Avon, 1999).

19. See, for example, William Graebner, *Coming of Age in Buffalo: Youth and Authority in the Postwar Era* (Philadelphia: Temple University Press, 1990).

20. The rise of teen consumerism is effectively linked to consumerism in general in Gary S. Cross, *An All-Consuming Century* (New York: Columbia University Press, 2000). See also Lizabeth Cohen, *A Consumer's Republic: The Politics of Mass Consumption in Postwar America* (New York: Knopf, 2003).

21. See Palladino, *Teenagers*.

22. On the role of the Cold War in shaping postwar American culture and contributing to concerns about youth, see Elaine Tyler May, *Homeward Bound: American Families in the Cold War Era* (New York: Basic Books, 1988).

23. See Altschuler, *All Shook Up*, for a more detailed discussion of these trends.

24. Robin D. G. Kelley, *Race Rebels: Culture, Politics, and the Black Working Class* (New York: Free Press, 1994).

25. Bertrand, *Race, Rock, and Elvis*.

26. See John D'Emilio and Estelle B. Freedman, *Intimate Matters: A History of Sexuality in America* (New York: Harper and Row, 1988).

27. The contrast between Presley and Boone was made explicit in a prominent magazine article. See Thomas C. Ryan, "Rock 'n' Roll Battle: Boone vs. Presley," *Collier's*, Oct. 26, 1956, pp. 109–11.

28. See, for example, "Elvis—a Different Kind of Idol," *Life*, Aug. 27, 1956, pp. 101–109.

29. On Presley's appeal to blacks, see Brian Ward, *Just My Soul Responding: Rhythm and Blues, Black Consciousness, and Race Relations* (Berkeley: University of California Press, 1998).

30. Quoted in Jerry Osborne, *Elvis: Word for Word* (New York: Harmony Books, 2000), p. 48.

31. Quoted in Guralnick, *Last Train to Memphis*, p. 320.

32. See Bertrand, *Race, Rock, and Elvis*.

33. Quoted in Guralnick, *Last Train to Memphis*, p. 379.

34. Parker's deal with Saperstein provided Elvis's critics with yet more evidence of the supposedly cynical calculations behind his rise to stardom. See Chester Morrison, "The Great Elvis Presley Industry," *Look*, Nov. 13, 1956, pp. 98–104.

35. For more on the origins of the fan clubs, see Doss, *Elvis Culture*.

36. Quoted in Guralnick, *Last Train to Memphis*, p. 289.

37. Marsh, *Elvis*, pp. 86–92.

38. Quoted in Guralnick, *Last Train to Memphis*, p. 407.

39. Ibid., p. 417.

4. THE NEXT JAMES DEAN?

1. The literature on celebrity is enormous and has been written by journalists and cultural critics as well as academics. See, for example, Richard Schickel, *Intimate Strangers: The Culture of Celebrity* (Garden City, N.Y.: Doubleday, 1985); Leo Braudy, *The Frenzy of Renown: Fame and Its History* (New York: Oxford University Press, 1986); Joshua Gamson, *Claims to Fame: Celebrity in Contemporary America* (Berkeley: University of California Press, 1994); P. David Marshall, *Celebrity and Power: Fame in Contemporary Culture* (Minneapolis: University of Minnesota Press, 1997); and Ponce de Leon, *Self-Exposure*.

2. Quoted in Osborne, *Elvis: Word for Word*, p. 14.

3. See June Juanico, *Elvis: In the Twilight of Memory* (New York: Arcade Books, 1997).

4. On Parker's attitudes toward Elvis and women, see Nash, *The Colonel*, pp. 205–206.

5. Quoted in Guralnick, *Last Train to Memphis*, p. 346.

6. Quoted in Guralnick and Jorgensen, *Elvis: Day by Day*, p. 98.

7. *Memphis Press-Scimitar*, March 23, 1957.

8. For a thoughtful and evocative discussion of Graceland and other important sites in Presley's life, see Marling, *Graceland*.

9. Alan Fortas, *Elvis: From Memphis to Hollywood* (Ann Arbor, Mich.: Popular Culture Ink, 1992), p. 58.

10. See Nash, *Elvis Aaron Presley*, pp. 80–87, on the development of Presley's entourage.

11. Fortas, *Elvis: From Memphis to Hollywood*, p. 74.

12. Quoted in Nash, *Elvis Aaron Presley*, p. 129. See also Dundy, *Elvis and Gladys*.

13. Quoted in Guralnick and Jorgensen, *Elvis: Day by Day*, p. 103.

14. Quoted in Guralnick, *Last Train to Memphis*, p. 479.

15. See Nash, *The Colonel*, on Parker's lack of interest in touring abroad. Though Nash's claim that Parker was seeking to avoid prosecution for a violent crime committed in the Netherlands is unpersuasive, her larger point about his unwillingness to endanger his situation in the United States makes sense.

16. Quoted in Guralnick, *Last Train to Memphis*, p. 438.

17. Ibid., p. 355.

18. Ibid., p. 451.

19. *Memphis Press-Scimitar*, March 24, 1958.

20. On pseudo-events, see Daniel J. Boorstin, *The Image* (New York: Atheneum, 1962), and Neal Gabler, *Life: The Movie* (New York: Knopf, 1998).

21. See "Private Presley's Debut," *Life*, April 7, 1958, pp. 117–18. On the importance of the military in postwar America, see Michael S. Sherry, *In the Shadow of War: The United States Since the 1930s* (New Haven, Conn.: Yale University Press, 1995), and Tom Engelhardt, *The End of Victory Culture* (New York: Basic Books, 1995).

22. Quoted in Osborne, *Elvis: Word for Word*, p. 123.

23. Quoted in Guralnick, *Last Train to Memphis*, p. 478.

24. See Dundy, *Elvis and Gladys*, for a detailed discussion of the impact that Gladys's death had on her son.

25. Quoted in Osborne, *Elvis: Word for Word*, pp. 121, 122, 125.

26. For a detailed account of Elvis's life in Germany, see Andreas Schröer, *Private Presley: The Missing Years, Elvis in Germany* (New York: Morrow, 1993).

27. See Joe Esposito and Elena Oumano, *Good Rockin' Tonight: Twenty Years on the Road and on the Town with Elvis* (New York: Simon and Schuster, 1994), and Elisabeth Mansfield and Rex Mansfield, as told to Marshall Terrill and Zoe Terrill, *Sergeant Presley: Our Untold Story of Elvis' Missing Years* (Toronto: ECW Press, 2002).

28. Priscilla Beaulieu Presley with Sandra Harmon, *Elvis and Me* (New York: Putnam, 1985), p. 35.

29. Quoted in Guralnick, *Careless Love*, p. 21.

30. See, for example, "Dear Fans," *Photoplay*, March 1960, pp. 21, 73.

31. See "Farewell to Priscilla, Hello to U.S.A.," *Life*, March 14, 1960, pp. 97–98.

5. MATINEE IDOL

1. Quoted in Osborne, *Elvis: Word for Word*, p. 159.

2. Marsh, *Elvis*, p. 141.

3. For details on the reasoning behind Parker's strategy in the early 1960s, see Nash, *The Colonel*, pp. 200–201.

4. Quoted in Guralnick, *Careless Love*, p. 86.

5. On changes in the movie industry during the 1960s, see Connie Bruck, *When Hollywood Had a King: The Reign of Lew Wasserman, Who Leveraged Talent into Power and Influence* (New York: Random House, 2003).

6. The American public's penchant for mood-altering substances during the postwar era has been noted by numerous historians, including several of the contributors to Peter Braunstein and Michael William Doyle, eds., *Imagine Nation: The American Counterculture of the 1960s and '70s* (New York: Routledge, 2001).

7. See Peter Biskind, *Easy Riders, Raging Bulls: How the Sex-Drugs-and-Rock-'n'-Roll Generation Saved Hollywood* (New York: Simon and Schuster, 1999), and John Gregory Dunne, *The Studio* (New York: Farrar, Straus and Giroux, 1969).

8. See Nash, *The Colonel*, p. 209.

9. Quoted in Guralnick, *Careless Love*, p. 171.

10. Esposito and Oumano, *Good Rockin' Tonight*, p. 144.

11. This is a principal theme in Nash, *The Colonel*, and Vallenga and Farren, *Elvis and the Colonel*.

12. Esposito and Oumano, *Good Rockin' Tonight*, p. 144.

13. For details about Presley's private life in this period, see Nash, *Elvis Aaron Presley*.

14. Fortas, *Elvis: From Memphis to Hollywood*, pp. 118–19.

15. Quoted in Nash, *Elvis Aaron Presley*, p. 83.

16. Quoted in ibid., p. 208.

17. Quoted in Guralnick, *Careless Love*, p. 174. See Larry Geller and Joel Spector with Patricia Romanowski, *"If I Can Dream": Elvis's Own Story* (New York: Simon and Schuster, 1989).

18. Geller and Spector, *"If I Can Dream,"* p. 100.

19. Presley, *Elvis and Me*, p. 115.

20. Quoted in Guralnick, *Careless Love*, p. 183.

21. Presley, *Elvis and Me*, p. 234.

22. On the fallout from Presley's wedding, see Nash, *Elvis Aaron Presley*, pp. 426–36.

6. THE KING OF ROCK AND ROLL

1. Quoted in Guralnick, *Careless Love*, p. 211.

2. The literature on the Beatles is even more extensive than that on Presley. For an excellent appraisal of their careers and cultural impact, see Devin McKinney, *Magic Circles: The Beatles in Dream and History* (Cambridge, Mass.: Harvard University Press, 2004).

3. Susan Sontag, "One Culture and the New Sensibility," in *Against Interpretation* (New York: Farrar, Straus and Giroux, 1966), pp. 303–304. See also Morris Dickstein, *Gates of Eden: American Culture in the Sixties* (New York: Basic Books, 1977).

4. For a thoughtful discussion of this phenomenon, see Greil Marcus's essay "Presliad" in *Mystery Train*.

5. The best history of this transformation is Miller, *Flowers in the Dustbin*. See also Szatmary, *Rockin' in Time*.

6. See McKinney, *Magic Circles*.

7. Quoted in Nash, *Elvis Aaron Presley*, p. 297.

8. On the emergence of an artistic consciousness among rock musicians in response to examples like Presley, see Miller, *Flowers in the Dustbin*.

9. Quoted in Nash, *Elvis Aaron Presley*, p. 383.

10. Quoted in Guralnick, *Careless Love*, p. 298.

11. On Parker's objections to the program, see Nash, *The Colonel*, pp. 234–35.

12. Quoted in Marsh, *Elvis*, p. 177.

13. Marcus, *Mystery Train*, p. 145.

14. Quoted in Guralnick, *Careless Love*, p. 317.

15. James Kingsley, "Relaxed Elvis Disks 16 Songs in Hometown Stint," Memphis *Commercial Appeal*, Jan. 23, 1969.

16. Marsh, *Elvis*, p. 188.

17. *Rolling Stone*, Aug. 23, 1969.

18. On the connections between country music and rock and pop during the 1960s and 1970s, see Malone, *Country Music, U.S.A.* The growing popularity of country music during this period is discussed in Bruce J. Schulman, *The Seventies: The Great Shift in American Culture, Society, and Politics* (New York: Da Capo, 2001).

19. On the emergence of taste cultures, see Herbert J. Gans, *Popular Culture and High Culture: An Analysis and Evaluation of Taste* (New York: Basic Books, 1974), and Michael Kammen, *American Culture, American Tastes: Social Change and the 20th Century* (New York: Basic Books, 2000).

20. Guralnick, *Careless Love*, p. 343.

21. Ibid., p. 348.

22. Ibid., p. 351.

23. Marcus, *Mystery Train*, p. 142.

24. Quoted in Osborne, *Elvis: Word for Word*, p. 256.

25. *New York Times*, June 18, 1972.

26. Quoted in Guralnick and Jorgensen, *Elvis: Day by Day*, p. 310.

27. See Ward, *Just My Soul Responding*.

7. LIVING LEGEND

1. Quoted in Guralnick and Jorgensen, *Elvis: Day by Day*, p. 290.

2. Quoted in Osborne, *Elvis: Word for Word*, p. 232.

3. Quoted in Guralnick, *Careless Love*, p. 362.

4. Presley, *Elvis and Me*, p. 280.

5. Esposito and Oumano, *Good Rockin' Tonight*, p. 219.

6. Quoted in Guralnick, *Careless Love*, p. 391.

7. Quoted in Nash, *Elvis Aaron Presley*, p. 539.

8. Quoted in Osborne, *Elvis: Word for Word*, p. 240.

9. For a lucid account of the rise and transformation of the social and political movements of the 1960s, see Terry H. Anderson, *The Movement and the Sixties: Protest in America from Greensboro to Wounded Knee* (New York: Oxford University Press, 1995). On their role in inspiring conservatism, see Maurice Isserman and Michael Kazin, *America Divided: The Civil War of the 1960s* (New

York: Oxford University Press, 2000), and Rebecca E. Klatch, *A Generation Divided: The New Left, the New Right, and the Sixties* (Berkeley: University of California Press, 1999).

10. Quoted in Nash, *Elvis Aaron Presley*, p. 530.

11. Quoted in Guralnick, *Careless Love*, p. 502.

12. Fan commitment to Elvis is a major theme in books and magazines catering to his subculture and remains a principal preoccupation of fan clubs. See Doss, *Elvis Culture*, for a subtle exploration of this.

13. See Nash, *The Colonel*, pp. 286–88, for details about this incident.

14. Alanna Nash has been most explicit about this. See her book *The Colonel*, pp. 33–44.

15. Esposito and Oumano, *Good Rockin' Tonight*, p. 198.

16. Ibid., p. 207.

17. Quoted in Guralnick, *Careless Love*, p. 600.

18. Quoted in Nash, *Elvis Aaron Presley*, p. 177.

19. Esposito and Oumano, *Good Rockin' Tonight*, p. 219.

20. Quoted in Nash, *Elvis Aaron Presley*, p. 594.

21. Quoted in ibid., p. 586.

22. Quoted in Guralnick, *Careless Love*, p. 504.

23. Quoted in ibid., p. 607.

24. Quoted in ibid., p. 617.

25. On tabloids, see S. Elizabeth Bird, *For Enquiring Minds: A Cultural Study of Supermarket Tabloids* (Knoxville: University of Tennessee Press, 1992).

26. Quoted in Nash, *Elvis Aaron Presley*, p. 668.

27. Quoted in ibid., p. 711.

28. Quoted in ibid., p. 255.

29. On developments in the immediate wake of Presley's death, see Neal Gregory and Janice Gregory, *When Elvis Died* (New York: Washington Square Press, 1980), and Charles C. Thompson II and James P. Cole, *The Death of Elvis: What Really Happened* (New York: Delacorte Press, 1991).

Acknowledgments

THIS BOOK IS a work of synthesis, and in the course of writing it I have relied on countless books, articles, and critical essays written about Elvis Presley over the past fifty years. Indeed, I have been fortunate to have been able to draw on recently published works that are exceedingly reliable, insightful, and thought-provoking. They have been crucial in enabling me to understand Presley and present his story in a coherent form. Peter Guralnick's two-volume biography is a masterpiece from which I have drawn extensively, and I would urge anyone interested in the details of Elvis's life to read it. A work of prodigious research, it will remain the definitive account for years to come. I have also learned a great deal from Michael T. Bertrand and Erika Doss, who have written smart, incisive books on Elvis's social and cultural impact. Pete Daniel's pathbreaking work on the American South has also had a tremendous influence on me, revealing ways in which I could link Presley's story to the main currents of U.S. history. I have drawn from the work of many other scholars as well, and I am grateful to all of them for having done the essential spadework that allowed me to produce a book of this kind: an *interpretive* biography that seeks to place Elvis in context, to connect the life to the times.

I am also grateful to Greil Marcus, Dave Marsh, Lester Bangs, and the other rock critics that I avidly read as a teenager and college student. I was never an Elvis fan during his lifetime, but their writing about him convinced me of his importance, and when I went to graduate school in the mid-1980s, I remained interested in the largely unexplored connections between rock music and the major themes of American history. Writing this book provided me with an excuse to think more systematically about these connections and tell Presley's story in a way that also allows the reader to learn something about the South, race relations, working-class culture, popular culture, show business, and celebrity.

I also owe a debt of gratitude to my family, who were very patient with me while I was conducting research and writing. The warm, supportive atmosphere they provided made it much easier for me to see this project to its completion, and I hope that my children, Caroline and Christopher, will not only read the book but also feel as though they contributed to it in their own way. At the very least, I hope they have fond memories later in life when they are channel surfing and happen upon an Elvis movie, or when Christopher, already a discerning rock fan at age ten, hears a song from *The Sun Sessions* on his iPod or the radio. My wife, Lynn, was her usual steadfast self, always thinking about how she could be of assistance, even while attending to her myriad professional responsibilities. The importance of such support should not be underestimated. My parents also deserve thanks for introducing me to the joys of music, which always filled our home when I was young—and for putting up with me when my tastes ran to the likes of the Clash and the Sex Pistols.

I must also acknowledge my friends and colleagues at Purchase College, who helped to create a vibrant, nurturing professional environment for me. Purchase has been an ideal place for my development as an intellectual, and I can't imagine having written this book had I not come here eleven years ago. My colleagues in the School of Humanities have been especially supportive and interested, and I want to extend special thanks to Michelle Stewart, Nina Straus, Casey Haskins, Elise Lemire, Aviva Taubenfeld, Alfred Hunt, Frank Farrell, Lee Schlesinger, and Gari LaGuardia for offering suggestions and enduring conversations with me about Elvis or issues related to the book. The administration and staff have been equally encouraging, offering me opportunities to discuss my work with faculty colleagues, alumni, and students and publicizing my professional activities to the community at large. I also benefited from often lengthy conversations about Elvis and rock music in general with friends, including Carl Potts, Michael Fields, Michael Hodes, Andy Martino, Steve Canino, and Zachary Daly. My students at Purchase have also been an inspiration to me. Their curiosity and abiding interest in music and popular culture have reaffirmed my own interest in these subjects and convinced me of the merits of taking them seriously.

Louis P. Masur was the person who encouraged me to undertake this project, and I want to thank him for giving me this opportunity and for recognizing my potential to write a book in a more popular vein. I can only hope it meets his expectations. At Hill and Wang, June Kim has been wonderful, the quintessence of courtesy and efficiency. Susan Sherwood and the staff at Graceland and Elvis Presley Enterprises were also very cooperative and professional. My biggest thanks, however, must go to my editor, Thomas LeBien. Thomas has been an absolute joy to work with, and his input and editorial suggestions have been extremely helpful every step of the way. In the course of my research, I learned a lot about Elvis, but it was Thomas's gentle yet insistent prodding that finally allowed me to figure out what I wanted to say. If this book makes sense and inspires readers to better understand Elvis, Thomas deserves much of the credit. For any shortcomings I will happily accept the blame.

Index

Printed in the USA
CPSIA information can be obtained
at www.ICGtesting.com
LVHW091131150724
785511LV00001B/78